William John Charles Moens

English Travelers and Italian Brigands

A Narrative of Capture and Captivity

William John Charles Moens

English Travelers and Italian Brigands
A Narrative of Capture and Captivity

ISBN/EAN: 9783337204662

Printed in Europe, USA, Canada, Australia, Japan

Cover: Foto ©ninafisch / pixelio.de

More available books at **www.hansebooks.com**

ENGLISH TRAVELERS

AND

ITALIAN BRIGANDS.

A Narrative of Capture and Captivity.

BY W. J. C. MOENS.

With a Map and Several Illustrations.

NEW YORK:
HARPER & BROTHERS, PUBLISHERS,
FRANKLIN SQUARE.
1866.

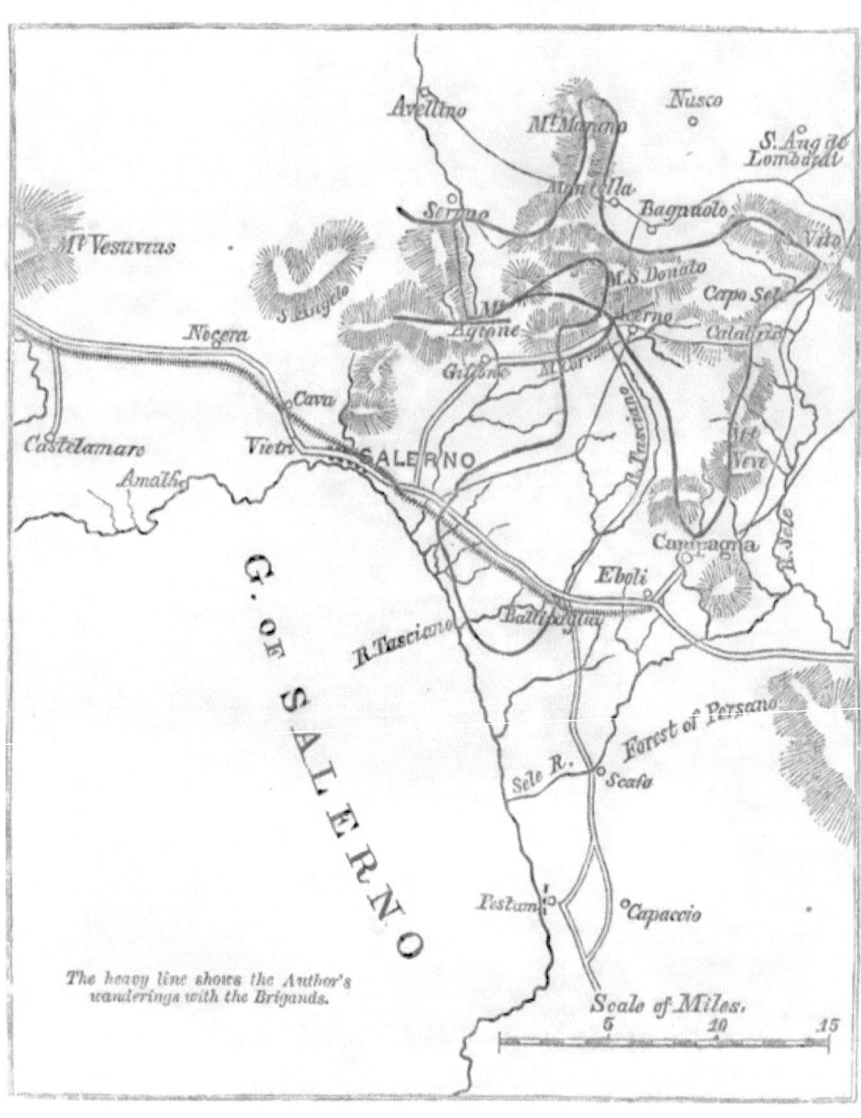

PREFACE.

THE great interest manifested in the misfortune with which the Reverend J. C. Murray Aynsley and I met during our visit to Southern Italy in the spring of this year (1865), coupled with the request of many of my friends that I should publish some account of my experiences there, induces me to hope that a description of my adventures in the mountains near Salerno may not be unacceptable to my countrymen, particularly as little is known in England of the "domestic" life of Italian brigands, very few (if indeed any) Englishmen having had such an opportunity of observing brigand manners as has fallen to my lot; and I sincerely trust it may be long before any of my countrymen has the misfortune to become so intimately acquainted as I have become with the mode of life followed by these free companions.*

The book which I venture to offer to the public has no pretensions whatever to literary merit of any sort. I have endeavored to describe, as simply as possible, what took place from day to day during my captivity, and I trust that the many shortcomings of the work may be considered as atoned for in some degree by the novelty

* Since my release, it has been announced that five other persons have been taken by my captors—none of them, however, Englishmen.

of, at all events, some part of what I have attempted to describe.

To make the narrative complete, my wife has supplied from her diary an account of what my friends were doing for me outside my prison; and we have prefixed three chapters recounting our visit to Sicily, which, as having taken place at the time Mount Etna was in active eruption, and also as having introduced us to Sicilian brigands, I hope may not be entirely without interest.

I have also ventured to add a few general remarks on Neapolitan brigandage, and the only cures which my experience enables me to suggest for it. If the truth has obliged me to make any remarks on this subject which put the state of brigandage under the present government in somewhat unfavorable contrast with what it was under the Bourbons, it must not be thought, on that account, that I am at all inclined to favor the latter. From the bottom of my heart I wish well to United Italy; but, for all that, while fully appreciating the difficulties of the new government, I must not seek to conceal its shortcomings in dealing with the dreadful scourge which deprives the glorious peninsula of half its charms.

Many incorrect rumors having been circulated with regard to the ransom paid for Mr. Aynsley and myself, I may here state, once for all, that the sum actually received and divided by the brigands was 30,000 ducats (or £5100), one half of which has been contributed by each of us.

And, while on this subject, let me express my gratitude to all those—many of them comparatively strangers to me—who volunteered pecuniary assistance in getting me liberated, assistance of which it was my good fortune not to stand in need.*

I take this opportunity also of returning my most hearty thanks to all those who, during my long captivity, so kindly interested themselves in various ways in my misfortunes, and especially to those who assisted my wife with their comfort and advice. Where all have been so kind, it may appear invidious to specify names, but I can not refrain from mentioning Edward Walter Bonham, Esq., C.B., her majesty's consul general at Naples, whose exertions in my behalf were indefatigable; Signor Elia Visconti, of Giffoni, near Salerno, who ran the risk of compromising himself and his family with the Italian government in order to assist my friends in transmitting the ransom to the brigands; my generous friend S—— W—— S——, who, on receiving a telegram from my fellow-captive, Mr. Aynsley, announcing that £8500 was required, without hesitation, and on his own sole responsibility, placed a credit for that amount in the hands of Messrs. Cumming, Wood, and Co., of Naples, at a time when a few days' delay might have cost me my life; Richard M. Holme, Esq., of the house of Cumming, Wood, and Co., who, in addition to other invaluable and unwearied exertions of his firm on my behalf, went to and fro between Salerno and Giffoni at very great personal risk, making the necessary arrangements for the transmission of the money to the brigands, and frequently

* Among other kind offers, the following deserves to be specially mentioned. Rajah Byjenath, having heard from my brother at Bareilly, in Rohileund, that a large sum of money was required for my ransom, immediately offered him a draft for a lac of rupees (£10,000) to effect my liberation.

carrying the gold about his person; Signor Michele di Majo, of Salerno, who generally accompanied Mr. Holme on these excursions, and who frequently went alone to Giffone for us, rendering us also, in other respects, the most invaluable assistance; and my friend H. Cowie, who came out specially from England, and bore a most important part in concerting the measures which ultimately led to my release.

I am also bound to acknowledge the kindness of the officials at Florence, and at the Foreign Office in London, who sent telegrams at all hours to my friends whenever there was news to communicate, and who were always ready to do whatever lay in their power to assist me; and also the great kindness of the prefect, and the general in command of Salerno, who invariably showed every disposition to exert themselves to the utmost in my behalf, the latter being ably seconded by the gallant officers and men under his command.

When I calmly reflect upon the truly noble and unselfish acts that have been done in my behalf by so many persons, I feel inclined to rejoice in my past sufferings and misfortunes. Looking back on them through the bright atmosphere of the sympathy and generosity which they have called forth from my friends and acquaintances, I may well afford to treat my pecuniary loss as nothing in the scale; and thanking God for his mercy in restoring me to my friends with a whole body after all the trials and hardships to which I was exposed, I can say from my heart, now that they are past,

"Hæc olim meminisse juvabit."

CROYDON, *Dec.*, 1865.

CONTENTS.

CHAPTER I.
JANUARY TO APRIL.

Palermo.—Traveling Companions.—Lovers of Art.—The Catacombs.—Monte Pelegrino.—News of the Eruption of Etna.—Domestic Manners of the Sicilians.—The Priests.—The Bombardment in 1860.—The Vendetta.—The Monasteries.—The Grand Cemetery.—Expedition to Monte Pelegrino and its Caverns.—Sicilian Brigands.—The Way the Palermitans manage these Things.—Storm at Sea.—The Fishermen.—Victor Emmanuel's Government.—A Scientific Monk.—The Value of Sympathy.—The Tunny Fishery.—The Campo Santo.—Manner of Burial.—Great Mortality among Children.—More about Sicilian Brigandage .... Page 19

CHAPTER II.
APRIL 3 TO 11.

Messina.—Italian Hotels.—How to avoid Disputes.—Shaving at Messina.—The Environs of the Place.—The Camera taken for an Infernal Machine.—The Prison.—Taormina.—View of Etna in Eruption.—The active Craters at Night.—Our Servant.—A Wedding at Taormina.—A truly volcanic Soil.—Linguagrossa.—The Albergo di Etna.—First Ascent of the Mountain.—Our Guides.—The moving Lava.—Destruction of the Forests.—Inquisitiveness of our Guides.—The Brigand Signs 41

CHAPTER III.
APRIL 12 TO MAY.

Linguagrossa.—Second Ascent of Etna.—The Brigand Signs are made to our Guide.—The Snow-line.—The active Craters.—Photography under Difficulties.—My first Adventure with Brigands.—A narrow

Escape.—We change our Plans.—A little Disappointment for the Brigands.—Catania.—Good Friday.—Processions in Southern Italy.—Change at Naples since 1860.—Benedictine Monastery.—Syracuse.—The old Theatre. — The Cathedral. — The Catacombs. — Fruit and Flowers.—Girgenti.—The *Cattiva Gente*.—Kindness of the Consul.—Our Hotel.—The Excavations in the Neighborhood.—Dispute with our Host.—Unexpected Decision of the Referee.—Italian Officers and their Families *en voyage*...................... Page 53

CHAPTER IV.

DIARY OF MRS. MOENS.

Ride from Salerno to Pæstum.—Our Escort.—The Temples.—Forebodings.—"Many a true Word spoken in Jest."—Our Escort deserts us.—The Reason why.—The Brigands at last!—The Capture.—Conduct of the Italian Troops.—The truly Unprotected.—The Village Doctor.—A new Cure for Fright.—Two trying Days for Wives.—Release of one of the Captives.—Mr. Moens retained as a Hostage. 70

CHAPTER V.

DIARY OF MR. MOENS, MAY 15 TO 20.

The Capture.—The first Night's Sleep *al fresco*.—Delicate Attentions.—The Englishmen's Fellow-prisoners.—The Captain commences Business.—Value of Englishmen in Italy.—Choice of Hostage by Lot.—Release of Mr. Aynsley.—Skirmish with the Troops.—I am detached from the Band.—A wet Night in the Mountains.—Brigand Diet.—Two more Fellow-captives.—The Brigands' Dress and Arms.—The Ladies.—Sheep-killing.—Gambling.—The Brigands' Anxiety about my Health.—My Friends Pavone and Scope............................. 84

CHAPTER VI.

DIARY OF MR. MOENS, MAY 20 TO 27.

Brigands merry-making.—The Captain watches over me while I sleep.—His protecting Care.—Thoughts of Home.—A Storm.—The Ladies of the Band.—Doniella.—Carmina. — Maria.—Antonina.—Concetta.—Their Furniture.—They think I am a Milord.—The Government will pay for me.—A Night March.—A terrific Climb.—Method of selecting Sentries.—Threats of Mutilation 114

CHAPTER VII.
Diary of Mr. Moens, May 28.

The second Sunday.—Good News for Visconti.—More Letter-writing —An Attempt at Sketching.—The Englishman's Appetite.—Alarms. —The Soldiers.—A Tradimento.—Death of Luigi.—Thoughts of Escaping.—The drying Process.—Difficulty of Washing.—A wounded Brigandess.—Assistance given by the Peasants to the Brigands.—Description of the Band.—A regular Feed for once in a way.—Pot-luck. —Unpleasant Sleeping-quarters.—Sheep-stealers .... Page 132

CHAPTER VIII.
Diary of Mr. Moens, June 1 to 7.

Wood-carving.—The wounded Girl.—A tantalizing View.—Victims.— The Captives not introduced.—A Thunderbolt.—Rain, Rain.—Three under a Cloak.—Ill Treatment from Cerino's Band.—Their abject fear of Death.—A Blow from Cerino.—Consolation.—New Arrivals.— Screwing up.—A Scrimmage with Generoso.—The greedy Cerino.— An Installment of my Ransom arrives.—The Proposal to the Brigands to leave the Country in an English Ship.—The Lesson of the "Aunis." —What became of the 10,000 francs.—Gambling.—Visconti is appointed my Agent.—Pleasant Position of his Family.—I am the only Captive.—Quarrels.—The *Argumentum Baculinum.*—I am invited to Gamble 151

CHAPTER IX.
Mrs. Moens's Letters, May 17 to June 18.

Return to Naples.—Hôtel de Genève.—The Coppersmiths.—Telegrams to England.—Letters to the Brigand.—Milords or Photographers.—First Letter from the Hostage.—A noble Reply to a Telegram.—The second Letter.—Imprisonment of the Brigand's Relatives.—Arrival of H.M.S. "Magicienne."—Omniscience of the Italian Government.—Sunday in Naples.—Our Message stopped.—The Brigandess's News.—Another Letter from the Hostage.—A second Installment prepared.—Letter to the *Times.*—A Visit from a supposed *Manutengolo.*—I hear of a Friend coming from England.—His Arrival 170

CHAPTER X.

Diary of Mr. Moens, June 7 to 28.

Thieving Propensities of Cerino.—Generoso's Conduct worthy of his Name.—I am again left with five Guardians.—The *Magicienne*.—A Three Days' Rest.—New and very unpleasant Companions.—Small Amount of Washing done in the Mountains.—A long Rest.—Bread Diet.—Its Effect.—A Peasant Visitor.—Wood-carving.—A Message with Letters.—A second Installment and warm Clothing.—I write again.—My new Treasures.—The Luxury of a Comb .... Page 186

CHAPTER XI.

Diary of Mrs. Moens, June 18 to July 31.

The second Installment received.—Scheme to ascertain the Hostage's own Views.—Journey from Salerno to Giffoni.—The Fire-eating Corporal.—Kindness of the Authorities.—An English Letter from the Hostage.—An Attempt to reduce the Ransom.—A third Installment sent to Giffoni.—The Palazzo Serracapriola.—Signora Q.—Her History.—Political Persecution.—The Questor.—His Kindness.—The Press.—The Rigors of the Troops.—The Neapolitan Detective.—Result of the Ladies' secret Scheme.—Life in Ischia.—The Vendetta 202

CHAPTER XII.

Diary of Mr. Moens, June 21 to 30.

On the Move again.—Without excess of Luggage.—The dépôt of Provisions.—We join Cerino's Band again.—Effect of the Arrival of H. M. S. *Magicienne* on the Amount of the Ransom.—A new Hat.—"Brigands supplied" by London Hatters.—The Charcoal-burners.—The Troops again in Sight.—Sheep-stealing.—Meat once a Fortnight.—Scope's Treatment of me.—Pavone's History.—Generoso at Death's Door.—Cold.—I have to Write more terrible Letters.—I am left with Eight or Ten of the Band.—Harsh Treatment.—Tantalizing View.—Wine and Rosolio.—I become very Ill.—Andrea's Heart softens.—Letters from my Friends, but no more Money.—My Ears in Danger.—I am made to Write again.—Cerino's Band go off with the Letters 219

CHAPTER XIII.
Diary of Mr. Moens, July 1 to 17.

Waiting for an Answer.—The Soldiers again.—We Retreat.—How they encouraged me to move on.—A narrow Escape.—News of Giardullo's Capture.—How it was effected.—Gambling again.—I lend my Comb.—Place aux Dames.—Orchard Robbing.—A Meal of Onions.—Pavone steals my Socks.—The Fame of Crocco and Borjès.—Telescopes.—Sheep-stealing.—Another Night Walk.—I write more Letters.—Guange offends Manzo.—Manzo enforces Discipline.—Feeling of the Band toward him.—Scarcity of Water.—Sentonio's Water-bottle.—Mysterious Disappearance of the Contents.—Lorenzo physics himself.—I am threatened by all.—I think seriously of cutting my Ears myself.—Proposal to Emigrate under my Leadership.................................Page 240

CHAPTER XIV.
Diary of Mr. Moens, July 17 to 22.

A good View of the Country.—A real live Wolf.—A good Omen.—Striking a Light with a Percussion Cap.—A Brigand Bivouac.—Cooking Scene.—The first Whisper of a Reduction in the Ransom.—Pasquale's kind Advice to the Captain.—Manzo leaves me again.—Scope's Gun goes off.—I venture to chaff him.—A fair Challenge.—His Revenge.—Visitors from Giardullo's Band.—Their Adventures.—Manzo's Return.—A Skirmish with the Soldiers.—The Band is divided.—Awkward Position of my Party.—I am in great Danger.—Thoughts of Escape.—I hesitate to kill two Sleeping Men 260

CHAPTER XV.
Diary of Mr. Moens, July 22 to 31.

My Guardians are without Money.—A bad Look-out.—My Penknife put to a new Use.—Meat and Fuel, but no Fire.—Necessity is the Mother of Invention.—The Attack of the Soldiers explained.—Failure when Success seemed certain.—Scarcity of Water.—An Attempt at Bribery.—A cheerless Spot.—They play me a shabby Trick.—Manzo arrives again.—An Abode assigned to me for the next Fortnight.—Traces of Giardullo's precious Tenancy.—An Attempt at Washing.—No Food for three Days.—A little raw rancid Fat.—A Bone.—I feed in a decidedly canine Manner.—Two more days without Food.—I am at the last Extremity.—Great Hardships.—Manzo joins us again.—I write once more at his Dictation.—Cerino's Discomfiture.................Page 279

CHAPTER XVI.
DIARY OF MR. MOENS, JULY 31 TO AUGUST 22.

Illness of Scope, my Bête Noir.—Starvation threatens again.—Scarcity of Water again.—The Brigands observe Fast-days.—Their religious Feelings.—Their Respect for my Talents.—Fearful State to which I was reduced.—The Soldiers once more.—We leave the Cave.—A Meal of Mutton and Potatoes.—I am sent away to meet Manzo.—In sight of Acerno again.—Rigors practiced by the Troops on the Peasantry. —Hard Work of the Women.—I hear that 6000 Ducats have been received.—Prospects of Freedom.—Antonio's new Suit.—More Gambling.—Two Days we live on Apples.—All the Money had at last.— Manzo's Behavior.—Division of the Spoil................................ 298

CHAPTER XVII.
DIARY OF MRS. MOENS, JULY 31 TO AUGUST 25.

News from the Band.—A Visit from Talarico.—*Otium cum dig.* after an honorable Career.—Talarico's Advice to the Captive's Wife.—His chivalrous Offer.—The five Brigands at Visconti's.—The last Letter from the Captive.—Reduction of the Brigands' Claim.—A gallant Priest.—Another Visit to General Balegno.—His Kindness.—Intense Excitement when the Ransom was all Paid.—Suspense.—Free at last. —Joy too deep for Words.. 313

CHAPTER XVIII.
DIARY OF MR. MOENS, *Concluded:* AUGUST 24 TO 26.

The sudden Reduction of the Ransom accounted for.—The Soldiers rather too near.—I am still in imminent Danger.—Manzo goes round with the Hat for me.—Parting Civilities.—Interchange of Gifts.—Pasquale's Generosity.—Pavone is affectionate.—I bid him a fond Adieu.—One more Night in the Woods.—Arrival of Tedesco, my Guide.—Manzo's Mother.—My parting Advice to Manzo.—My elegant Appearance.— Kindness of the Peasants.—Crosses on the Mountains.—In sight of Giffoni.—My Reception there.—Kindness of the Visconti Family.— Arrival of my Wife at Giffoni.—We return together to Salerno.... 323

CHAPTER XIX.
REFLECTIONS ON BRIGANDAGE: SOUTHERN ITALY.

The Ransom all paid to the Band.—No other Persons participate directly.—The exorbitant Prices charged for Food.—The Peasants the real Gainers.—Manutengoli.—The real Causes of the Success of Brigandage.—The Roots to be eradicated.—Measures proposed........Page 339

APPENDIX.

A. Notice posted up in the Hotel Vittoria, Salerno. .... Page 347
B. The Dangers of **Signor Visconti's** position 347
C. Reply from the Prefect of Salerno to the Inquiry whether his Government would pay any of the Ransom—addressed to Mrs. Moens.. 348
D. **Translation** of Signor Visconti's Letter to Mrs. Moens 348
E. **Translation** of Manzo's **Letter** to Signor Visconti 349
F. Were the Brigands connected with **Francis II. ?**...................... 349
G. A **Brigand Song** 350
H. **Letter** from the Captive to his Wife, dictated verbatim by Manzo 352
I. Letter by a celebrated Brigand Chief to Manzo **in behalf of the Captive**... 353
K. Copy of Manzo's Receipt, and Translation 353
L. Names of Brigands arrested, tried, and shot in 1865 in the Provinces of Salerno.. 354
M. The Names of the **Manutengoli who were arrested in 1865** 354
N. Number of Soldiers in **the two Provinces in March** and April, 1865 355
   Ditto in July and August... 355
O. Names of **Persons seized and held to Ransom in 1865 by Manzo** and Giardullo, and Amounts of **Ransom demanded and paid**... 355

LIST OF ILLUSTRATIONS.

PORTRAIT OF THE AUTHOR... *Frontispiece.*
MAP, SHOWING THE AUTHOR'S WANDERINGS WITH THE BRIGANDS .... *to face Preface.*
THE BASILICA AND TEMPLE OF NEPTUNE, PÆSTUM .... Page 72
THE CAPTURE AT BATTIPAGLIA 75
GAETANO MANZO 85
THE FIGHT WITH THE SOLDIERS ON MONTE CORVINO 92
GIARDULLO DI PESTO.. 243
BIVOUAC AT NIGHT NEAR CAMPAGNA 288

ENGLISH TRAVELERS
AND
ITALIAN BRIGANDS.

CHAPTER I.
JANUARY TO APRIL.

Palermo.—Traveling Companions.—Lovers of Art.—The Catacombs.—Monte Pelegrino.—News of the Eruption of Etna.—Domestic Manners of the Sicilians.—The Priests.—The Bombardment in 1860.—The Vendetta.—The Monasteries.—The Grand Cemetery.—Expedition to Monte Pelegrino and its Caverns.—Sicilian Brigands.—The Way the Palermitans manage these Things.—Storm at Sea.—The Fishermen.—Victor Emmanuel's Government.—A Scientific Monk.—The Value of Sympathy.—The Tunny Fishery.—The Campo Santo.—Manner of Burial.—Great Mortality among Children.—More about Sicilian Brigandage.

Palermo, January 15. On the 12th of January, 1865, we reached Palermo, after a quick passage of only forty-eight hours from Marseilles. The change from the fog and snow we left at Paris to this warm June weather is delightful. I feel my winter clothing quite oppressive, and my husband has discarded his great-coat.

Our voyage was a very pleasant one; the passengers on board the steamer were mostly Americans, very amusing and sociable; and the sea was so calm and smooth that we spent the greater part of the time on deck. The food and accommodation on board were excellent, though our last breakfast of black pudding, pigs' pettitoes, thrushes and blackbirds, was not very tempting.

I had long conversations with some American ladies from Philadelphia, who made my blood boil by the way in which they spoke of England and the English; they considered that a very few months would now decide the war; the Southern rebellion would then be crushed, and slavery be at an end. The North was fighting in a holy cause; they had put off the war too long, and Heaven had justly punished them by making it so terrible a one, etc., etc.

On our way we steamed past Caprera, a barren-looking rock, with Garibaldi's English yacht lying at anchor near his abode.

The Bay of Palermo is more lovely to my taste than the far-famed Bay of Naples. I stood at the head of the vessel as we approached the red and stupendous precipices of Monte Pelegrino, the city, with its campanile towers and churches, surrounded by its amphitheatre of mountains, coming slowly in sight as we rounded the corner of the bay. Mount Etna, though one hundred miles off, was plainly visible, its summit entirely covered with a glittering robe of snow.

I felt unpleasantly excited as the boats came round the vessel to carry our luggage to the Dogana, for we began to have serious doubts about our chance of obtaining rooms at the Hotel Trinacria (the best in the place), especially when we heard that the Americans had telegraphed from Marseilles for apartments.

One of these (an old man, shunned by his fellow-countrymen) landed with us. Both he and his old Scotch servant were characters: the master was very wealthy, having just amassed a large fortune at the oil springs, but he was as dirty and shabby as his servant, and that is saying a good deal,

and neither could speak a word of any language but **their own.** Their **first** intention on starting for their travels had been to go **to** Jerusalem, but, falling in with the American party on board, they had accompanied them to Palermo. The Scotchman seemed terribly upset by the change of plans, his imagination had been so excited by the idea **of** visiting the Holy Land. I pitied the poor old man, who looked wretchedly thin and ill; his master seemed to begrudge every penny he spent on him, and ordered him about as if **he had** been a boy of fifteen. He was generally to be seen sitting, a woe-begone image of patience, on the luggage, which consisted of three old carpet bags. He certainly had no greater appreciation of the fine arts than his **master, who** was once overheard telling Robert to go into the **Capitol** at Rome to see if there were any thing there that would repay him for the trouble of visiting it. He went, but returned in a few minutes, saying, "There's naething but a wheen naked men and women, sir, and I'm sure you've seen eneuch o' *them* lately; ye canna want to see ony mair." Robert's opinion was sufficient for his master, who did not even enter to look at the most celebrated statues in the world.

January 28. My husband's great amusement is in finding **out and wandering** over old churches. To-day I have been **sitting with him among some** very fine cloisters, dating from **the 12th century, which have lately been discovered. We** had to ascend to them **through houses, as** they had been entirely built up and concealed **by a high** wall; this wall having given way, the beautiful pillars were unveiled to view, and the cloisters are now all clear and open. We spent **some** hours there, enjoying the delicious balmy air, which is much **softer and** warmer than at Nice, or even at Mentone. I had a long **conversation** with the wife of the *custode* while W—— was climbing **over the old walls.** With the help of two men, who held a ladder supported on crumbling stones, he took some very good pictures. Yesterday I went down into the catacombs of the Capuchin convent; it was a sickening, horrible sight; we passed through long, narrow rooms, dimly lighted by windows high up in the walls. The walls are covered with shelves, on which are placed glass cases containing the dried and shrunken forms of men, women, and children, richly arrayed in ball-dresses, with wreaths of flowers around their fallen temples, and white shoes and gloves on their shriveled hands and feet. The bodies of men, suspended by the waist, hang round the vaults; ghastly rows of priests, in full canonicals, with their servants by their sides. The inferior station in life of the latter was denoted, even after death, by the rope round their necks. I clung to my husband's arm as we walked slowly through the ghastly place, startling the cats, which rushed from under the shelves in every direction as we approached.

What a sermon this scene silently preached to us! Can we believe that, in a few short years, we may present as revolting an appearance as these horrible grinning figures? The picture is too terrible to dwell upon. It is, indeed, in mercy and in wisdom that Scripture says, "Bury thy dead out of thy sight," consoling us, at the same time, with the assurance that "the spirit shall return to God who gave it."

W—— is never weary of his photography; all our fellow-travelers envy him this amusement. I sometimes pity them as I see them lounging idly about, while time passes only too quickly with us.

January 29. To-day, being Sunday, we were present at the English service, held in a large room at the consul's. The congregation numbered about one hundred. After church we walked in the botanical gardens, which are very lovely with their palm-trees and other tropical vegetation.

We sat and looked at the blue mountains towering in the distance.

A day or two ago we had a delightful expedition up Mount Pelegrino, to see a large natural cavern in the limestone rock: at the end of the cavern, in the darkest corner, stands an altar, under which, inclosed within a gilded grating, is the marble figure of St. Rosalie, represented as a lovely girl of fifteen, in a dress of solid gold, ornamented with precious stones. It was a striking scene—the dark damp grotto, the water slowly trickling from the roof, and the overhanging ferns, forming a contrast to the marble statue with its glittering ornaments, protected from spoliation by the veneration of the people. Once a year there is a grand procession of all Palermo to this shrine, St. Rosalie being the patron saint of the city.

January 30. We have just heard that an eruption of Mount Etna has broken out. A crater has opened at the north of the *Val del Bove*, in the district called Concazze, and the lava is steadily creeping down the declivity, destroying trees and vineyards. Etna is almost entirely covered with snow.

February 12. The Hotel Trinacria is most comfortable, and the landlord, Ragusa, very attentive. He is most particular about the people whom he admits to his table d'hôte. One Sicilian was turned away because, to my great disgust, he expectorated incessantly while sitting opposite to me at table. This filthy habit is common to all ranks in the island, from the nobleman to the lazaroni. An English friend of ours had basins placed all round her room, with this inscription, "*Qui si sputa.*" The Sicilians and English associate very little together. The latter complain that the former are such a narrow-minded set; they think there is no place in the world like Sicily, and no people to be compared to the Sicilians. The English colony at Palermo is composed of bankers, merchants, and exporters of Marsala wine. They are very amiable and hospitable, and some of them immensely wealthy.

The English clergyman called on us yesterday, and told us a great deal about the priests; some of them, whom he knew very intimately, were highly educated men, who had traveled a great deal, but were still most contracted in their ideas. He told me it was difficult to argue with them, as their education from childhood ran entirely in one groove, certainly not the Baconian one. They start from the old axioms of the fathers—every idea that runs counter to theirs must be wrong. A boy destined for the priesthood is placed in a seminary while still almost an infant, and taught to view every thing through the one-sided medium of a strictly theological education. I wish the Church of England would open a school here. It would be permitted by the Italian government. Why should we be behind the Scotch and the French, who are working away hard in the cause of education?

We visited the museum the other day, and saw some beautiful metopes, carved stones from the tops of temples built five hundred years before the birth of our Savior. There was a lovely statue, too, of Hercules as a young boy. We then went over the Observatory, where there is, among others, a magnificent telescope just arrived from Berlin. Two astronomers were hard at work. It must be a labor of love to watch the brilliant stars in the deep blue Sicilian sky!

January is considered the best spring month here; the thermometer in our room is at 60°; and we called yesterday on a lady who picked for me in her garden a lovely bouquet of roses, carnations, and heliotropes.

The Marina, the fashionable promenade of Palermo, about half a mile long, is crowded every afternoon with gay equipages. The Italians outvie one another in the gaudiness and bad taste of their carriages. I often think it a pity that the lord-mayor's and the sheriffs' state carriages, or that of the Speaker of the House of Commons, can not appear here. They certainly would be looked upon with envy, and create a very great sensation. My English friends tell me that many of the owners of these gay carriages have not a decent room to receive a friend in, and that some of the splendidly-dressed ladies would be sadly embarrassed were a visitor to call upon them in the morning, as neither they nor their houses are then fit to be seen. No one dare venture beyond the gates of the city for fear of the brigands, so their drive is a very limited one—about two miles and a half up and down the town and the Marina. It gives me a fit of *ennui* to look at the paraders, who seem to sacrifice every thing for the sake of a little display in public.

I scarcely wonder at an earnest-minded man, or woman either, retiring in disgust from the hollow worldliness of such society, and seeking a refuge in some religious house; though, perhaps too often, alas! destined to find more hollowness there than they leave behind in the world which wearies them.

One thing often astonishes me—why the inhabitants suffer themselves to be prisoners in their town. Why do they not spend some of their surperfluous time and money in clearing their environs from the brigands who infest them?*

We spent an evening with the English consul. He was most kind and hospitable, and we thoroughly enjoyed his English tea and his English fireplace. He told us some in-

* When I wrote this, I little thought how deeply interested I was fated to become in the subject of brigands.

B

teresting stories of the siege of Palermo, by Garibaldi, in 1860. He was the only Englishman who remained in the town during the bombardment.

He one day received letters from two abbesses, begging him to come and see the mischief that had been done to their convents by the shells and shot during the storming of the town, that he might report it to the Queen of England, and ask her for redress. The consul was delighted at the invitation, as it gave him an opportunity of seeing the interior of the convents.

The religious houses occupy the best situations in the town, and it will be the greatest possible benefit to Palermo when they are all suppressed, as they infallibly will be some day. There are 10,000 monks and nuns in Palermo! There is a great want of good houses in the place, and I am not the least surprised at cholera breaking out among the overcrowded, ill-ventilated habitations. I was horrified to see the places where the children grow up; the streets are high and narrow, and there are neither back windows nor doors to the houses, ventilation being entirely disregarded. Among the deaths in the obituary, half are those of children; and poor people will generally tell you that they have lost five or six children by fever. The shopkeepers pass their time lounging at their shop doors, scarcely caring to serve a customer, and not taking the trouble to bring him different articles for selection. You must point to the shelves for what you want, and then they hesitate about taking down the article.

February 26. The weather for the last month has been wet and stormy—for one week it rained incessantly; yesterday was clear and bright, and we walked five miles off toward Bagaria, to a cliff to gather fossil shells. We quite enjoyed being able to leave the hotel. Our Italian lessons, which we have been taking three times a week, are a great resource to us; but we find it very difficult to understand the Sicilian dialect, which is a mixture of Arabic, French, Spanish, and Italian. All the Italian o's are turned into u's, and the first or last half of the word is clipped according to the fancy of the speaker.

Our Italian master described to us a scene he had witnessed yesterday, which strongly illustrates the Italian character. He was in a church, where lay on a bier the body of a murdered man; the widow was kneeling by its side, with her little child of three years old in her arms. After a burst of frantic weeping she joined the child's hands together, and made him repeat after her a solemn oath to the effect that when he grew up he would take deadly vengeance on the murderer's nearest relative. She ended by a solemn and fearful curse on the child should he fail to keep the vow he had taken over the dead body of his father. It is this spirit of revenge which makes it difficult to bring a malefactor to justice; no one will assist in convicting him for fear of the punishment that so doing might entail on the informer or his nearest relatives.*

March 13. We are beginning to prepare for the *giro*; two or three parties have already started, who will prepare the way for us. The party at the table d'hôte diminishes daily. We have had travelers from all parts of the world; last week some Brazilians arrived, who assured us that there is no scenery to be compared to that of Rio de Janeiro. Yesterday a Canadian sat by me at dinner, and told me that he was mortified at finding that the English knew so little of his country. One English lady had actually asked him if the Mississippi did not run through Canada! He will go

* For instances of the length to which the *vendetta* is carried in the Mediterranean, Murray's Corsica may be consulted.

back and declare that Englishwomen are so ignorant—a contrary opinion to that entertained by Italians, who have, generally speaking, **a high** respect for our countrywomen, on account of their **superior education.**

March 16. **How interesting to observe the** wonderful diversity of opinions on religious matters! One lady told me not long ago that Rome was a sink of iniquity—a collection of whited sepulchres; and yesterday another, who has joined the Church of Rome, gave me as a reason for her conversion that she had seen Rome, and that was enough, for it was impossible to resist the influence of a place so calm, so holy, so full of prayer!

Yesterday we sailed across the bay to see the stratum of fossil shells in the face of the cliffs exposed to the wearing of the sea; we collected numbers of them of different kinds. **We then** walked to an old monastery, **but** the monks would **not admit** me, though I said to them in "what I am pleased to think" my best manner, "Non posso far male." They were very polite, however, and brought me a present **of citrons and limes.** Many rich **Sicilians are buried** in large pits here, **into which the body is lowered by the monks;** quicklime **is thrown over it, and in two or three days it** is consumed. I read the inscriptions of many monumental tablets, but not one contained a text from Scripture. How thick a darkness broods over the Roman religion, as professed by the lower orders in Southern Italy and Sicily, owing to the Bible—the true source of light—being **so carefully kept from them** by the priests! The grand burying-place of noble Sicilian ladies **is within the walls of a** nunnery in the town. **The corpse is conveyed** thither and given into the hands of the nuns, **who dress it in the habit of their order,** and then place it in their church, where it can be seen **for some** hours through the windows. It is then buried in the ground attached to the convent, to which no one is ever admitted. A Sicilian friend of ours told us that he had lost his mother two months ago. He and his brother, though poor, determined to show her every respect, and collected a sufficient sum to bury her in this place. We had a very interesting conversation with this gentleman on religious matters; he spoke very bitterly of the priests. We sent him our Prayer-book to read—he returned it with many expressions of admiration at the simple and "soothing" beauty of our services.

March 18. We have settled to make the *giro* of the island in about ten days. We hear a great deal of brigands, and are told that all the peasants carry guns, and the country round Palermo is in a most unsettled state; but Ragusa and the English consul assure us that we can go with perfect safety, as four ladies, unaccompanied by a gentleman, have just performed the tour. Before taking the grand tour, we intend making a small one round Monte Pelegrino.

March 20. Yesterday was beautifully fine. We stepped on to our balcony, saw that Monte Pelegrino stood out clearly against the blue sky, and made up our minds to start on an expedition at half past ten o'clock. I descended to the door of the hotel minus crinoline, expecting to mount a donkey there, but I found it was not considered *comme il faut* to ride through the town, so we had half an hour's row to the other side of the bay, where the animals were waiting for us. To reach Monte Pelegrino, which presents to the sea a bare precipitous face about 2000 feet high, we had to cross first a carriage-road, and then some fields, thickly planted with beautiful trees. The lowest slopes of the mountain are covered with spurge—there a full low shrub of a lovely green—and cacti with stems as thick as those of our fruit-trees. The road ends close by the English

cemetery. There is then only a rough bridle-path, and the
mountain seems advancing into the sea. All is rugged and
wild—no trees, no shrubs, nothing but masses of bare rock.
As might be expected, I was nervous about brigands, and
my heart bounded when I saw some men with guns advancing to us. However, they were only inoffensive sports-
men, and I could concentrate all my attention again on my
donkey, which stumbled at every step. We soon rounded
the point, and a lovely bay was spread out before us, with
high mountains in the distance, and a smooth turf beneath
us. We by-and-by came to a large flock of sheep and goats,
and the fierce dogs guarding them rushed out upon us.

The view here was exquisite, but I could not stay to enjoy it, for we saw perched high up on the side of the precipice the cave which was the principal object of our expedition. We dismounted, and began climbing the side of the
mountain. It was hard work, as the ground was covered
with large, loose stones, overgrown by creepers. W——
wanted first to examine a lower cave, but as we approached
it a huge dog sprang out at the entrance, and growled
fiercely at us. I steadily refused to face the enemy, and,
after a little dispute, of course had my own way, and recommenced climbing vigorously, holding on tight to the end of
W——'s umbrella. We heard some one calling loudly to
us, but could not understand what was said. A tall, handsome man, clothed in sheepskin, with the wool outside, soon
joined us, and offered to lead us to the cave by an easier
path. We soon reached it, and were well repaid for our
exertions. The arch of the cave was an enormous span
of I know not how many feet, and about 800 feet high.
Through a small opening at the top we could see the clear
blue sky, with two large eagles floating in it. Great stalac-
tites were hanging from the roof, and the sides of the cave

were tapestried with beautiful creepers and light green spurge. The blue sea was spread before us, and it was long before I could think of any thing but the beauty of the scene on which I was feasting my eyes.

I was startled by the sudden apparition of another man with a gun. Our guide, divining my thoughts, introduced him as "only my companion." We sat down to eat the few biscuits we had brought with us. This seemed to excite the compassion of our guides, for they immediately offered to lead us to *their* cave, which they did with tender care, breaking down all the creepers in my path, and making the way as smooth for me as possible. They placed rough seats for us, covered with their cloaks, and, spreading a pocket-handkerchief as a table-cloth, laid out upon it a loaf of bread and a kind of scalded cream called *racotta*. They entreated us to eat, and we sat by the fire enjoying the scene, surrounded by the four dogs and two men, who talked very readily to us. They remarked with wonder my complexion and W——'s as being so very different from their own. They told us they were shepherds, and this cave was their home. At last, with great regret, we left them, thanking them for their hospitality, and leaving the money, which they refused to take from us, on their pails. We then returned to our donkeys, and, riding through La Favorita (the king's gardens), reached our hotel about five o'clock. We brought away with us a few fossil teeth and small bones with which these caves abound. W—— employed two men a few days ago to dig up an enormous shoulder-blade for him, but it broke and cut his finger badly. The cut has since festered, which has damped his ardor in collecting fossil bones.

March. My fears were not unfounded. The day after our expedition, on the very road we had traversed with such pleasure and security, a Sicilian gentleman, driving with a friend, was carried off by brigands. He was quite close to the town, when a break with two horses drove swiftly past him, turned sharply round, and drew up right across the road, stopping his carriage. Eight men with guns jumped from the break, surrounded the carriage, and carried off the Cavaliere Guccia, telling the friend, whom they mistook for a servant, to return to Palermo and procure a certain sum for his master's ransom. The papers took scarcely any notice of this affair. They merely mentioned that Signor Guccia was sequestered by *malfattori*. He was liberated in a few days, either by payment of the ransom or through the interest of some rich proprietor said to have power over the band. I made many inquiries, but the whole affair was soon hushed up, and I could obtain but little information.

The indifference displayed rather shocked our English notions. I could not help thinking of the storm of indignation that would be excited in England were any gentleman in North Devon or Wales, or even in Ireland, to be unceremoniously separated from his family, and forced to pay half, or perhaps all his fortune, to be restored to them. These atrocious affairs seem to be matters of every-day occurrence here. Only a few weeks ago another case occurred (not mentioned by the newspapers), in which I was so much interested that I used to go almost daily to the consul's to hear if the poor man had regained his liberty. A Signor Salemi, returning from Monte Maggiore, near Bagaria, had gone two or three miles, attended by two *bordenari* in front, and his own armed servant behind, all on horseback. They were stopped by twenty armed horsemen. The two *bordenari* were allowed to escape, but Salemi and his man were blindfolded and taken half an hour's march into the country.

The man was then sent back with a message that 1500 ounces, or £750, were required by the band. Madame Salemi the next day collected half the amount, which was returned to her with a message that it was not sufficient. In a fortnight the required sum was procured. It was received, counted over, and a receipt sent back by the brigands. The next morning, at daybreak, Signor Salemi was placed in the middle of a field, blindfolded, and commanded not to remove the bandage until a signal was given. When he took it off he did not know where he was; but, seeing a cottage at a distance, he went to it and roused the inmates. They gave him food and a bed, and in the afternoon he was taken to Monte Maggiore. He was so weak that he could hardly stand, as they had given him nothing to eat but bread, herbs, and water. He had lived entirely in the open air, and was kept blindfolded the whole time.*

We have had several thunder-storms; and sometimes I get nervous about earthquakes, for Monte Cuccio, the highest mountain here, is an extinct volcano. At times rumblings and groans are heard, making one feel that it may break out at any moment. Yesterday there was a change in the appearance of the sky; a mist hung over the sea, gray as the heavens, but all was still and calm when the

* During the six months from January to June, several other gentlemen have been taken in the neighborhood of Palermo, and among them Signor Bergami, a most respected corn-broker, and a good friend to all the peasants, who was taken four miles from Palermo. When the brigands surrounded him Bergami drew his revolver, which missed fire, but at the same instant one of the thieves thrust at him with a dagger, wounding him in two places. That was the extent of the mischief done in his case, for the police turned up at this moment, causing the thieves to run away. Scarcely a week passed without a fresh instance, but not one fourth of the cases are ever heard of. It is only when a man of note is taken that any fuss is made.—W. I. C. M.

fishing-boats went out as usual in the afternoon. We were walking down the street, when there came on such a gale that we were forced to rush home immediately. We saw from our windows a most exciting scene: the sea was covered with enormous waves; all the little vessels were trying to come into the harbor; it seemed impossible for them to live in such a storm. The poor fishers' wives and children assembled on the beach, watching with fearful anxiety each tiny little bark. I was thankful when they one by one got into port, and the poor women went home rejoicing over the safety of their husbands and sons. A French Admiral Fitzroy had written to warn the fishermen of this coming Levanter, as these sudden storms are called, but they, too, like many of our own maritime and fishing population, are so self-willed that they gave no heed to the warning, and the storm found them unprepared.

It was the king's birthday a day or two ago; flags were hung out, but there was a very poor illumination. It is no great wonder if his government be not popular among the poor, as so many new taxes have been levied, and the young men are taken away for two years to serve in the army, though the last arrangement is greatly to their advantage, for they are kindly treated, taught to read and write, and to hold themselves erect. They see, too, a little of the world beyond the boundaries of their own town and village, and return to their homes, at all events, with less contracted notions than when they left them.

March 30. The storm has changed the weather; it is lovely to-day, and very hot. The thermometer is at 70° in my room. My husband has been out all day at Monreale, a beautiful old monastery, built in the year 1182 by William of Sicily, and Joanna, sister to our Richard Cœur-de-Lion. He has been taking photographs of the cloisters. I did not go with him, as no women are allowed to pass the gates of the monastery. The monks, of the Benedictine order, all belong to noble families. They lead any thing but a secluded life, as they keep carriages in which they drive about Palermo, and they take in all the newspapers, etc. They invited W—— to dinner. The wine, grown in their own vineyards, was, like the other constituents of the dinner, excellent. One monk, a very handsome, intellectual man, became a great friend of my husband's. One day I went up to Monreale, where I was introduced to him. We had a long conversation together, in the course of which he told me he never regretted becoming a monk. I asked him if he ever suffered from *ennui*. "No, never. I am constantly occupied when not engaged in the offices of religion. I employ my time in constructing a steam-engine, a machine to fly through the air, etc.; but this is a great secret, for not one of my brother monks knows of it." Happy man! to be so contented. I often think, with Goethe, that the happiest man is the cobbler, who sings at his work.

A titled English lady is working hard here, doing all the good she can, and trying to persuade the Sicilian ladies to visit their poor sisters, who have to struggle with poverty, sickness, and, too often also, with unkind and cruel husbands, and ungrateful children. Oh, if women only knew how often, by a gentle word of sympathy, a disheartened, broken spirit might be soothed, an embittered, overburdened heart softened, nay, even a soul rescued from despair, and strengthened to struggle again with renewed vigor in the hard battle of life! Hundreds in this world hunger and thirst after this little help, which could be afforded them with ease if women would but feel

"A sense of an earnest will
To help the lowly living.

And a terrible heart-thrill
If you have no power of giving;
An arm of aid to the weak,
A friendly hand to the friendless,
Kind words, so short to speak,
But whose echo is endless"—

noble words, in which rings an echo of the feeling that inspired the Preacher when he told the whole world that "Heaviness in the heart of man maketh it stoop, but a good word maketh it glad."

March 31. Palermo is like an Oriental town. The shops are open and without windows, and you may see the tailors, shoemakers, tinmen, etc., plying their several crafts almost in the open air. For nearly a month they have been selling strawberries, green peas, etc., in the streets. The climate far surpasses my expectations; it is exquisite, and so is the scenery. The only drawback is the difficulty of getting into the country, but this does not seem to trouble the inhabitants. No one, not even the cobbler's wife, walks. The great amusement of all is to be driven slowly up and down the town, which can be done for fivepence. They are all astonished at our English love of exercise. We started the other day to walk round Monte Pelegrino, but got caught in a heavy shower of rain at the little fishing village of Virgine Maria. The peasants asked us into a cottage about twelve feet wide, and very long, half filled with the tunny nets they were making and preparing for the arrival of the tunny fish in April.

The large nets are made of grass spun into the thickest string, which they net without needle or mesh, simply twisting it round their fingers. The nets, when set, extend for nearly a mile—sometimes farther. The tunny fish, which is a perfect monster of the deep, something like the porpoise in shape, and from four to eight feet long, is driven from chamber to chamber in the nets till it enters the *corpo*, or chamber of death. When the captives are all collected there, the work of death commences; all the boats of the fishermen for miles round, with much formality at first, but soon in indescribable confusion, surround the fish and slaughter them by hundreds with their spears, till fish, boats, and men are all half smothered with blood. We were told that it was one of the most horrid spectacles that could be witnessed.

On our way home we passed the Campo Santo, or common burial-place of the town. There is a sufficient number of vaults to allow of one being opened every other day. The dead, to the number of twenty or thirty (in a town of 200,000 inhabitants), are collected every day, and at twenty-two o'clock, or two hours before sunset, they are thrown in; quick-lime is scattered over them, and the vault sealed up till its turn comes round again in a year. We met several bodies being carried on the way to their long home. The coffins are not shaped like ours, but are simply oblong boxes, sometimes black, but generally red and green, with colored effigies of saints painted on them.

Half the deaths are among very young children. You may constantly see a man walking along very quickly with a small red oblong box slung behind his shoulders by a piece of cord; he reaches the dead-house, puts the box down outside the door, opens the lid, and takes the body carelessly out. If it has clothing on worth any thing, the attendant harpies seize it as their spoil, and then throw the corpse on the ground, while the box is carried back by the man who brought it. We saw one body being carried in a black sedan-chair by two men, who, before going up a little hill, left the body in the middle of the road while they went into a wine-shop to drink. After the dead are taken from their homes, the relatives never see them; there is no service read over them; the priest simply sprinkles the bodies with holy water before they are flung down a hole two feet square into the vault beneath, in a few hours after which lime resolves them into their primary elements.

The English burial-ground joins the Campo Santo, but is very different. It is filled with flowers, ornamental trees and shrubs, with a large stone opposite the gateway, on which are inscribed texts from the Holy Scriptures in English and Italian. The monuments, with their words of holy comfort and hope, give a very different impression to that of the Italian ones, where one never reads any thing but a long catalogue of the virtues, real or imaginary, of those to whose memory they are erected.

March 29. We intend starting for our *giro* to-morrow. Many of our friends have advised us not to go; others tell us that it is quite safe, as English people are never taken; but when I ask them "would you go?" they seem to think that is quite another affair. As I mentioned before, neither the rich Sicilians nor the English residents dare drive half a mile out of the town. I do not know why the tourists and people belonging to the hotels are safe. I sometimes think the hotel-keepers pay black mail to the brigands. The people stopping with us at the Trinacria took long expeditions over the mountains, and were never molested. W—— and I take long walks into the country and always return safe—a thing no Sicilian would do. The gardener of the Palazzo Serra di Falco told us that his mistress rarely came now to see the garden, in which she had formerly taken such delight, though it is not more than a quarter of an hour's drive from the town!

We were told the other day the story of the capture of

Mr. ——, an English merchant, two or three years ago. He was driving with his daughter about a mile from Palermo, when the carriage was suddenly surrounded by six men, who threatened to shoot him if he did not get out of the carriage quietly and go with them. He pretended at first not to understand them, and spoke to them in English; but they said "it is no use trying to deceive us; you can speak Sicilian quite as well as we can, Mr. ——; come with us directly." He, seeing resistance was useless, went with them, leaving his daughter in the carriage with the coachman, surrounded by men who kept pointing their guns at them if they dared to move. The bandits dragged poor Mr. ——, who is a large, stout man, over walls, fields, and ditches, until at last he fell through fatigue, and said he would go no farther. They then all sat down, and began steadily bargaining with him for his ransom. He was to sign a paper for £1000, but this he positively refused to do. They then asked £500, which he declared he would not give; then £200, and at last it was settled that he should bring £50 himself on the following morning, and deposit it on a certain stone in a field which they pointed out to him. He was then allowed to depart, after solemnly promising that the money should be forthcoming. Poor Miss —— sat in the mean time in the carriage in the most terrible anxiety, crying bitterly. The brigands hid themselves behind the wall, on the top of which the muzzles of their guns could be seen pointing at the carriage. She did not dare drive on, as the brigands told her if she did so it would be at the peril of her life. A priest and some other men passed, but took no notice of her. At last a cart drove up with several men armed with guns sitting in it. They stopped and asked Miss —— why she was in such distress. She told her sad story, and they advised her to drive home directly, as it was dangerous for her to stay outside the town. She tried to persuade them to follow the brigands and to rescue her father; but this they steadily refused to do. They kept entreating her to drive on, but she said she dared not do so, as the guns of the brigands were still pointing at her. She wanted to point out the guns to these men, but they immediately hushed her with gestures of great alarm, and drove away. She at last, summoning up courage to follow their advice, drove swiftly back to the town, to carry the sad news to her family; the soldiers immediately turned out and scoured the country. Mr. —— returned in the evening. Many men were taken up on suspicion and thrown into prison. Mr. —— was asked to go and try to identify them: this was endangering his own life, however; for, had he been the instrument of their conviction, their relations would have shot him; so he declared he knew none of them, and they were consequently released. In a few days several men called on Mr. —— to thank him, and his watch was returned to him.

CHAPTER II.
APRIL 3 TO 11.

Messina.—Italian Hotels.—How to avoid Disputes.—Shaving at Messina.—The Environs of the Place.—The Camera taken for an Infernal Machine.—The Prison.—Taormina.—View of Etna in Eruption.—The active Craters at Night.—Our Servant.—A Wedding at Taormina.—A truly volcanic Soil.—Linguagrossa.—The Albergo di Etna.—First Ascent of the Mountain.—Our Guides.—The moving Lava.—Destruction of the Forests.—Inquisitiveness of our Guides.—The Brigand Signs.

Messina, April 3. WE got very tired of Palermo, and as the weather was so bad that it was useless to attempt the *giro* along the roads, we took the steamer at five o'clock one afternoon, and arrived here at six o'clock the following morning. It has been raining hard to-day. We seem persecuted by bad weather, as in March it rained for twenty-four consecutive days. Our hotel (the Trinacria again) is comfortable, and the charges very moderate—twenty francs a day, including servants and candles, a sitting-room and bedroom. We settled the prices with the landlord before we agreed to remain. The only way to get on at the Italian hotels is to bargain beforehand. Those who pay the price demanded are despised as well as imposed upon.

This town is quite a modern one, as it has been frequently destroyed both by earthquakes and bombardments. It is now a thriving sea-port, full of life and activity; nearly all the steamers trading in the Mediterranean put into the harbor, which is sheltered by a strip of land in the shape of a crescent. The view across the straits, with the mountains of Calabria in the distance, is charming, and I am never tired of watching from my window the animated groups collected round the fine fountain on the opposite side of the road. Above the fountain is a colossal statue of Neptune, calm and majestic, looking as if he had just risen from his watery realm. His large beard is dripping, and at his feet, chained, lie two large female figures, representing Scylla and Charybdis, with faces distorted by passion.

The barbers here ply their busy trade, and seem hardly to have time to attend to their numerous customers, every coachman, tailor, and beggar of the town coming here in turn to be shaved. The dirtiest old beggar, with only a few straggling gray hairs on his head, his body covered with filthy rags, will sit down in the sun, and, with upturned face, give himself up to ten minutes of thorough enjoyment while a gentle and dexterous hand lathers his withered cheeks, and with a sharp razor removes all "superfluous" hairs, and sends him back again to society, if not a better, at least a cleaner man.

April 4. We have just returned from a delightful expedition to a very old Norman abbey, built in the middle of a torrent, about three miles from the town. The water has washed such a quantity of rubbish into it that its beautiful doors and pillars are nearly buried. On each side of the torrent rise high walls of rock, overshadowing the building. We sat here for two hours, and I amused myself by watching the women climb the steep sides of one of these mountains, with large baskets on their heads, their heavily-laden mules following them. To my dismay, I was told that, when the pictures were taken, I should have to climb quite as steep a hill. While W—— was photographing, several young men passed, and I asked them to stand to enliven the pictures, but they all declined, and evidently thought that the camera, on which they looked with the greatest fear, contained an evil spirit. They had never seen such an apparatus before. At last I persuaded one bolder than the rest, and W—— took his portrait standing against the picturesque old building. When the pictures were all satisfactorily taken, the basket containing the apparatus was put on the back of a donkey, and we began to ascend the hill. It was a regular clamber, but I was well repaid by the magnificent view when we reached the summit.

The Straits of Messina, the snow-capped mountains of Calabria, and the town, with its strong fortresses, were all mapped out before us. On the other side was the blue Mediterranean, stretching far away to the horizon. Stromboli and the other Lipari Islands were plainly visible, the former puffing up tall columns of smoke. I sat down to rest on the short sweet turf, and could scarcely tear myself away from the lovely scene. Our carriage met us here, and we drove back to Messina by a zigzag road down the mountain, catching at intervals the same beautiful view, while on one side of the road were large groups of trees, banks of moss, and wild flowers in profusion, cyclamens, enormous violets, and quantities of white heather. The air was perfumed by the sweet scent of the flowers.

April 5. Yesterday we visited a very old tower called Rocca Guelfonia, and had to go through part of the prison to reach it, four or five soldiers escorting us. It was a sad sight to see the prisoners staring at us like wild beasts from behind their iron gratings, which are often double. Some were walking up and down for exercise on a very small roof with iron railings all around. Many of the faces made one shudder, every evil passion seeming to have set its seal upon them. The soldiers had all honest, open countenances and gentle manners, and would not accept the money we offered them, neither would they allow the porter at the gate to take any. I saw such young children, not more than five or six years old, working hard at breaking stones, or leading horses, and engaged in many other kinds of work.

Taormina, April 7. We have engaged a very good carriage, with three horses, for twenty francs a day, which is to include all expenses, and in this vehicle we have driven along the coast. The road, which winds close to the sea, is very lovely, bordered by orchards, some in full leaf, others in blossom, their pink flowers standing out in bright relief against the snowy background of the mountains. The country is thickly populated, and we drove through numbers of villages, the houses generally of stone, two stories high, but without glass in the windows, which were closed with wooden shutters only. The people looked very happy and industrious, with honest, good-natured faces; the young girls had all fine features, but very dark complexions. We went into one house where they were making vases and jars; my dress, as I went in, upset two large ones at the doorway. I expected to hear the smash, but, on looking round, saw that the jars had merely altered their shape, and were all bent on one side, the clay being still wet and pliable. Our hotel has only just been opened in the centre of the town; the accommodation is miserable, but the view magnificent, with Mount Etna exactly opposite the window; but, alas! the pleasure to one sense is counterbalanced by the misery to another, for one of the black streams so common in Sicily, into which runs all the drainage of the town, flows down the middle of the street, just under our windows.

We can get no meat here, nor any thing eatable except macaroni. The town is eight hundred feet above the level of the sea, the road up to it is a very steep ascent, and was only made a year ago by the command of Prince Humbert. The view from it is very fine, and we were fortunate in having a clear day, which allowed us to see Mount Etna towering in its lofty grandeur to the height of eleven thousand feet, its summit and great part of its base covered with snow, and volumes of smoke ascending from the crater. We saw two new cones, which looked at night like huge bonfires. This view of the mountain is most sublime; it seems to fill nearly the whole horizon, standing alone in all its unearthly might. We could scarcely sleep the first night, but stood at the window watching the flaming cones.

We spent yesterday at the old Greek theatre, which is built on a high hill; the pillars are of granite, which must have been brought from Egypt, as there is none in Italy. We have engaged a servant, who speaks tolerable English; he is most handy and useful, and generally looks neat, although he contrives to travel without any luggage, carrying not even a small bag.

The dirt is terrible, but so it is every where in Sicily. We carry our own sheets with us, made in the shape of bags to tie round the throat. Without this precaution we should never have been able to sleep at all, nor would there have been much of us left by this time.

April 9. The town was in a state of great excitement to-day on account of the marriage of the richest man in the place with a young girl who came straight from the convent to the church. After the ceremony she changed her dress, and putting on a gay red jacket, a hat with feathers, etc., paraded, with the bridegroom, up and down the town, her friends walking in procession behind her. We met them, and bowed to the bride, who was not at all pretty.

We have just returned from a lovely walk. The sun had

sunk behind the hills, but still lighted up the top of Mount Etna, gilding the transparent smoke which rose from the crater, and floated away in fantastic wreaths above the clouds which hung in dark masses below. We were walking in a deep valley, between the mountains, covered with trees and vineyards. A stream ran far beneath us to the sea, which was of the loveliest and deepest blue, the white sails of the boats looking like large sea-birds floating over the surface. The blackbird, now heard for the first time since I left England, was singing sweetly; all else was hushed and calm. I can not describe the soothing influence of the lovely hour and scene. On reaching the water, the charm was broken by the horrible smell rising from it, or rather from the mud and water-plants which grew by it, whose fetid odor often occasions destructive fevers.

This side of the island is most fertile and densely populated. After the lapse of years has rendered the lava brittle and easily pulverized, vegetation will spring up luxuriantly, and villages are built over the ashes of former ones, the inhabitants thinking little of the ruin that may, at any moment, overwhelm themselves.

On every side of the mountain are corn-fields and vineyards, and luxuriant groves of olive and almond trees, planted on land entirely reclaimed from the lava, which crops out now and then in all its hideous blackness and sterility, either in low mounds or huge rocks, whose bare and rugged sides mark the course which the river of molten fire took centuries ago, destroying ancient corn-fields and vineyards as fertile and beautiful as those which now rejoice the eye with their luxuriant growth. "Every where by the side of present happiness and wealth we see the phantom of past desolation and misery, making us tremble for the future." Trouble and sorrow are so like this lava; they sweep over the human heart, leaving it to all appearance bare and scorched like the sides of the mountains. Years roll by, and as from the lava-covered plains rich fruits spring up in all their luxuriant beauty, so, "though now chastening seemeth not to be joyous, but grievous, nevertheless afterward it yieldeth the peaceable fruits of righteousness."

April 11.* Having determined to make a close inspection of this new eruption, which had broken out during the month of January, and had continued incessantly ever since, we started from Taormina at six o'clock in the morning, in a carriage with three horses harnessed abreast, according to the custom of the country. We had been strongly advised not to stop at Piedimonte (where most of the people who had visited the new craters had taken up their quarters), but to go four miles farther, to an equally miserable town rejoicing in the name of Linguagrossa, supposed to be derived from the rustic dialect of its inhabitants.

The course the lava was now taking rendered it necessary for all those starting from the former town to go round to the westward of the district devastated by the fiery stream; and to do this, the four miles of road to Linguagrossa had to be traversed, which we thought might be done more comfortably in a carriage than on the backs of mules. At Linguagrossa we took up our quarters at the Albergo di Etna, and we soon came to the conclusion that Linguagrossa was the most miserable looking collection of houses we had ever seen. Not only were the houses black from being built of lava, but every thing was black, land and all; the soil was nothing more than the lava pulverized by the action of the weather on it for centuries. One hill, however, to the north of the town, was an exception, being

* The narrative is here taken up by me from my diary.—W. J. C. M.

composed of red lava, which only served to make the rest of the land around look blacker.

Our arrival seemed to afford great amusement to the crowd lounging about the door of the hostelry. They were especially **diverted with the weight of my** wife's portmanteau, **which required two men to carry it, as it** was half filled **with glass ready** for pictures, my dutiful wife having, in a **most** exemplary manner, sacrificed half the space allotted to her wardrobe for the sake of her husband's negatives.

We had been rather dismayed at the hotel at Taormina, but on entering the Albergo di Etna I confess my heart sank, and A—— looked the picture of despair. We had the choice of two rooms, each of which had beds in all four corners; and we were told that if more travelers came we should have to share our room with the new-comers, but this we declared impossible; so the spectacled landlord said as there was a lady in the case he would break his rule for once. The best room, looking into the street, was declared uninhabitable on account of the fearful smell of burning fat occasioned **by cooking on a** *braciera* **or pan of live charcoal, which is the only fire used by the natives of Sicily.** A table **was carried into the other, and we waited** impatiently for our dinner, which was being cooked, while the landlord was ordering and preparing the mules and guides to the *nuovo fuoco*, as the place of the eruption is termed.

We arrived at 12 30, and by two o'clock we **had dispatched** part of the tiny saddle of mutton we **had** bought *en route*. (It never does to trust **to the resources of a** town in this part of the world **on the first day** of an arrival.) On the announcement that the **mules were** ready, we descended into the street, and found four animals and three guides— the head guide, we afterward learned, was a brigand, under whose care our party was considerately placed by the landlord, who told him he would be held responsible for our safety. He was a most villainous-looking fellow—of most abhorred aspect, "by the hand of nature marked, quoted, and signed to do a deed of shame." He was accompanied by a boy, and a very good-looking youth about twenty years of age, who devoted himself to A—— all the time.

The first three quarters of an hour we passed between lava walls, the land on either side cultivated in a rough style as corn-fields, filbert-woods, or vineyards. We noticed, too, that although the vines at Taormina were beginning to show the new shoots, here, at 1800 feet above the level of the sea, they did not give the slightest signs of the approach of summer. We passed along deep ravines, or lava-nullahs (if I may be allowed to use such a word) chiselled out by the fiery torrents in days gone by, the appearance of the country growing blacker still, and wilder, as we ascended. The winter torrents had, in places, cut the solid lava into curious ridges parallel to each other, while scattered about were many craters that had caused devastation hundreds of years ago.

Sixteen hundred feet above Linguagrossa the woody region begins, the forests consisting of enormous oak-trees. Here were congregated a number of charcoal-burners, who lived in rude huts, on which were placed branches of fir-trees to keep off the rain, and outside each hut was a large block of snow placed on a slab of lava; the water from the snow, as it thawed, dripped into a barrel. The men were exceedingly wild-looking, and had very large axes, which they were wielding vigorously, but all ceased their labors to watch our cavalcade pass by. I observed that they had fierce dogs for their companions, like the men on Monte Pelegrino.

The *scorza*, or track, was here so steep that A—— had at

times to cling to the neck of her mule. We now saw firs mingled with oaks. The latter, according to my aneroid barometer, did not grow at a higher altitude than 2600 feet above Linguagrossa (or 4325 feet above the level of the sea). Some of these oaks were very large, being fifteen feet in circumference. The firs were also of great size, being nine feet round, and rising straight up to a great height.

After continuing our adventurous way through this lonely region for the space of two hours and a half, we heard the noise of more wood-cutters hard at work. These proved to be men engaged in saving the trees that were in the line of the lava's course. The stream was now moving fast down the mountain, having advanced one hundred yards since yesterday. My barometer at Linguagrossa reported 28·50, my thermometer 58°; here the former showed 25·60, the latter 42°, indicating that the spot where the molten stream had arrived was about 4725 feet above the sea level.

The first sight of the moving mass of lava was truly marvelous, and baffles description. In some places it was a mile wide, and about twenty-five feet high, and from the main stream ran a number of smaller ones, like huge railway embankments. The surface of the side toward us was black in color, and as the mass swept on in its remorseless march with horrible crackling sound, lighting up the grand old trees before devouring them, the upper surface was gently raised by the molten matter running underneath, and the *scoria* fell over the sides, emitting a fearfully lurid glare.

It was difficult to approach very close, on account of the intense heat. I detached a piece of red-hot lava with a long stick, and forced a franc into it to keep as a memento of our visit, but in one minute it swelled up, and, passing off in fumes, disappeared, while all the natives laughed at our looks of dismay.

We saw several large firs that had been enveloped by the fiery stream, and as we watched we saw them fall with a crash, their trunks having been eaten through by the hot lava, and they were then carried with the stream on the top of the scoria. I noticed that when the lava lost its red heat it was still impossible to break it, from its tenacious character; but as it grew cold it was quite brittle. The scoria here was not in very large pieces like that of Mount Vesuvius, where it is in shape of slabs, but was in roundish lumps from six inches to a foot long. Just above where we were the lava had taken a sharp turn, and it was expected to run down a valley full of large trees; the owners of the wood were here with fifty men, cutting down and dragging the stems out of the expected course of the devouring element. Oxen were attached to the log in a curious way; a bar was simply placed under their humps, and to the ropes from this were fastened large spikes, which were driven into the wood. The faces of the proprietors showed their distress of mind, and they complained bitterly of the ill fortune that had overtaken them; luckily, however, they had buyers for the wood they were cutting, as the new railway from Messina to Catania required large quantities of it for sleepers.

It was with great difficulty that we tore ourselves away from this scene of new sensations; but we were getting faint with the great heat, and it was late, and we did not wish to run the risk of being out in the dark in this wild region. Before leaving, however, we quite made up our minds to visit the mouths of the new craters the next day, which were two hours' climb higher up the mountain, the lava having already run about ten miles from the mouth of the fissure, where it issues from the mountain side. It was twenty minutes past five when we turned our faces homeward; we soon experienced the discomfort of riding down places almost as steep as a staircase, but the mules were sure-footed, and we could only hold on tight and trust in Providence.

On our way down the head guide explained to me the brigands' signs, which are always made to each other in meeting. The eyes twisted to the left, and a slight toss of the head upward, show that the travelers are of the same trade, and that some work is in hand; the hand extended, with the fingers turned up, meant "take him prisoner;" the same, with the fingers turned down, signified "kill him." Our guides were curious to know whether the *signorina* was going up to the *bocce* to-morrow—which route we should take, and where we were going afterward. I was annoyed when I heard that our man, Giuseppe, had told them to Randazzo. We had contented ourselves with saying Catania, to which town there were two roads, without informing them that we intended to choose the one through Randazzo.

It was dark an hour before reaching our resting-place, but a moon nearly at the full helped us on our way, and, arranging for fresh mules the next day, we went early to bed in order to prepare for the hard work before us.

CHAPTER III.

April 12 to May.

Linguagrossa.—Second Ascent of Etna.—The Brigand Signs are made to our Guide.—The Snow-line.—The active Craters.—Photography under Difficulties.—My first Adventure with Brigands.—A narrow Escape.—We change our Plans.—A little Disappointment for the Brigands.—Catania.—Good Friday.—Processions in Southern Italy.—Change at Naples since 1860.—Benedictine Monastery.—Syracuse.—The old Theatre.—The Cathedral.—The Catacombs.—Fruit and Flowers.—Girgenti.—The *Cattiva Gente*.—Kindness of the Consul.—Our Hotel.—The Excavations in the Neighborhood.—Dispute with our Host.—Unexpected Decision of the Referee.—Italian Officers and their Families *en voyage*.

April 12, 1865. THE next morning we were up by five o'clock, having spent rather a sleepless night from the excitement of seeing what we had talked about so long and with so much interest. We made as good a breakfast as we could manage to procure, and at about six started again over the same ground as yesterday. There was to-day another mule, on which was placed the square basket containing my photographic apparatus, which was at last secured, after great wrangling among the four men who accompanied us. Two of the guides were the same as yesterday, and the others were brothers of the good-looking youth (by name Pepi) who attended so carefully to my wife's safety.

When we had been on our way about half an hour—passing numbers of women carrying heavy loads of wood—we met two men carrying axes in their hands. I saw them make the signs to Pepi which I had been taught the day before, including the extended hand, whereupon I laughingly said "All three alike." They looked rather surprised, and replied, "You know too much." I did not like this at all; but as the two men were going toward the town, I determined to go on, keeping, however, a sharp look-out all the way up. About two miles from the spot where we had seen the lava yesterday afternoon, we turned off a little to the right, passing through the dense forest of fir-trees; and here we first noticed the ground covered with a fine black dust, which had been carried by the wind from the new craters. We now came to the snow-line, and great care was necessary in passing the ravines, all of which were full of soft snow, in which the mules sank to their knees, and it required great exertion on the part of the guides to extricate them and get them over safely. The dust got thicker and thicker as we ascended. We passed a large tract where all the branches of the trees had been consumed by fire, leaving the gaunt stems blackened by its action.

At about ten o'clock we reached Monte Crisimo, an old crater about 150 feet high, and very steep. On ascending this, the scene of devastation and fury of the elements burst on us; it was a fearful sight, and the awful roar proceeding from the then active craters completely deafened us. The smoke rose in dense masses, but fortunately a northern wind blew both it and the stones and dust, which were constantly being thrown up, away from us in the opposite direction.

About one hundred yards from the crater on which we were was the lava that had already destroyed all in its course. Here the mass was from forty to sixty feet high, and, according to our guide, extended one mile across. It was a curious sight, its whole surface cracked and distorted into all kinds of shapes, bearing upon it numerous trunks of trees that had succumbed to the force of the fiery stream, and now lay extended like giants on its cooled surface.

The longer we looked the more awe-struck we became; the two nearer craters were belching forth steam and smoke, making a noise like that of great waves breaking on a shingle shore, or like the noise of all the engines in the world letting off their steam, while a lambent sulphurous vapor kept playing over various circular patches on the northern sides. This vapor appeared by daylight a yellowish color, but at night we were told it was a dull red flame.

The smoke was not constant, but rose every five or ten minutes. It would come up in dense clouds and curl round the craters, and then in two or three minutes rise in the air, leaving the two mouths visible, which were in the form of perfect circles with one side depressed. I took two views from this spot, using the water which the men had brought up with them (as they thought for drinking purposes). As I was finishing the second picture, I saw, to my dismay, the two men we had met before with axes approaching, but now they were armed with guns. I immediately sent Giuseppe, our servant, to A——, who, on seeing the new-comers, retreated to the top of the old crater. The two men now came up and began whispering to the guides. I at this put my hand in my side-pocket, so as to be ready to use my revolver at a moment's notice if requisite; and, not to appear afraid, I approached the new-comers and said a word to them, when, to my delight, they said "good-day," and left us.

I now took another picture, and A—— came down from the hill to me. In a few minutes who should appear but the men who had just gone away, but this time they had five or six more with them, all armed as the others, and wearing belts round their waists. These men all came and

stood close behind me as I had my head under the black
cloth, while developing the view of the lava I had just taken,
and I do not think a photograph was ever taken under
more disturbing influences. I really did not know what to
do; and, to get them away from the position they had taken
close to me, I made Giuseppe, who was in an awful fright
and pretended to be asleep, tell them to sit down a little
way off, while I, without their knowledge, took a capital
picture of them.

A——, fortunately, had not the slightest idea what these
men were, and as a joke she sat down by them, pretending
to be a captive in the hands of brigands. Little did she
think that, instead of a joke, it was reality, and that these
men had come up all this way on purpose to rob and murder us, thinking I was an engineer because of my photographic apparatus and barometer. In this part of the world
all engineers are considered millionaires, for the ignorant
people think that they are the persons who employ so many
hundreds of workmen, and that they make the railways
with their own private funds. Fortunately, as we afterward found out, our guides had felt the weight of our luggage at the inn in the town below, and Giuseppe having
told them that we were going to Randazzo, they thought it
would be more profitable to take us, luggage and all, the
next day, while on our road in the carriage. We now had
luncheon, and when this was eaten, I had the satisfaction of
seeing our new friends depart, but only after a great deal
of confidential talk with the men who had come up with us.

I now insisted that we should be taken nearer to the
mouths of the craters, to which at first the men would not
agree; but on my persisting, we started off on foot, two of
the guides carrying the photographic box. We walked
along the side of the lava for nearly a mile over the snow

which here lay on the ground, though covered with the black dust from the eruption to the depth of from four to twelve inches. The first layer of dust had been live ashes, some of them an inch each way in size. It was very closely packed, and would probably keep the snow from thawing all the summer. Pepi and I supported A—— between us, all three of us sometimes sinking in the snow to our knees. At last we found out that it was only where the dust was wet that the surface was unsafe, and after this discovery we got on better.

As we got closer, the wild grandeur and thunder of the months increased, and the noise was fearful, quite stopping all conversation. A little to the west of the two most active craters was a hill, or rather mountain, 1000 feet high, that had been thrown up (as we were told) in two or three days at the commencement of the eruption. This was quite black in color, with patches of yellow (probably sulphur) in several places. From the summit of this large crater light vapor was always ascending, and every now and then enormous black clouds of smoke would cover the top. The wood in this direction had suffered much, only the tall stems of the fir-trees being left, where the lava had not utterly destroyed them. It was a most wild and desolate sight, and made fine studies for my camera, by the aid of which I secured, with great difficulty, some very striking views.

The work was most fatiguing, for I had to go to expose the plates at least 300 yards from where I had put up the developing box, and running over the treacherous surface of snow and dust was most tiring. I do not think that any amateur ever worked harder. I felt, however, that I should never have such a chance again, and was stimulated by the knowledge that no one but M. Andrieu, whom we had met at Messina, had ever photographed such a scene, and by the wish of sustaining the honor of England, by getting, if possible, better negatives than those which my rival had shown me. On completing my labors, I was so exhausted that I drank with avidity a little distilled water which I found among my chemicals, and I would gladly have given a Napoleon an ounce for some more. It was now time to return, but before doing so we took one more look at this wild and fascinating scene. Behind the great crater to the left Mount Etna raised its lofty head, about 5000 feet higher than the spot where we were, covered with the purest snow, listening in majestic silence to the roaring of its youngest born.

The new eruption had taken place just at the termination of the woody region. Five craters in all, we were told, had given vent to the subterranean fires, but, at the time of our visit, two of them had ceased to be active.

We now hurried back to our mules, and packing all our *impedimenta*, mounted, and began our course homeward.

The excitement of the craters had in the interval made me forget the brigands, who, I felt sure, were not far off; but the behavior of our guides now renewed my apprehensions. Instead of talking to me continually as before, they were quite silent, and would hardly answer my most trivial question, and they were constantly wandering on each side ahead of the party. I do not think I ever spent a more uncomfortable time; for uncertainty is worse than reality; and my anxiety was not made more pleasing by one of the men saying to me, "*Mi piace molto la signorina!*" It was a great comfort to me that A—— had not the slightest idea of my fears, which I did not tell her till our arrival at Catania next day. At 7 30 we reached our little inn, and, after having supper, we were soon fast asleep.

April 13. When we first arrived at Linguagrossa we had arranged with our coachman for a visit to Randazzo and the other towns at the back of the mountain. We were talking about this expedition after our return from Mount Etna, when our man, Giuseppe, entered the room, and closing the door mysteriously behind him, as if afraid of being overheard, entreated us, in a whisper, to give up our projected visit to Randazzo, as he had heard that the men whom he had seen the day before were brigands, and that they had arranged a plan to take us and our luggage on the road. The poor man turned white with fear as he spoke. We told him, laughing, that he need not be alarmed, as the brigands only captured Italians, and never English travelers. He then ran over a long list of the people who had been taken, and told us that even the inhabitants of Linguagrossa knew we were very rich persons, for "all could see that the Englishman was an engineer, or the next thing to it, viz., a nobleman! for was not the white turban he wore round his hat a sign of his riches or rank?" The landlord added his advice to Giuseppe's entreaties, telling us plainly that he could not guarantee our safety unless we took an escort of soldiers. Being determined not to let any one know the road we were to take, I dismissed them with these words: "Tell the coachman to be ready to start at eight o'clock to-morrow morning." They both left the room, shrugging their shoulders at the madness of the Englishman. I, however, from the moment I had been surrounded by the men near the crater, had resolved to return to Catania by the coast, and to give up the expedition round the mountain.

The next morning, early, Giuseppe came again to implore me to drive to Catania, but all that he could get from me was the order to tell the coachman to get the carriage ready for the luggage. Poor Giuseppe obeyed with many a doleful sigh and shrug. The carriage drove round; the horses' heads were turned toward Randazzo; the bells had been taken off, that no warning of our approach might be given; the coachman looked pale and nervous, watching the crowd that assembled to see us off; I stood on the balcony while the luggage was being packed, and when all was ready we descended and stepped into the carriage; and then, standing up, I said to the coachman, "Turn the horses' heads, and drive to Catania." A loud roar of laughter broke from the crowd as we drove furiously away, feeling sure that no intimation of our change of purpose could have been conveyed to the brigands in time for them to interfere with us. They probably spent this day in lying in wait for us in some dark wood, or convenient angle of the rocky road between Linguagrossa and Randazzo.

April 13.* We arrived at Catania on the 13th. The drive from Linguagrossa was beautiful, but the distant view of Catania, which is on a flat plain at the foot of Mount Etna, did not prepare us for the beauty of its splendid buildings. It forms in this point a striking contrast to many of the Sicilian towns we have seen, which are generally lovely at a distance, from their picturesque situations, but dirty and miserable when once the gates are passed. Catania is a comparatively modern city, having been built about two hundred years ago, after the overthrow of the old town by one of the many earthquakes which are always threatening the towns and villages around the giant mountain whose smoking crater is to be seen towering above from every street. The houses, which are really enormous, are entirely built of lava and stuccoed over, and the wide streets are paved with it. Catania is a flourishing, thriving place, and the trade will be immensely increased when the railroad is finished round the coast, connecting all the principal towns.

* From Mrs. M——'s diary.

Englishmen will probably then find that this is a charming winter residence, as it is very healthy, and the country round is lovely.

There are very interesting remains of the old Greek and Roman city disinterred from the lava, especially the remains of the theatre and the catacombs; but we were not able to visit the latter, neither could we make any of the usual expeditions round the mountain, for which Catania is the starting-point, on account of the ill health of my husband, who was almost entirely confined to the hotel during our stay in the place.

On Good Friday, at six o'clock in the evening, there was a grand procession of the senators, monks, noblemen, and principal people in the town. They first assembled in the Cathedral, which was brilliantly lighted up, and assisted at a solemn requiem. The general public were not admitted, so we took our stand on the grand piazza outside, and after waiting a short time, the great doors of the Cathedral were flung open, and the procession slowly defiled from it, headed by the bishop and canons in quaint copes and hoods lined with ermine, with long fur trains. A crown of thorns was the only head-dress worn, and every one carried an enormous wax taper, the monks chanting a solemn dirge the while. In the centre of the procession was a wax figure of our Savior lying on a bier, the blood slowly trickling from his side. For two hours they slowly marched about, while a solemn silence reigned around; awe and devotion were imprinted on the features of the crowd, almost as if they were present at the awful event itself instead of its scenic representation. The most striking incongruity in this solemnity was the conduct of the street-boys, who ran in and out of the procession, picking up and carefully treasuring the pieces of wax that dropped from the lighted candles.

The popularity of these processions is a sort of measure by which to gauge the moral and intellectual progress of the people. Among the ignorant population of the remote towns of Sicily they are frequent, and are considered to bring a blessing on both town and people; whereas in Southern Italy, even in Naples itself—once the abode of the most abject superstition—these ceremonies are becoming every day rarer. The entry of Garibaldi into the latter town was the first ray of the flood of light, which is destined, I trust, to illuminate all the dark places of this lovely land. Instead of processions, he gave the people schools, which are eagerly attended by a people so long systematically kept by their rulers in the grossest ignorance. I was grieved to hear that the Church of England, both at Palermo and Naples, is doing little or nothing, while the Lutherans and Presbyterians have established Sunday-schools, dépôts for the sale of Bibles, etc.

But I have wandered too far away from Catania and its churches. We paid a visit the other day to one of the largest in the world—that belonging to the Benedictine monastery. It is unfinished, as, on account either of an earthquake or of some fault in the building, the pillars have sunk, and the foundation is considered insecure. We heard high mass, and I was rather amused at seeing the care the priests took to avoid cold in their numerous prostrations. Every time they lay flat on the floor (a ceremony I had never before observed in any Roman Catholic Church), a rich carpet, with a velvet pillow, was spread on the ground, while the poor and scanty congregation were compelled to content themselves with the hard, cold stone floor.

After the service we walked round the church, and I stopped to admire two magnificent bouquets of the loveliest flowers on one of the altars. The priest, seeing my admiration, stepped forward, and, to my surprise, politely invited me to take any I liked. I hesitated to do so, and he collected for me a bouquet of the most splendid roses, heliotropes, white tulips, violets, etc. In the mean time W—— visited the museum. I was only allowed to enter the chapel. The monastery is extremely rich, but there are very few monks. We then visited the ruins of the old theatre. Curiously enough, they have discovered that under the Roman theatre was an old Greek one, the excavators having laid bare the enormous blocks of stone characteristic of Grecian architecture. We saw little else in the place on account of my husband being attacked with illness; and directly he was well enough to travel, we took the steamer for Syracuse, where we arrived on the 20th.

Syracuse, April 24. We are now in far-famed Syracuse. I am enchanted with the place. No wonder that the Greeks, with their keen love for the beautiful, built their city here, for the situation is so striking, and the harbor splendid. There is every probability that it will be the chosen station for the fleet of United Italy. This town brings the power of ancient days vividly before me. The Cathedral is built out of an old temple to Minerva. The enormous Doric columns, built six hundred years B.C., are still to be seen imbedded in the walls. No modern columns can be compared to these, so gigantic and severely grand. Once or twice the earthquakes have striven to dislodge them, and have succeeded so far that some have been thrown on one side and off their base. Every where a column, a ruin, an old wall, tells of the days when the Greeks were lords here.

We met the other day an English clergyman, the Rev. J. C. Murray Aynsley, and his wife; and yesterday, after reading the morning service of the Church, we all went for a long ramble, and, when tired, rested close to the shore, under the shade of enormous fig-trees, through whose clustering branches we could see the deep blue sea. Above us a nightingale was singing most melodiously, and the ground was every where enameled with flowers of the most brilliant hues. At our feet—for we sat on a little hill—were the ruins of the Baths of Diana. Columns, statues, white marble steps, all lay scattered about. We sat and gazed till my heart seemed to overflow with thankfulness at having been permitted to see such a lovely scene.

We left it with deep regret, and then continued our walk, in the course of which we descended into the catacombs, which extend their subterraneous ramifications for miles and miles. There were but few inscriptions and only one or two frescoes. They are larger and more regular than the catacombs at Rome. The walls in the galleries have large arched openings at regular intervals, leading to passages cut far into the limestone rock, and containing numbers of stone recesses of all sizes, once covered by slabs, which have all disappeared. This city of the dead awed and chilled me to the heart. After the long, damp passages, the sepulchral gloom, the thick, close air, I was glad to ascend again into the land of the living, to bask in its warm, bright sunshine, to breathe the sweet perfume of its flowers and trees.

"We rested again in a very bower of Arcadian sweets, where Flora was still in her prime." The ancient quarries are turned into gardens—and such gardens! Here, for the first time, I saw the orange and lemon trees in their natural growth, not topped and trimmed to produce fruit, but trees of a splendid size, covered with bloom and fruit. The air was deliciously scented by these and the beautiful rose-trees (really *trees*), geraniums, and fig-trees. Surrounded by cliffs hung with creepers of every bright and lovely hue, we lingered long in this sweet spot, until evening, creeping softly and slowly over the landscape, warned us to return home.

Girgenti, April 27. We left Syracuse on the 26th by the weekly boat. Mr. and Mrs. Murray Aynsley traveled with us, and after a smooth passage of twenty-four hours we came in sight of the harbor of Girgenti, which is not deep enough to admit the steamer, so we were forced to land in a little boat—to my eyes dangerously overladen with the weight of the boatmen, our four selves, the luggage, and Giuseppe and his personal belongings (consisting of a pair of socks we had given him) tied up in a pocket-handkerchief.

As we approached the pier, three or four wild-looking men sprang into the boat and almost overset it. A regular fight now began for our luggage; fortunately, the boatmen took our part in the dispute that ensued. I stood a little apart, keeping close to two of the gens-d'armes, whose loaded revolvers bore witness to the truth of what we had been told at Palermo—that whoever comes to Girgenti must expect to meet *cattiva gente*. The luggage was at last put on a truck and wheeled toward the Dogana, but here, as elsewhere, owing to the credentials kindly given to us by the Marquis d'Azeglio, it was not examined, and W——'s negatives escaped the rough handling of the custom-house officers.

We now looked round for some means of conveyance to the town, which we saw proudly towering on a hill about four miles off. Its appearance at this distance, with its castellated buildings and lordly mansions, enchanted us—a charm soon to be cruelly dispelled on a nearer view. We heard at the Dogana that there was no carriage here, and that we must send to Girgenti for one. Poor Giuseppe, greatly against his will, was dispatched on this errand. I do not know whether the long walk up the hill or the fear of brigands weighed most on his mind. He started at twelve o'clock, and we sat on chairs placed in the open air for us, and whiled away the time talking to the head of the Dogana, who, like all other officials we met with, seemed thoroughly discontented with his position. One o'clock came, two, three, four; we grew wearied and hungry, and the gentlemen went in search of food, while we kept guard over our boxes. They returned with a little bread and cheese, and then wished to go in search of Giuseppe, but we were too much afraid of brigands to allow them to leave us. Five o'clock came—no Giuseppe; but at six, just as we were giving up all hopes of his appearance that night, we saw him coming slowly toward us with a doleful face, and the unpleasant information that there were but two carriages in the town, and both these were engaged. The hotels, too, were full, and not a room to be had in the place. We were fairly at our wits' end, when, happily for us, the consul drove by, and, seeing our disconsolate position, offered to take us to the town, while our husbands walked with the small cart which had been secured to carry the luggage.

After a wearisome drive up the steep hill, we entered the old gateway, and, passing through the crowd of people lounging round it, drove to the consul's through the filthy streets. After fruitless endeavors to get apartments at one of the hotels, we accepted the offer of an old man to let us two rooms. We were led down a narrow alley, and picked our way in disgust through black pools of water emitting the most villainous odors. The rooms were dirty and miserable, but we were so worn out with fatigue that we were thankful for any shelter. Just, however, as we were discussing how we should manage, Giuseppe came to tell us that a guide, to whom W—— had shown some kindness at Palermo, offered to give up his room at the hotel to us.

Thinking we should be more comfortable there, we accepted the offer, but were not much better off, for the window looked into an alley similar to the one which led to the old man's house, and the door opened into the salle-à-manger, where eating was going on all day long, and into which, when supper was over, the servants brought planks, turning it into a well-filled sleeping-room, so that our chance of obtaining fresh air was very small. We were obliged to remain, as the steamer called at Girgenti only once a week, and we were told it would be madness to attempt a land journey across the island to Palermo. We could only do it by engaging a very large escort of soldiers, and even then there would be every probability of our being attacked and perhaps taken by the brigands; so we made the best of our situation, and engaged a carriage to take us early every morning to the Temples, where we spent the whole day, enjoying the pure air and exquisite scenery. I used to lie down among the red clover, feasting my eyes on the beautiful ruins, all of which are on rising ground commanding a view of the sea on one side, and the wide plain thickly planted with almond-trees, just then in their tender spring beauty, on the other, the picturesque town crowning the summit of the lofty hill, and forming a fitting background to the picture.

May 2. We invited the consul and his family to a picnic yesterday, and passed a very pleasant day. The town, despite its dirt and smells, is very amusing, for the inhabitants live in the streets, where they discuss their own and neighbors' affairs with the utmost energy. To-day we went to the sulphur mines; but I, having learned by former experience in Tyrol to dread the atmosphere of a mine, declined accompanying the others in their descent. They came back horrified at the sight of children of from six to twelve years of age toiling under loads of from 70 to 100 lbs. We afterward visited the excavations carried on by Mr. Dennis. Nothing of any importance had been discovered, though tombs and rows of houses are scattered all over the fields in the neighborhood of the town.

Our week passed quickly, and the morning of our departure arrived. We began to think we should have a little trouble about settling our bill, as we had not been satisfied with the conduct of the landlord, and W——'s great-coat had been stolen from the hotel. Our fears were verified; a most exorbitant bill was brought, every thing being charged half as much again as we had paid at the best hotel in Palermo, and many things put down which we had never had. Mr. Aynsley and my husband determined not to be imposed upon; but, to their surprise, the landlord, at the first objection made, said, "Refer it to the English consul." They accordingly went, but were surprised at this gentleman's supporting the landlord in his attempt at imposition. They would not give in, and returned to the hotel, where we were waiting in the carriage. They then laid down the proper amount, due according to the tariff of prices established every where in the island, and, as the coachman refused to drive on, and a crowd assembled round us, we got out and walked, our luggage having been sent on in the morning. We had not got half way down the zigzag path cut in the hill when we saw the landlord and some of his men pursuing us. They came up with us, vociferating and gesticulating fiercely, and some one, pretending to be an official, stopped our luggage; we appealed to the vice-consul, who took our part; but, fearful of losing the boat, the gentlemen consented to pay an extra Napoleon, and we embarked, feeling that the reputation of the inhabitants of Girgenti was a well-earned one.

The boat was crowded with soldiers, officers and their

wives, the latter all young and very pretty, and it was most amusing to see one mamma after another, when tired of her baby, handing the little creature over to a great, tall soldier, who walked away with a grim smile of satisfaction overspreading his countenance as the baby clutched vigorously at his mustache and gay cap. I heard afterward that these soldiers were the only nurses the babies had, and most efficient and tender ones they proved.

I could not help thinking that this certainly was an advantage for the soldier. His being brought into such near contact with ladies and children must humanize him. The enlistment of the young men for soldiers, instead of being, as the ignorant peasants think, a great hardship, is, on the contrary, a very great benefit for them. The poor ignorant boy is taken away from his village, where he has grown up in perfect ignorance, and, besides having his mind opened by contact with others, fares altogether far better than if he were to remain all his days at home.

Soon after this we left Sicily for Naples, where we arrived without experiencing any adventures worth recording.

CHAPTER IV.

Diary of Mrs. Moens.

Ride from Salerno to Pæstum.—Our Escort.—The Temples.—Forebodings.—"Many a true Word spoken in Jest."—Our Escort deserts us.—The Reason why.—The Brigands at last!—The Capture.—Conduct of the Italian Troops.—The truly Unprotected.—The Village Doctor.—A new Cure for Fright.—Two trying Days for Wives.—Release of one of the Captives.—Mr. Moens retained as a Hostage.

May 19. WHEN we had been a few days at Naples, we thought of starting again on our tour, and accordingly, on the 14th of May, we traveled by rail to Salerno, intending, if possible, to pay a visit to the renowned ruins of Pæstum. We put up at the Hotel Vittoria, and next morning we started on our proposed excursion about 8 A.M., having received the most positive assurances, both from the authorities at Naples and the hotel-keeper at Salerno, that the road to Pæstum was perfectly safe,* and guarded by soldiers throughout.

Our party consisted of Mr. and Mrs. Murray Aynsley, my husband and myself. As I got into the carriage, I said in English, "I hope we shall escape the brigands." To my surprise, the porter answered me in my own language—"Oh, no fear, lady, the road is safe; parties are going every day from here to visit the temples." I had no real fear for myself, but merely made the observation in joke, as I had always done when starting for any of our expeditions in Sicily.

* In Appendix A will be found copies of the notices which were posted up in the Hotel Vittoria.

THE BASILICA AND TEMPLE OF NEPTUNE AT PÆSTUM.

The road from Salerno to Pæstum is most uninteresting; no hills—nothing but a dusty plain. We had three horses to our carriage, with the usual accompaniment of jingling bells. How I hated the sound of bells afterward! They always brought back to my mind this dreadful day. We were escorted the whole way to Pæstum by soldiers, who joined us on the road when a little distance from Salerno, asking our coachman where we were going. Although they thus accompanied us, they did not warn us of any danger, notwithstanding that (as we afterward discovered) they were fully aware of the presence of a band of brigands in the neighborhood, two Italian gentlemen having been captured by them a week previously. We arrived at the temples at eleven o'clock, and spent the whole day among them, my husband amusing himself in taking photographs of them, one of the carbineers being all the time in the temples in attendance on us.

The day was hot and sultry. I could not walk a step without feeling ill from the intense heat. We occupied ourselves in trying to find relics of the past in a place where some workmen were excavating. Mr. Aynsley picked up a ring and some marble fragments. Two Germans here joined us, and we formed a plan for returning together, but, fortunately for them, this plan was frustrated by the willful delay of our coachman. After we had taken tea, it being then half past four o'clock, and the carriage having been ordered at three, the gentlemen grew tired of waiting, and went in search of the coachman, while I reclined on one of the large piles of stones, and admired the extreme beauty of the scene before me, with which at first I had not been so much impressed. I looked through the massive columns of the ruined temples at the wooded plain beyond, with the mountains towering in the distance; but a dark cloud seemed over all.

D

A feeling of melancholy crept over me—a foreshadowing, I suppose, of some coming sorrow.

The carriage at last arrived, and we were all glad to get into it and drive away. The road was quite deserted, our escort of the morning having disappeared—in fact, we did not see a single soldier, and the authorities allowed us to return without any warning or guard, although they knew the danger we were running in so doing. We heard afterward that the troops were drawn off on purpose to allow negotiations to be carried on with the band of a brigand named Giardullo for the ransom of Signors Bellelli and Magnone.

We soon began talking about the brigands again, and Mrs. Aynsley and my husband kept trying to frighten me by pointing out dangerous places. However, I never for a moment felt that there was real cause for alarm, and so we talked and laughed about the brigands just as careless, unthinking people talk about their own death, never realizing the possibility of its being at hand. Mrs. Aynsley and W—— were in high spirits, and at last, tired of teasing me, told me that we had passed all the dangerous places, and one wood in particular that had been always notorious as an ambush.

I was very tired, and so fell asleep, but was suddenly roused by hearing Mrs. Aynsley exclaim, "Here really are the brigands at last!" I started up and saw, as it seemed to me, the fields on both sides of the road covered with armed men, some like serpents creeping through the standing corn, and advancing swiftly to the carriage; others rising in all quarters—from out of the corn, and from behind the tall hedges. They all closed noiselessly round the carriage, pointing their guns at us. One man seized the horses' heads, and turned them across the road. The coachman did not attempt to drive on. No one spoke. We were com-

THE CAPTURE AT BATTIPAGLIA.

pletely surrounded. There could not have been less than thirty men! I whispered to my husband, "Give me your watch. I can hide it." This watch, which he much prized, he slipped behind the cushions of the carriage without answering me. Still not a word was spoken. I said something, I know not what, to the man holding the horses' heads. He did not reply, but the brigands all made signs to my husband and Mr. Aynsley to get down. Silently the coachman descended and let down the steps, saying "*scende*." Silently my husband and Mr. Aynsley got out: the armed men surrounded them, and quickly marched off with them, one of the brigands whispering to the coachman to stay there for a quarter of an hour. Till then I had been bewildered, looking on what was taking place as a dream.

I now first realized what was happening, and a strong determination came over me that I would not be separated from my husband. I sprang out of the carriage and rushed after him for about twenty paces, but the brigands instantly formed a line to prevent my following, and my husband and Mr. Aynsley, turning round, implored me to return. I felt powerless, and two brigands gently and courteously led me back to the carriage, begging me not to be afraid, as they would return with my husband in a quarter of an hour.*

Once back in the carriage, my head reeled, and I nearly fainted. Mortal fear came upon both Mrs. A—— and myself. All we did at first was to pray; then we looked at one another and asked what we were to do. We hoped and thought the brigands would carry our husbands behind a house not far from us, take their money, rings, etc., make arrangements for paying a ransom, and then send them back to us. We had heard that this had been done with Mr.——

* The brigands afterward told my husband that my conduct was "madness."

when he was taken by brigands at Palermo some years ago. We kept gazing at the house, and constantly saw people coming toward us. Alas! they were only peasants, more than a hundred of whom passed while we were waiting in fearful expectation, but no one took the slightest notice of us.* My heart seemed to stand still.

About a quarter of an hour had passed, when suddenly we saw a cloud of dust along the road, and heard the feet of horses galloping furiously. "The soldiers!" exclaimed our coachman; and, as they were passing us, we stopped them with the terrible news, "The brigands have taken our husbands!" "Which way?" they asked. We pointed to the house, and away galloped about thirty soldiers in hot pursuit. We now thought that as the brigands were on foot there must be an instant encounter, and our husbands would be restored to us.

Half an hour passed—then an hour—but no signs of the soldiers; nothing but peasants passing along the road on their way to their homes. Hope began to leave us. It was now seven o'clock; the night was drawing on, and at last we reluctantly made up our minds to leave the spot, and to drive on to Battipaglia, the nearest village; there we stopped to consult about our going on to Salerno, as the coachman was very averse to our proceeding farther that night. I, too, thought it better to stop, if possible, where we were, as I had a large number of circular notes about me, my husband having the letter of indication. A crowd surrounded our carriage, but none showed signs of sympathy. We asked the most respectable-looking man if there was any place where we could pass the night. He pointed to a wretched-looking house—one of the stations built to accommodate the soldiers and their horses.

* At least fifty were looking on when the brigands surrounded us.

There was a room over the stables which we were told we could have, and we were advised to pass the night there. I must confess that by this time my own nerve had given way, and I longed to hide myself from the gaze of the curious crowd. We asked every one, "Have you informed the soldiers?" "Have you alarmed the country?" We were assured that messengers had been sent in every direction with the news.

One man, the best dressed in the crowd, kept talking vehemently to Mrs. Aynsley. I could not hear what he said, but I thought that he was perhaps the owner of a good house, and was offering us shelter for the night. Mrs. Aynsley rebuffed him, and, when we had driven into the stables, I asked her "why she spoke so crossly to him." She told me he was the village doctor, and so importunate in his entreaties to be allowed *to bleed us* that she was at last obliged to speak sharply to him. I looked at her colorless face, and felt that mine presented the same appearance, and thought bleeding a very unnecessary operation. The Italian doctors, however, would seem to be disciples of Doctor Sangrado, as they always have recourse to his favorite operation after any great excitement.

A kind old peasant woman now advanced to show us the way to our room; we mounted a ladder, and found ourselves in a loft, half filled with hay, with a large heap of Indian corn in one corner—in another a hen sitting on her nest. There was but one small window, which I opened directly, as the room felt oppressively hot and stifling. Our hostess gave us water with snow in it, which was most refreshing, and brought some clean sheets and a night-dress for Mrs. Aynsley, who immediately went to bed. Three or four women came to us; among others, a poor creature whose own husband had been taken, and who came, as she said, "to mingle her tears with ours." I reciprocated her kind feelings, and would gladly have talked with her, but the presence of strangers was irksome to Mrs. Aynsley, who begged me to get rid of them; so I told them the signora was ill, and they all quietly retired. I then tried to make some tea with Mrs. Aynsley's apparatus, when the door again opened and some men came in. Among them I saw the sullen face of the coachman, whom we afterward strongly suspected of having been in league with the brigands. They gave us the good news that the brigands were surrounded and could not possibly escape.

They went away, and were succeeded by two young officers, with several of their men. How our hearts sank when the first question they asked us was, "Which way did the brigands go?" We answered, "Why we told you at the time, round by the white house." "We can not find them," was the reply. "We have scoured the country, our horses are worn out, and we must rest two hours before we go out again." "Have you alarmed the country?" we asked. "Are the soldiers guarding the roads to the mountains? Have you sent intelligence of what has happened to Salerno and Eboli?" Over and over again they assured us that every thing had been done; that telegrams had been sent; that the mountains were well guarded; all the soldiers called out; the brigands could not escape, etc.; but they failed to convince me, and my heart sank. I wept bitterly, as all hope of seeing my husband left me. The officers were kind-hearted men, and tried to comfort me. They begged us to keep up our courage as they wished us good-night, promising to go out again in two hours' time in search of the band.

I could neither lie down nor sleep, but sat at the window, looking at the scene outside. The soldiers were leading their horses to the water, or sitting in groups, smoking and talking together. A wandering musician, with a concertina, went from group to group, listening to their conversation, and after a time crept quietly away. I firmly believe that this man was a spy of the brigands, as I noticed that he did not play any tune correctly; he was only trying to discover what were the plans of the soldiers for the morrow. After a time the soldiers retired to rest, and Mrs. Aynsley asked me to read to her. I had Fénélon's *Conseils* with me, and read a chapter or two to her. (This small book I sent afterward to my husband.) She fell asleep, and I returned again to my window.

It was a lovely night; the stars were clear and bright. At about three o'clock the soldiers led out their horses, and after about an hour's preparation they mounted and galloped out of sight. Still too wretched to sleep, I sat at my window, thinking that the morning would never dawn. I could see the roads to Pæstum and Eboli, along which numbers of peasants passed, either on foot or in the rough country carts. At last the stars disappeared one by one, and the welcome sun arose. I extinguished our curious old lamp, and we prepared for our return to Salerno. The officers had promised us an escort, and we waited some time for it; but, as no soldiers appeared, we determined to proceed alone. The broad daylight, the numbers of people passing, renewed our courage, and we again took our places in the carriage, after thanking and rewarding our kind hostess.

On our way we met two or three carriages, the occupants of which we warned of the danger attending their expedition to Pæstum. They of course gave it up, and turned back.

We determined, notwithstanding our dusty condition, to drive direct to the general's at Salerno. The coachman at first demurred; but, as we firmly insisted, he was obliged to take us. We trusted that the general would be able to give us some news of our husbands; we never for a moment suspected that we should be the first persons to convey to him the intelligence of their capture, after seventeen hours had elapsed since it took place. We were shown into a large drawing-room, and in a few minutes General Balegno appeared. He looked rather surprised at seeing two ladies, who could hardly speak for weeping. We told our story, and great was our dismay when we found that he was utterly ignorant of the fact of two Englishmen having been carried off in broad daylight on the high road from Salerno to Pæstum—a road supposed to be perfectly safe, and guarded by the soldiers under his command. He instantly rang the bell, summoned two of his staff officers, and gave orders for such and such detachments of soldiers to be sent out in pursuit, and not to return until our husbands were free, or the brigands prisoners. Having dispatched these officers, he turned to us, and begged us to be comforted, as all would soon be well.

In the evening we had many visitors, coming to offer their help and sympathy. A deputy of the Italian Parliament entreated us to send a telegram to Florence to rouse the Italian government, and to beg for help against the brigands. Another gentleman, a resident at Salerno, came to comfort us by telling us that he too had been taken by the brigands, and had escaped from them unhurt by paying a ransom. We were just retiring for the night when a messenger arrived with a letter for Mrs. Aynsley, containing the joyful intelligence that her husband was free, and would be with her early the next morning, the brigands having liberated him to raise the ransom for my husband and himself.

I was dressing the next morning when Mrs. Aynsley

rushed into my room, exclaiming, "Good news! good news! they are *both* coming! I have seen them in the carriage." I rushed out into the passage; the stairs and landing-place were crowded with people. I saw Mrs. Aynsley in her husband's arms. I gazed, oh! how eagerly, into all the faces that were turned toward us, but I did not see the one I looked for, and I returned into my room with that deadly feeling of disappointment which makes the heart sick. I sank on the sofa. Mr. and Mrs. Aynsley came into my room, but for some time I could not speak to them; at last I managed to shake Mr. Aynsley's hand warmly, and congratulated him on his escape; but I had not the heart to ask him how it was that he had returned alone, and that my husband was still with the brigands.

He then proceeded to tell us his adventures, which will be found fully detailed in my husband's diary.

CHAPTER V.

Diary of Mr. Moens, May 15 to 20.

The Capture.—The first Night's Sleep *al fresco.*—Delicate Attentions.—The Englishmen's Fellow-prisoners.—The Captain commences Business.—Value of Englishmen in Italy.—Choice of Hostage by Lot.—Release of Mr. Aynsley.—Skirmish with the Troops.—I am detached from the Band.—A wet Night in the Mountains.—Brigand Diet.—Two more Fellow-captives.—The Brigands' Dress and Arms.—The Ladies.—Sheep-killing.—Gambling.—The Brigands' Anxiety about my Health.—My Friends Pavone and Scope.

May 15. We had ordered the carriage to be at the temples at three o'clock, but it did not come till four. We had nearly reached Battipaglia, observing, to our great astonishment, that there were no soldiers about as in the morning, when all at once, about five miles from Scafa, the ferry over the River Sele, we saw a number of men creeping out of the corn on the east side of the road; they pointed their guns at us, and, quickly coming up to the carriage, turned the horses across the road. More men now advanced, and the coachman got down, opened the carriage door, saying *Scende.* Mr. Aynsley and I had to get out, I having instinctively taken off my watch and left it in the carriage.

We were dragged away at once, but, on looking back, I saw to my grief that A—— had jumped out and wanted to come with me; she was stopped by the brigands, who said to her, "*Non avete paura, Signorina, non avete paura.*" I wanted to return for a minute, but the brigands would not let me. We were hurried away up a lane on the west side of the road toward the sea, past a house. (The carriage was stopped near wood-carts, on the top of one of which a man was placed to give notice when we were coming. We had passed these carts near the river in the morning.) Almost immediately after leaving the high road, Luzzo, a proprietor living at Battipaglia, was taken by the brigands, and a minute after a young man, who was seen about 200 yards off in a field, was also captured.

We were then pushed along at a fast pace toward the sea, over fields and through thickets, the best path always being left for us. When at last we were allowed to rest a little, the captain of the band (whose name I found to be Gaetano Manzo) gave us each a very large cloak, called a

GAETANO MANZO.

capote, usually worn by the peasants, to sit on. We took this opportunity of asking the captain what he wanted with us. He rubbed his right thumb and finger together, and said "*Denaro; non temete.*" I asked how much farther we had to walk. The answer was "*Lontano, lontano assai.*" I, joking, said I hoped he had horses to carry us. He nodded his head, "*Si, si.*" They were all very kind in their manner, always addressing us as "Signori," putting a strong accent on the last syllable. We rested about ten minutes, and Luzzo, shivering a great deal, asked for a *capote*, saying there was much malaria about. We also put on our *capotes*.

Soon after starting again we had to pass several wet places. It was getting dark when we came to a river (the Tusciano) running very fast, about ten or twelve yards wide. They carried us over on their shoulders, and we rested again on the other side and drank some water. Here I tore up my letter of indication, as well as a letter of introduction to one of the principal bankers at Naples, and other letters, thinking it more prudent to do so than to keep them about me. I put the pieces into my gloves, and threw them away as opportunity offered.

On we went again, passing over swampy ground and deep ditches, which we jumped easily, much to the amusement of the brigands, who can not jump. They laughed heartily at our agility, and still more heartily when one of their own party fell into a ditch. When we were near the sea we passed a house, and one man who was sent to visit it brought back a quantity of dark-colored, hard dry bread, in shape like small penny rolls. These were distributed, and we walked on again for some time, and presently came to cultivated land. It was very dark now, and we could not see our path by the side of a running brook, so they gave me a long stick, which was a great help. We passed near some houses, dogs barking as we approached. Two or three men were sent on in advance, and we were placed in the centre of the band, who all walked in Indian file.

The advanced guard were making signals continually. The brigands' peculiar call-note is made by uniting the tips of thumb and forefinger of left hand, and then kissing loudly the third joint of the forefinger. We were often stopped till the road was considered secure. As it was getting toward midnight the caution increased, and when we neared the main road still greater vigilance was exercised, and we halted while the great highway was examined. We were then taken across. The same precautions were used when we approached the Eboli road, after crossing which we came upon a patch of cabbage and onions. "*Pigliate*" was the command from the captain, and the spot was soon stripped. A little hard cabbage was handed over to me, with some garlic, which I put in my pocket.

On we went past a large farm-house. I looked out for a chance to escape, but they saw as well by night as by day, and had we attempted to have left the ranks our fate would have been to have had a few shots sent into us, which would have left our bodies a prey to the worms. We halted before daybreak on the banks of a rapidly flowing stream, and we were told to lie down and go to sleep among some osiers. The ground was very damp, so we objected, and were allowed to sleep on the dry bank; but at daybreak we were made to descend and conceal ourselves with the band. Branches were stuck in the ground to make the cover thicker.

As I was lying fast asleep, I was awakened and startled by feeling a man's hand pass over my chest and ribs. My moving disturbed the man, and he left me. I mentioned this to Mr. Aynsley. We did not like it at all; I was so tired, however, that I soon fell sound asleep again. Mr. Aynsley was not so fortunate. He told me the next morning he could not sleep after this incident. I believe now the man was trying to find if I had a pistol. My first night's rest in the open air was excellent. I little thought how many I should have to pass far less comfortably before I saw a bed again.

The first operation in the morning was to collect all the bread and then divide it into shares. We were treated like the rest. The bread was so hard that they soaked it before eating it. They now continually asked us about our property. At about eleven o'clock we made a move, and walked in Indian file through a highly cultivated country.

After two hours there was a halt, and the captain asked us how much money we had at Salerno. We told them our stock of gold, but they would only believe in our being rich lords. They wanted also to know what was the matter with my hands. I explained to them that I had been photographing all day long at Pæstum, and the chemicals had stained my hands, and that if I had been a lord I should have had somebody to do it for me. One brigand said, "Look at his hands; they are black, indeed; his trowsers (they were gray flannel), too, are like what prisoners wear, and they are all worn out, *povero uomo!*" The captain and the rest seemed rather disappointed, but said, "We will see; wait."

They offered us a little piece of hard sausage called *super-sato*, but, after discussing its digestible qualities together, we told them that it would not agree with us. They laughed, and the captain said, "They will like it by-and-by," which truly came to pass. I never heard the end of this; the brigands never forgot the two Englishmen discussing the wholesomeness of the sausage. We started again, passing by some men, an old woman, and two girls; the old woman was sent for water, which she brought in a broken fiasco. We were very thirsty, for it was a very hot day. We rested continually, Mr. Aynsley always lying down at full length on his back. A little farther on we found a spring, and here they filled a wide-awake and brought it to us. At last, about four o'clock, we reached the top of Monte Corvino, the highest mountain in the neighborhood; a road ran along its base. We were placed under the shade of bushes close to a little spring: on the merits of this stream the brigands expatiated eloquently.

The captain asked me what I should like to eat. I answered like Sancho Panza, "Some meat, bread, wine, and eggs." He told me I should have them; but, alas! like Sancho Panza, I was doomed to disappointment. For the next three days we had scarcely enough to keep body and soul together—only a mouthful each day of Indian-corn bread. There was a goat tethered near us ready to be killed, and the remains of the fire which they had left when they had descended from the mountains on their way to the plains.

The captain now got out paper and pen, and commenced business. He took poor Luzzo in hand first. He was shivering with fear, and shrugging his shoulders when we looked at him. All the band began by raving at him, the captain shrieking at him and threatening him with all kinds of horrors, and told him that 12,000 ducats was his price. Manzo wrote a letter, which he gave me to read, but I told him he had only asked for twelve ducats, so I was requested to write it again for him, which I did. The other poor captive was now brought forward—8000 ducats was his price; they both sat wringing their hands, declaring that such sums were quite out of their power to give. They met with nothing but ridicule and threats from the brigands.

It was now our turn; but there was at once a difficulty —"Whom to write to?" We said it was no use writing to our wives, they could do nothing in a foreign land. We had no money in Naples and no friends; one of us must go to get what money we could. When we heard the sum demanded, we looked at each other with horror—100,000 ducats, equal to £17,000. After a few minutes' conversation with Sentonio, a tall, clumsy ruffian with black eyes, hair, and beard, Manzo reduced it to 50,000 ducats, or £8500. This sum, we said, was ridiculous—out of the question; but we were told, in spite of our protestations to the contrary, that we had 2,000,000 ducats each, and that we were great lords. We declared it was no use to trust to our wives to raise the money, as they did not speak the language, and that there were few English people at Naples, and no one would trust them as foreigners.

They then agreed to let one of us go for the money, and wanted us to decide which it should be; but we, knowing that whichever offered himself would be kept back, were silent. At last we proposed to draw lots; so I took a small twig and broke it in two pieces, a short and a long piece, and we arranged that the holder of the short one was to remain with the band, and the holder of the longer piece was to go and get the money for both. I took the pieces of wood, and holding out my hand before me, I said to Mr. Aynsley, "Draw." He drew one, and left the other (which was the shorter of the two) in my hand. I must confess I felt as if I had been drawing for my life, and I had lost.

I had to make up my mind to my fate at once. Mr. Aynsley told me he did not know whether he could pay so much. I told him that I could, and that I would advance his half for him till arrangements could be made. I told him to apply to a friend whom I named, a member of the Stock Exchange, for £2500, which I had left in his hands. I gave him other little directions, and told him to do all he

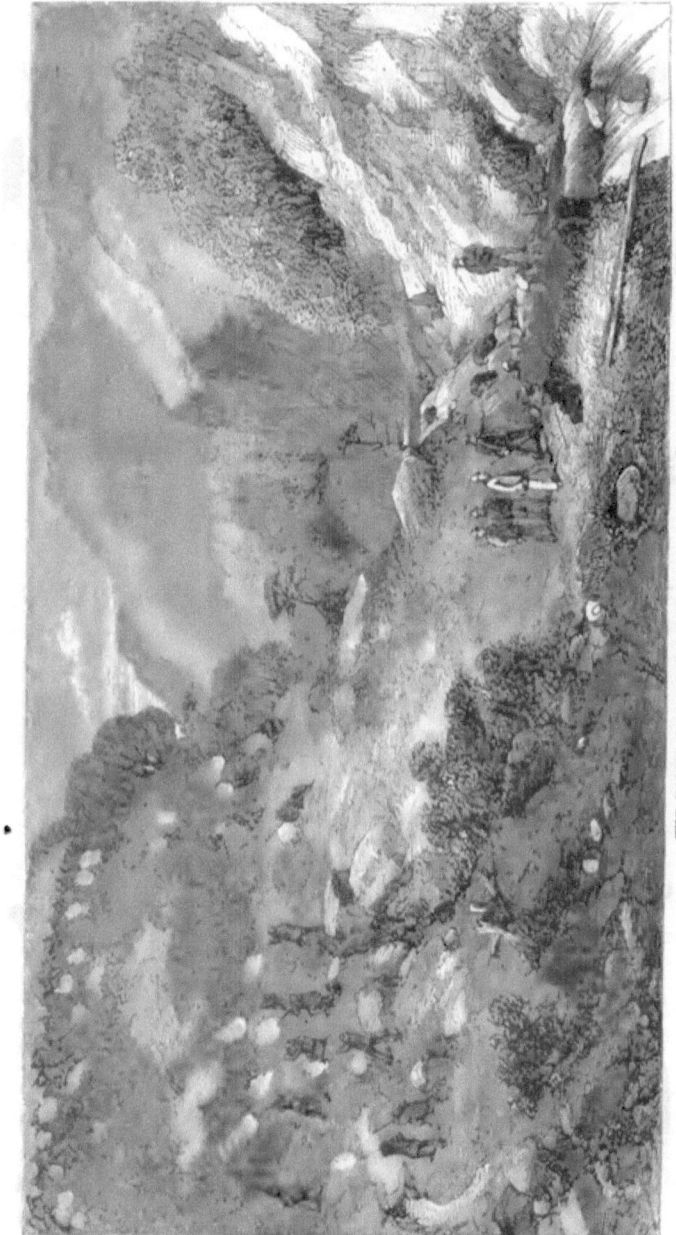

THE FIGHT WITH THE SOLDIERS ON MONTE CORVINO.

could for my wife, placing her under his care. Our conversation was interrupted by the captain being called by the sentinel to come and look at about 100 soldiers walking along the road below. After a few minutes, Mr. Aynsley and two men, to whom the letters of Luzzo and the other captive were given, were hurried away. His last words were, "Remember, whatever is paid, we each pay half."

I was put under charge of four or five men, and ordered off to the rear. I turned round and saw Mr. Aynsley and his two guides walking down the hill. It was a trying moment. I was now driven on at a fast pace, and in a minute heard the report of a gun, the bullet whizzing over my head. This was from the soldiers whom Mr. Aynsley met almost immediately after leaving us. The brigands answered this, and there was a brisk fire. I tried to go off to the right, thinking an escape possible, but was turned immediately; my foot slipped, and I fell down some depth, for the mountain was very steep, and all the stones loose. I was very much shaken, and I thought my arm was broken. I could hardly move it, but I was made to get up, and to the cry "*Corre, corre,*" on we went.

The hill was very high, the base of it covered with trees. I looked up, and saw the rest of the band lining the top of the hill in skirmishing order, firing as fast as they could. The shots of the soldiers now came rattling round us as we passed from bush to bush one by one, and for a quarter of an hour we had to run the gauntlet. At last we got to the bottom of the mountain, where we found a rushing torrent ten yards wide; the fire was too hot for hesitation, so one by one the brigands waded over. I had to follow; on I went, the water up to my waist, rushing, foaming over the stones, and the bullets splashing into it on all sides of me. I do believe the soldiers took special aim at me, the tallest of the party. My death would no doubt have saved them considerable trouble. Had it not been for my stick, I should have been carried away by the force of the stream; as it was, I had to cross in an oblique direction, landing on the other side only two yards above a waterfall of some height. The brigand who followed me was washed down, and went head over heels over the fall, but he was not much hurt, and scrambled out below. The others passed over safely, and we hurried up the steep ascent over the other side for some considerable distance till we were concealed among the trees, and safe from the fire of the troops. I thanked God for my escape from my rescuers, and felt any thing but charitably disposed toward their rulers, who ought years ago to have cleared their country from these ruffians, instead of leaving them alone till they carried off an Englishman.

We rested among the trees until nightfall. At sunset we saw about two hundred soldiers in a body ascending the opposite bank by a path from the stream. They cheered as they marched along. I turned to the brigands and said, "You have lost some comrades." They did not choose to admit this. After dark some more shots were heard, and the band was surprised again. The other prisoners managed to escape. Lucky fellows, they were but small fry, and were forgotten in the excitement of the fight; but the greatest care was taken of me. I was never allowed a chance for a moment. When it was dark, we saw the bivouac fire of the troops. We had no fire, but lay down under our capotes, I lying between two men. We soon forgot our fatigue in sleep, and an hour before sunrise I was waked up, stiff from the cold and wet, for the passage through the river had thoroughly soaked me. The walking, however, warmed us, and after an hour's march, by which time the day had dawned, we reached a spot hidden by broom, all golden with the yellow blossoms. It was a lovely place, the ground mossy, and covered with luxuriant creepers, graceful ferns, and foxgloves. Here we rested, a murmuring stream running below.

The ferns were at least ten feet high. I laid down and tried to sleep, but my thoughts would not allow me. I kept thinking of the desolate situation of my wife, and of the anxiety that would be felt by my family in England. I looked round for a chance of escaping, and edged off as far as I could from the men, but the slightest movement caused them to look after me with the cry *Che fate?* We were on the edge of a hill, at the base of which ran the rivulet, crossed by a rude bridge formed of the trunk of a tree. We saw soldiers passing at intervals all day in small bodies, eight or ten at a time, over the bridge and along a bridle-path near. It struck me that I might run off and cry out to the soldiers; but it was soon intimated to me by the brigands (they must have divined what was passing in my mind) that if I attempted to escape I should be shot at once. I noticed that the soldiers looked like mites, thus showing the great height of the mountain, and the distance we were from them. I now turned my attention to nearer objects, looking at the violets and forget-me-nots. I then read my Prayer-book, which I had found in my pocket. This was a great find, and afforded me the greatest comfort throughout my captivity. I read some of the Psalms, which brought tears to my eyes. The brigands soon perceived this, and entreated me not to be down-hearted, as they would not hurt me if they got the money soon. I told them that it was not fear, but grief for what my wife was suffering on my account. Talking, however, was not my humor then, and I would say no more to them, but returned to my sad meditations.

A little animal now came to make friends with me. I heard a slight rustle in some broom by my side. I looked round and saw the sleekest little mouse perched on the branch of a shrub of broom. It was of a fawn color, with the brightest black eyes, and apparently very tame. As long as I looked at it it never moved, and only stirred when I put my hand near it, and then it only ran down the stem, but soon returned again. I felt very friendly to this little creature when I saw how beautifully and perfectly it was formed. I then thought of its Creator, who had called it into being, and who, as a benevolent Deity, had provided, as might be expected, for its nourishment. I drew consolation from this thought of God's care. My attention was drawn off from my little friend by the soldiers, and when I looked again he had gone, and did not return. I felt very hungry, for I had had no food since yesterday. I kept asking for bread, but was told that it was impossible to get any on account of the troops who were continually patroling round us; but I kept asking all day, for I felt it was nothing to me what risk they ran in getting food. At last my friend Justi, who always pitied me, said he would go and try to get some. "There are kind hearts every where." He asked me if I had any money. I gave him a two-franc piece, but he said that was not enough, so I gave him five francs, and off he went. In about an hour he returned with something tied up in a cotton handkerchief, which proved to be Indian-corn bread broken in pieces. It seemed delicious, for I was almost starving. I had no scruple about eating more than my share, and I put some into my pocket, but a very small portion, as the whole quantity brought was very little, and I was obliged to leave some for them. The old proverb is very true, "Hunger is the best sauce." No gourmand ever enjoyed his perigord pie as I did my dry crusts in the mountains. The flavor was exquisitely nice. It was now getting late in the afternoon, when some more soldiers passed. When once they were out of sight, we began to descend the mountain, keeping as much under cover as we could. I now saw how little chance I should ever have of escaping from the brigands. They ran down the mountain like goats, while I had to be careful to pick my way at every step. How could I hope to run away under these circumstances?

Accustomed to mountains from their earliest youth, they were as sure-footed as the goats, and had eyes like cats; darkness and light, daytime or night, made not the slightest difference to them. Their hearing, too, was most acute. This sense they had cultivated to such a pitch, that, like the red Indians, the slightest rustle of the leaves, the faintest sound, never escaped their notice. Men miles distant working in the fields, or mowing the grass, they could distinguish with the greatest ease. They knew generally who they were, young and old, and to what village they belonged; when I, perhaps, could barely distinguish living beings, they could describe all their motions. We crossed the stream again at dusk, and walked along the path lately traversed by the troops for some distance, and then turned off to the left, through a very thick wood, ascending for some hours. At last we reached the summit; the brigands now stopped, and there was hesitation and doubt in their manner. I could perceive that they did not know the road exactly. The direction we were pursuing, namely, N.W., would have led us to a sheer precipice. After a little consultation, a divergence to the westward was pronounced feasible. I declared it impossible; but, seeing two of them descend, I, for the honor of my country, followed.

It was so steep that we had to descend by aid of our

E

hands, with our faces to the mountain; in fact, I turned myself from a biped into a four-legged animal. The old adage came to my mind, "You never know what you can do till you try." Without the assistance of the bushes and trees that grew there, it would have been impossible to descend. After a tiresome descent of an hour in the dark (for there was no moon), we reached the bottom. As far as I could make out, it was a curious, picturesque spot, the mountains rising all around, and on the south side a great square block of stone jutting out like a castle.

On the northwest side, the sloping side of the mountain looked as if covered with snow. This effect proved to be produced by a kind of white limestone broken in small pieces. I put some in my pocket, but found, after some time, that specimens of geology and natural history were very inconvenient to carry, and they were all thrown away. By degrees, as our marches became more fatiguing, we walked over the broken limestone, and kept passing up and down hills, over most difficult and pathless places, where every spot had to be felt carefully by the foot before the weight of the body was trusted on it. I constantly trod on loose stones with my foot, and was in continual danger of spraining my ankle as I walked on in the dark. It was "Mind your steps, sir," at every moment, and woe betide me if I did not. We continued this march until daybreak, when we rested and endeavored to sleep. I found out, to my annoyance, that during this march I had lost a signet-ring I much valued. I had put it in my pocket for security, and this pocket had got torn in our scramble down the side of the mountain.

May 18. I slept till eight or nine o'clock, and, on awaking and looking round, I found we were just above the dry bed of a stream that in winter ran down the mountain-side. We were facing the west, and at about half a mile off ran a stream like a delicate little silver serpent, twisting in and out of the bushes and green banks; on the other side of it was a bridle-path. We saw several bodies of troops pass during the day, who were always watched with the greatest interest, and the merits of the different sorts of soldiers were freely discussed. I tried to get as far away from my guardians as I could, and then began to think over some plan of escaping. I propped up my straw hat on a peg, so that the men, who were all below me, might think I was sleeping, and then tried to edge off and to be ready for a run when more soldiers came; but one, who was very wary, and who turned out to be one of the four brigandesses, changed her position so as to see the place where I was.

The day seemed very long. I read my Prayer-book. Seeing some "Forget-me-nots," they reminded me strongly of happy days in England, and, for want of any thing better to amuse me, I picked one and fastened it in my Prayer-book with a little piece of a postage-stamp I had in my pocket. Very curiously, without knowing it, I placed it just over the Gospel for the fifteenth Sunday after Trinity. Our Savior there draws lessons from the flowers of the field. The little flower that I had plucked always afterward spoke volumes to me in my solitude, and I drew intense comfort from the thought that God, who cares for the lilies of the field, would not forget me, and felt convinced that I should be saved in time; but I felt very wretched when I thought I might never again see those who were dear to me.

I was dreadfully hungry, and found in my pocket a piece of the Indian-corn bread as large as a walnut; this soon went, and I turned out all my pockets, and discovered to my joy the little cabbage I had put away on the 15th. I ate that raw, and thought it any thing but disgusting. I now found two roots of garlic: one satisfied me, the flavor being rather strong—(how soon I was cured of all daintiness! Before I was with the brigands the smell of garlic alone was nauseous to me, let alone the taste)—the other I put again into my pocket. We had had some water to drink during the night, and with this I was obliged to be satisfied till the evening. A village was near, for we heard the bells of the church chiming the hours. I fancied we were near Castellamare; but, on asking one of the brigands if it were so, he replied "Yes," and I knew then at once that it could not be, for it is always the brigands' principle to deceive their captives as to where they are. At dusk we started again, finding it much farther to the river than I imagined; the stream was full of water, and running down very fast. We stepped from stone to stone and got over dry-footed, followed the path some way, and then, as yesterday, diverged over mountains and through woods for four or five hours, till, having reached an open part at the summit of a mountain covered with grass, there was a halt, and we lay down to sleep. The night was very cold, wet, and foggy—in fact, we were actually in the clouds. Every night hitherto I had been allowed a *capote* to myself, but to-night some of the brigands growled at the cold, and one came to share my cloak with me. I did not approve of this, but I had to submit; the other three slept under another *capote*.

May 19. We woke up an hour before daybreak, stiff from the cold; I could not move till I had rubbed my knees for ten minutes. We started again down hill, and then along a path up another mountain. Walking by daylight for once in a way was a great treat to me, not only on account of the light, but also from having a path. As the sun got up we grew very thirsty, for we had only dared to stop half a minute for a drink the evening before, on account of the place being dangerous, and we had passed no streams during the night. After some time a search was made for snow, and at last, in a most unlikely place, under leaves, some was found. It was most delicious, and as we walked on I kept eating it. The brigands laid down on the ground and lapped up the water that had thawed, and was running among the decayed leaves. I thought of fever, and preferred the snow. Soon after this we passed a spring, where we stopped to rest and drink at about eleven o'clock.

I was here told that we were near the main body of the band, and on emerging from the trees we saw the captain and about twenty-five of his men reclining on the grass in a lovely glade, surrounded by large beech-trees, whose luxuriant branches swept the lawn. Several sheep and goats were tethered near, cropping the grass. The men, with their guns in their hands, their picturesque costumes and reclining postures, the lovely light and checkered shade of the trees, made a picture for Salvator Rosa. But I do not believe that Salvator Rosa, or any other man, ever paid a second visit to brigands, however great his love of the picturesque might be, for no one would willingly endure brigand life after one experience of it, or place himself a second time in such a perilous situation.

The band all rose, and looked very pleased at seeing me, for we had been separated from them since the fight on the 17th, and they were in great fear that I might have escaped, or have been rescued by the troops. I stepped forward and shook hands with the captain, for I considered it my best policy to appear cheerful and friendly with the chief of my captors. He met me cordially in a ready way, and asked me how I was. I said I was very tired and hungry, so he immediately sent one of his men off, who returned in a few minutes with a round loaf of bread, and another loaf with the inside cut out, and packed full of cold mutton cut into small pieces and cooked. I asked for salt, and was told it was **salted.** When cooked the meat tasted delicious to me, though it was awfully tough, for I had not had meat since luncheon on Monday, in the temples of Pæstum, four days before. I ate a quantity, and then asked for water, which was brought to me in a large leathern flask, with a horn round the top, and a hole on one side serving to admit air, as the water was required for drinking. I had observed a large lump of snow suspended by a stick through its centre, between two forked sticks; the water dripping from it was collected in flasks, and then drank. There were two or three of these flasks. The captain asked me if I was satisfied. I answered " Yes."

I was then told that there were two more companions for me. I was taken through a gap in the trees to the rest of the band, about seventeen in number. Here I found those who were destined to be my companions for the next three weeks. A young man about twenty-eight, with a black beard of a month's growth, dressed just like Manzo's band, who was introduced to me as Don Cice, *alias* Don Francesco Visconti, and one Tomasino, his cousin, a boy of fourteen years old. I shook hands with them, and condoled with them on our common fate, which Don Francesco described as fearful. I was told to sit down on one side, which I did, and looked around me.

The spot seemed perfect for concealment. We were at the top of a high mountain, entirely surrounded by high trees, excepting two small gaps serving for entrances, opposite to each other. The surface of the ground was quite level. About twenty yards away, on the side opposite to where I entered, there was a quantity of snow, from which they cut the large pieces for drinking purposes. I saw five or six men bringing a fresh block, which they had just cut, and slung on a pole. It was now a little before midday, and they were preparing a caldron full of *pasta* (a kind of macaroni), which was ready by twelve o'clock. Some was offered to me, which I accepted. One brigand proposed putting the *pasta* into a hollow loaf, but another brigand brought forward a deep earthen-ware dish of a round shape. I thought milk would be an improvement, so I asked for some. Two men went to the goats and brought some in a few minutes. The *pasta* was very clean and well cooked. What with the meat and bread, and this *pasta*, I made an excellent dinner, and felt much better. The *pasta* was all devoured in a few minutes by the band, who collected round the *caldaja*, and dipped in spoons and fingers. I had now leisure to examine the men; they were a fine, healthy set of fellows.

Here the two divisions of the band were united, thirty men under the command of Gaetano Manzo, and twelve under Pepino Cerino. The latter had the two prisoners, who had been taken on the 16th of April near the valley of Giffoni, at five o'clock in the afternoon, as they were returning from arranging some affairs connected with the death of a relative.

The smaller band had four women with them, attired like the men, with their hair cut short—at first I took them for boys; and all these displayed a greater love of jewellery than the members of Manzo's band. They were decked out to do me honor, and one of them wore no less than twenty-four gold rings, of various sizes and stones, on her hands at the same moment; others twenty, sixteen, ten, according to their wealth. To have but one gold chain attached to a watch was considered paltry and mean. Cerino and Manzo had bunches as thick as an arm suspended across the breasts of their waistcoats, with gorgeous brooches at each fastening. These were sewed on for security; little bunches of charms were also attached in conspicuous positions. I will now describe the uniforms of the two bands. Manzo's band had long jackets of strong brown cloth, the color of withered leaves, with large pockets of a circular shape on the two sides, and others in the breasts outside; and a slit on each side gave entrance to a large pocket that could hold any thing in the back of the garment. I have seen a pair of trowsers, two shirts, three or four pounds of bread, a bit of dirty bacon, cheese, etc., pulled out one after another when searching for some article that was missing. The waistcoats buttoned at the side, but had gilt buttons down the centre for show and ornament; the larger ones were stamped with dogs' heads, birds, etc. There were two large circular pockets at the lower part of the waistcoats, in which were kept spare cartridges, balls, gunpowder, knives, etc.; and in the two smaller ones higher up, the watch on one side and percussion caps in the other. This garment was of dark blue cloth, like the trowsers, which were cut in the ordinary way.

The uniform of Cerino's band was very similar, only that the jacket and trowsers were alike of dark blue cloth, and the waistcoat of bright green, with small round silver buttons placed close together. When the jackets were new they all had attached to the collars, by buttons, *capuces*, or hoods, which are drawn over the head at night or when the weather is very cold, but most of them had been lost in the woods. A belt about three inches deep, divided by two partitions, to hold about fifty cartridges, completed the dress, which, when new, was very neat-looking and serviceable. Some of the cartridges were murderous missiles. Tin was soldered round a ball so as to hold the powder, which was kept in by a plug of tow. When used the tow was taken out, and, after the powder was poured down the barrel, the case was reversed, and, a lot of slugs being added, was rammed down with the tow on the top. These must be very destructive at close quarters, but they generally blaze at the soldiers, and *vice versâ*, at such a distance, that little harm is done from the uncertain aim taken. Most of them had revolvers, kept either in the belts or the left-hand pocket of their jackets; they were secured by a silk cord round their necks, and fastened to a ring in the butt of the pistol. Some few had stilettos, only used for human victims. Many wore ostrich feathers with turned-up wide-awakes, which gave the wearers a theatrical and absurd appearance. Gay silk handkerchiefs round their necks and collars on their cotton shirts made them look quite dandies when these were clean, which was but seldom.

At last, tired of watching the band, I lay down and fell asleep. I slept for some hours, during which a poor sheep was dragged into the inclosure, killed, cut up, cooked in the pot, and eaten. I must have slept until near sunset, for when I awoke another sheep was being brought forward, and I watched the process of killing and cutting up the poor beast. The sheep was taken in hand by two men, Generoso and Antonio generally acting as the butchers of the band. One doubled the fore legs of the sheep across the head; the other held the head back, inserting a knife into the throat, and cutting the windpipe and jugular vein. It was then thrown down and left to expire. When dead, a slit was made in one of the hind legs near the feet, and an iron ramrod taken and passed down the leg to the body of the animal; it was then withdrawn, and the mouth of one of the men placed to the slit in the leg, and the animal was inflated as much as possible and then skinned. When the skin was

E 2

separated from the legs and sides, the carcass was taken and suspended on a peg on a tree, through the tendon of a hind leg; the skin was then drawn off the back (sometimes the head was skinned, but this rarely). The skin was now spread out on the ground to receive the meat, etc., when cut off the body; the inside was taken out, the entrails being drawn out carefully and cleaned; these were wound round the inside fat by two or three who were fond of this luxury — Sentonio, and Andrea the executioner, generally performing this operation. These delicacies, as they were considered, being made about four inches long and about one inch in diameter, are fried in fat or roasted on spits. It was some time before I could bring myself to eat these, but curiosity first, and hunger afterward, often caused me to eat my share, for I soon learned it was unwise to refuse any thing.

While these two men were preparing the inside, the other two were cutting up the carcass. The breast was first cut off, and then the shoulders; the sheep was then cut in half with the axe, and then the bones were laid on a stump and cut through, so that it all could be cut in small pieces. One man would hold the meat, while another would take hold of a piece with his left hand and cut with his right. As it was cut up, the pieces would be put into a large cotton handkerchief, which was spread out on the ground; the liver and lungs were cut up in the same way; the fat was then put in the *caldaja*, and, when this was melted, the kidneys and heart (if the latter had not been appropriated by some one) were put in, cooked, and eaten, every one helping himself by dipping his fingers in the pot. The pieces of liver were considered the prizes. All the rest of the sheep was then put in the pot at once, and after a short time the pot was taken off the fire and jerked, so as to bring the under pieces to the top.

They liked the meat well cooked; and when once pronounced done, it was divided into as many equal portions as there were numbers present; the captives being treated as "companions"—the term they always used in speaking of one another—I soon found that the sooner I picked up my share the better. If there was no doubt about their being plenty for all, the food was never divided. Then they dived with their hands, whoever ate fastest coming off best. I could only eat slowly, having to cut all the meat into shreds, as it was so tough; so I always took as much as they would let me, and retired to my lair, like a dog with his bone. If I finished this before all was gone, I returned for more, it being always necessary to secure as much as possible, as one was never sure when more food would be forthcoming, and it is contrary to brigand etiquette to pocket food when eaten thus. When it was divided, I might of course do as I liked with my share, but even then it was prudent not to allow them to know that I had reserved a stock in my pocket, or I was sure to come off short on the next division taking place. The skin was now taken and stretched out to dry, and then used to sleep on. I now had a talk with Visconti, who told me he had been with the brigands more than a month, having been taken by Pepino's band of twelve men close to his house in Giffoni, with his little cousin Tomasino. 40,000 ducats was the price asked for him, of which 9000 had already been paid. He complained woefully of the life and the scarcity of food, though he had never really suffered from want, the band having laid their hands on twenty sheep at once while he was with them. The length of the days troubled him much. He had not had much walking, and had been eight days in the present encampment. He had suffered from fever for some days, but was now better. He looked very white and puffy in the face. Little Tomasino was as fat as possible, and seemed to enjoy his life like a child, not reflecting on the danger of his situation. He was a great favorite with the band, and was already half a brigand. While talking, we were startled by an accidental shot from one of the brigand's guns; this made a great stir among the band, and called down the severe displeasure of the captain, who scolded the delinquent most warmly. It now grew dark, and the captain came round and told me to lie down on two sheepskins which had been assigned to me. A wallet was given me for a pillow, and also a *capote*. I was very tired, notwithstanding my sleep in the afternoon, and soon fell asleep. The captain and ten or twelve men went down the mountain in the mean time to watch. About eleven o'clock we were awakened by firing, and there was soon a volley, by which we knew they had fallen in with the troops. After a time all was quiet again, and toward the morning the captain returned with the news that one of the men had been shot while carrying bread and sundries in a handkerchief on his gun over his shoulder. He fell immediately. (Signor D—— afterward told me that it was his act.) There was great lamentation; and, at an hour before sunrise, the whole band was collected, and started off in flight.

On the 20th we did not march very far, only walking about two hours in the shade of the wood till we got lower down, where we rested for the day. A great deal of gambling went on all day long. Pepino's band were the players, for they had lately received 9000 ducats of Visconti's ransom. Their game was something of this sort: three or four men sat round a handkerchief spread on the ground; three half Napoleons were then put into a wide-awake, the lining being first torn out. The hat was then shaken, and turned over, so as to drop out the coins, which were then concealed by the hat. Money is now staked on the *croce* or *capo*. All day long it was a perpetual "*cinque a cinque capo, vint' a vinte*," and so on. I was always apprehensive of danger when the gambling was going on, for after a few minutes there was sure to be a quarrel, and when their passions were roused they were always more inclined to treat me badly. Loud voices would be heard, those making the greatest noise demanding silence, and the captain, who was as inveterate a gambler as any of them, would storm and rage at his men in the most furious manner. The gambling would often be carried on in the most dangerous places, even when the soldiers were known to be near, and when the risk attending a quarrel among themselves might easily have been fatal to the brigands.*

No fire was made to-day on account of the proximity of the soldiers, who disturbed the band last night. Bread in small quantities was divided among us, but there was no water. Two hours before sunset we started again, there being great groans from Visconti and many of the band on account of the long walk before us — seven or eight hours' march; for, though always walking, the brigands dislike and dread much of it. Soon after starting it began to rain hard. I turned my flannel trowsers up to my knees and put on my *capote*, thinking it better to endure a little cold than get my trowsers wet. This horrified the brigands, who were most anxious that I should put them down again, saying that it was very injurious to expose the knees. I told them it was the Scotch fashion, and Scotland had plenty of rain, and the people were renowned for their courage, strength, and good sense. The grass and trees were

* "It is worthy the observing, that there is no passion in the mind of man so weak but it mates and masters the fear of death."—*Bacon's Essays.*

very wet, and our boots and socks were soon wet through. In a short time we left the wood, and falling on a path, we pursued our way with the greatest caution, the captain being always in advance, and the others following in Indian file. The captives had to march toward the rear, with about four or five men behind them; one man, Pavone by name, being especially charged to take care of me. He was responsible for me, and if I had escaped his life would have been forfeited. Another, called Scope,* who was also charged never to leave me, was behind me. These two never left me, day or night. Scope, with two others, came from Acerno, and had only joined the band a few days before we were captured. He had been a *zappatore*, or laborer in the fields; his nature was most brutal. He was always with me, and invariably ill-treated me. He grudged me every morsel I had to eat, and whenever he gave me any food he always threw me my portion as if I had been a dog. He was a tall, spare man, about twenty-two years old, with a long, thin face, with large nose and large eyes. His eyes had always a mournful expression, and were constantly fixed on the ground. Remorse for some fearful deed of murder was clearly written on his countenance, as though he were already suffering for it. I often used to charge him with thinking of his victim, but he would never admit it—a shake of the forefinger or contemptuous tap on the head being all the answer he would deign to give me. We now came to a long stripe of open ground, the forest of large beech-trees skirting it on the left, and the mountain, with a gentle slope, rising on the right. Some of this ground was cultivated, and had just been plowed and sown with maize, or *granone*, as they call it. We were cautioned against speaking, or walking on the soft ground, and were

---

* Abbreviated from Scopecchio.

told to tread upon the grass, so that we might not leave any traces to betray our track to the troops, or to any of that class called by the brigands *infame*—the term they use for informers, and all those who are not well-disposed toward them, and would give any notice or information to the authorities. After walking some hours' time we passed several *pagliatte*, or straw conical huts. Some little distance from us there was a light in the last of these, arising from a wood fire in front. We were halted while some of the advance guard went up to reconnoitre. One brigand went forward to speak to the occupants, who proved to be shepherds; they had put out the fire as the band approached, and after a short conversation the two shepherds were brought down to the captain, who had remained with the band under a large spreading oak-tree. I stepped forward, longing to see an honest face, but was roughly pulled back, and told to stop where I was. My blood boiled for a moment, but I restrained myself, and endeavored to show indifference by a shrug of the shoulders. It was their invariable practice to prevent their captives from seeing or speaking to the peasants. I inquired why this was so, and was told that the peasants object to it, for fear of being recognized and denounced afterward when the prisoner has been ransomed and is free. The captain asked me if I should like some milk. I cheered up a little at the prospect of a drink at last, and a large pailful having been brought to me, I took it in my hands, and did not take it from my lips till I felt I had had enough. This was the first opportunity they had of observing my milk-consuming powers. They were rather astonished, and I explained that "*Latte me piace molto*," as it did all English people. I did not know when I should have a chance of drinking again, and acted on Captain Dugald Dalgetty's plan of laying in a stock when I had the opportunity. The two Viscontis hardly drank any, being of opinion that it was unwholesome; they are like their countrymen—they rarely touched milk. (In Rome it is a common sight to see written in English, "Milk sold here," English people being the principal consumers of that beverage.) After a halt of about half an hour we continued our walk. Pavone asked me if I knew where Salerno was, and was annoyed at my pointing without any hesitation toward it. Then followed a question as to where Pæstum (or Peste, as they call it) was. I pointed correctly as before, and also showed them the directions in which lay Rome, Apulia, and, lastly, England. They did not know the north star, which was now shining brightly, the rain having left off and the sky being quite clear; and my knowing the way, as they said, always, both by day or night, in any part of the mountains, puzzled them immensely. They never got over it, continually asking me throughout my captivity how it was that I obtained this wonderful knowledge.

On this particular occasion, my extraordinary cleverness, as they termed it, was their topic of conversation all night. The ground we were now traversing was more cultivated, and we passed another river, the Viscontis and I being carried across on the shoulders of some of the band. The path then grew better and ran between hedges. It was now very dark, and I had great difficulty in following, not being able to see an inch before me, and was obliged to take hold of the man walking before me, and to feel every step before I ventured to put my foot to the ground. Sometimes I lagged a little, and those behind now and then gave me a rap, and were in a great rage with me, Pavone indulging in a few oaths at the same time. After five hours' walking our captors began to get very tired, and poor Visconti was very foot-sore. I fortunately had a pair of well-fitting strong boots on, and, excepting that my right ankle felt a little warm, I was well enough, and ready to walk on for some hours more. I inquired how much longer we should be walking. Some said half an hour, others four or five hours; the good-natured ones of the band always shortening the time to encourage us, the others doing the reverse. It was almost an impossibility for them to tell the truth at any time, on any subject. Another hour brought us to a place where our approach disturbed some dogs, which barked most furiously till we were again far away from them. We were now told that we were getting near our sleeping-place; the district got more wild and rocky, and we heard the rushing sound of a mountain torrent, and, after following it some little way, we came to a place with rocks rising on each side, the river running between them, and leaving a small level space between it and the rocks on one side.

CHAPTER VI.

DIARY OF MR. MOENS, MAY 20 TO 27.

Brigands merry-making.—The Captain watches over me while I sleep.—His protecting Care.—Thoughts of Home.—A Storm.—The Ladies of the Band.—Doniella.—Carmina.—Maria.—Antonina.—Concetta.—Their Furniture.—They think I am a Milord.—The Government will pay for me.—A Night March.—A terrific Climb.—Method of selecting Sentries.—Threats of Mutilation.

May 20. The edge of the stream was fringed with bushes, two or three trees growing by the side of the rocks on the right of the level ground. As soon as we arrived at the camping-ground, the band gave themselves up to mirth and merriment, as they always did on coming to any place where they considered themselves perfectly safe. This encampment being below the level of the surrounding country, and the noise of the turbulent stream drowning the sound of their voices, made them now feel themselves quite secure. All but two or three burst out into one of their favorite songs; the others set to work to collect dead wood for the fire, and to cut a curved branch, which was driven into the ground near the fire, and on which was suspended the *caldaja* or caldron, containing one of the sheep that were killed when we left the top of the mountain in the morning. The fire soon burnt up; a quantity of wood was piled on, and we all crowded round to warm and dry ourselves, it having rained so heavily during our night's march. The favorite song of the band was now sung by all, and the light shining on those standing and sitting round the fire, as well as lighting up the little amphitheatre, made the whole scene most picturesque. I walked two or three steps to the river, in order to bathe my right ankle, which felt a little warm. Immediately there was a cry of "*Dove andate?*" and it was with some difficulty that I persuaded those who came to look after me to allow me to put my foot into the icy cold water. They tried to persuade me that it was most injurious, and that I should do myself some serious harm, and they eventually made me come back to the fire long before I had had time enough to bathe my foot.

In a few minutes the meat was cooked enough to please them, and divided into forty-five parts upon one of the *capotes;* three parts were given to the captives, the others coming forward to take their share. All the bread had been eaten during the day, so that we had to devour the lumps of tough mutton alone. Two other fires were now lighted up, and I tried to dry my *capote* and boots as much as possible, but in a few minutes I was shown the place allotted to me for the few hours that remained before sunrise.

The two Viscontis and I lay down together. I was on the outside, with the captain close to me. To make doubly sure, he put one leg over my chest; I tried to shake it off, but he would have it so; and, being very tired, I tried to forget all, and was soon asleep.

May 21. It seemed only five minutes when I was roused up, hearing a stern voice say "*Alza!*" which is their word for "get up." There was no denying them, so up I got, grieving over our fate at having to start again, for I had hoped, and fully expected, that we should have stopped some time at this place. We climbed up the rocky bank, and soon began to ascend a mountain covered with beech-trees, the branches of which we had to bend on one side in order to make our way through them. A tremendous thunder-storm now broke over us, with drenching rain, and after getting thoroughly wet, we reached a grotto where we rested. Here I heard, to my horror, that the two poor proprietors whom we had seen captured by the brigands, and who had been our companions during the first night's walk and the next day till the attack of the soldiers, had been murdered on that occasion when trying to escape. (I afterward found out that this was not true. Luzzo had complained of the cold on the evening of the 15th, and Manzo generously lent him his own jacket. This Luzzo had on when he escaped, and in it was a pocket-book containing papers, some of which were accounts of large sums of money expended for the band, while others were said to compromise certain neighboring proprietors.) This filled me with anguish and anxiety as regarded my poor wife; for if she had heard that some of the *ricattati* had been killed, she would at once fear for me. I asked Manzo where Luzzo was, in order to be certain whether what I had heard was true; for one of the principles of brigandage is never to tell the truth, and the only way to ascertain any thing was to ask several of my captors the same question, when I had an opportunity of doing so alone, without the others hearing me, and then, from the various answers, I would glean an approximation to the truth. Sometimes six or seven of them would give me quite different answers. The reply I got from the captain was "*Non c'è*," and that my letters and money were not to be sent to Luzzo's house, but that other arrangements had been made. He took paper out of his pocket-book, and unscrewed a little black tin ink-bottle, in which was steel pen and some cotton waste; a little water was added to this and stirred up; the water now became black and served for ink; a large, flat, round loaf was brought me to write on, and the captain began to dictate a letter for me to write to our consul general at Naples. The composition went on very slowly, by reason of my having had very little practice in writing Italian, and the Neapolitan dialect being so unlike the Roman, which is always spoken by Englishmen.

When this was done, the letter to my wife, which I had written on the 19th, at the place where I joined the band, was given back to me, to add a postscript, stating that all letters and money were to be sent to the house of my fellow-sufferer's father at Giffoni.

At twelve o'clock, noon, some *pasta* was cooked, which, with a little bread, and still less raw fat bacon, constituted our dinner. I now remembered that to-day was Sunday, and I thought of home, and the many happy Sundays we had spent there; and of the little church, where I felt that many silent prayers were being offered up on my behalf (and where, as I afterward learnt, I was prayed for by name, all those weary months that I remained in the hands of my captors). I read all our beautiful Church service; how different it appeared to me now, in my lonely and terrible position, to what it did when read in churches—the prayers and psalms seemed as though written *for me!* What confidence and trust they gave me, that by the grace of God I should be delivered from the hands of those wicked men! From this day till I was set free, I never missed reading through the whole of the morning service and litany. I generally chose the afternoon about two o'clock, when the band (like all Southerners), with the exception of the sentries, all slept, and thus gave me a quiet interval from the swearing, gambling, and disputing that were always going on around me.

At about two o'clock the captain and ten of the band went off with my letters, and the others with us climbed higher up the mountain. Soon after starting the sky grew very dark, with every appearance of another storm, which fortunately did not break until we were under the shelter of a grotto—about an hour's walk from where we had spent the morning. The grotto was very small, and only afforded room sufficient for Visconti and myself, little Tomasino creeping in behind us. About five or six feet in front of the cave was a large heap of snow that had remained unmelted in consequence of a quantity of earth having fallen upon it from the rocks above. I was about to eat some, but they would not allow me because of the earth over it, which they said generally made the snow injurious by means of poisonous matter washed from it. The cave was very damp, and the sides covered with green mould; the part between it and the bank of snow was very uneven and sloping, so Sentonio (who, though the oldest, yet was always the most active of the band) borrowed my stick, and with the point of it dug up the upper part, and in a short time made a level space large enough to accommodate the brigands with us. The storm now broke, accompanied by a most furious shower of rain that lasted about half an hour, after which it became fine again. This was the sort of weather we had for at least six weeks, though all the time it was fine and without a drop of rain in the plains of Naples and Salerno. Toward the evening a larger and drier grotto was discovered by those who went for water, a little lower down on the right; so we were moved to it after some hesitation on the part of Sentonio, who had worked so hard in order to level the ground; and we soon got wet again. How I hated these changes after we had settled down quietly! Three fires were, however, lighted on arriving at our new place of shelter, and we did our best to dry our boots and *capotes*. Our supper consisted of *pasta* again. The captain and men came back during the night with bread, some large sugar-plums, which they call *confetti*, and two bottles of *Rosolio*, which is a sort of sweetened rum. The captives had a share of these, and we thoroughly enjoyed them, having been without any luxury of the kind for a week.

May 22. To-day we had a repetition of the wet and thunder of yesterday, and, to my horror, we went down to the glen where we were yesterday morning, thus wetting my boots through again.

Here I discovered that five of the band were *brigandesses*. They were dressed exactly like the men, and their hair was cut short, the only peculiarity in their clothing being small boneless articles, which, I believe, ladies call corsets. They exhibited none of that sanguinary and savage character which I had always heard belonged to lady-brigands; all were part of the goods and chattels of their respective masters. They were considered by all as the *ultime compagne* of the band; they had no share in the ransom money, and were often beaten and ill-treated by their lords. Two of them carried guns, and the other three revolvers. Two were tall, fine, strong young women; the third had a melancholy thin face, but the largest oval eyes I had ever seen; the fourth was an ugly, sulky girl, who always appeared to refuse food or any thing offered to her, and the fifth was very much like her.

Doniella, the partner of Pepino Cerino, the *capo* of the small band of eleven men, who had taken Don Francesco and his cousin Tomasino, was a strapping young woman about nineteen years old, with a very good figure and handsome features, a pretty smile and splended teeth. She and her husband were both very greedy, and always managed to secure a double share of food, which made them very unpopular, and was eventually the cause of Pepino being deposed from his office of captain. She would sometimes give us *confetti*, but always refused us any of the extra share of food which she always had in her pocket. I often wondered how it was that she was generous enough to give me a *capuce* or hood, of blue cloth, which she did during our night's march of the 19th; but after six weeks I found out that it belonged to Cerino, who, to my grief, came to claim it when his band parted from Manzo's. This *capuce* was the greatest comfort at night. I always tied a cotton handkerchief, which they gave me, round my head, and then drew on this hood of double cloth half over my face, keeping off all wind and wet.

Carmina belonged to Giuseppe, a good-looking man, with red fuzzy hair of prodigious length; he was the dandy of the band, and had the reputation of being rich—that is, of possessing 4000 ducats. Many were the rings and gold chains on their persons and in their pockets, for a *festa* or some grand occasion was necessary to draw out of the little tin boxes that served them for jewel cases the wealth they contained. Carmina was very good-natured, and would nearly always give me any food she could spare.

Maria was the sulky girl. She hardly ever spoke to anybody, and when any one addressed her, a nod or shake of the head was all the response she would deign to give; she would never give me any thing, or do any thing for me.

Antonina was the lotus-eyed damsel. She possessed a cheerful disposition, and was always willing to do any thing she could for me in the mending way. She attached herself to Generoso di Salerno, who fully carried out the import of his name. Many a time, when food was very scarce, would these two share with me the little that they had saved from the previous day. I considered that all was fair in war, and never lost an opportunity of securing whatever I could lay my hands on. Many a time I endeavored to impress on them that, as an Englishman, I required double the quantity that would suffice for them; but I regret to say that this had little effect, except in giving them the idea that I had an insatiable appetite.

Concetta belonged to Cicco Guange, and was very similar in disposition to Maria.

All these women had about them needles, scissors, cotton and silk of various hues, as well as bits of cloth, and they were always ready to do any repairs that were needful; and when a fresh supply of handkerchiefs (or *maccatore*, as they were termed) arrived, they would all sit together and steadily work away till they were done. During a thunder-storm they would always cease working—out of some religious feeling—and at every clap of thunder cross themselves. Sunday was the same as other days as regarded working. I tried to explain to them that they should rest from labor on that day, but always without effect.

On the western side of this glen, in which we remained all day, there was a high bank of earth, with the roots of the large beech-trees protruding from it. In the winter the glen served as a water-course; but it was now quite dry, and served as a capital place of concealment, though on that account it was all the worse for us. The dense forest of beech-trees that clothed the whole side of the mountain prevented us seeing beyond a very little way, and the ground was every where covered with dead leaves, six inches deep, packed closely together by the weight of the snow in winter.

I looked round to discover something that might perchance serve to pass away the weary hours; flowers there

F

were none, but suddenly my eye rested on a twisted root, about five inches thick. It struck me that I might be able to manufacture a spoon, to be my own, so that it would not be necessary to use one that had just been in the mouth of a murderer. I got up, took the **hatchet,** and began with gentle and silent strokes to cut a piece about six inches long; three or four of my guardians soon inquired what I was doing, and told me not to make a **noise.** After five minutes Pavone came up, and with two or three cuts, much more violent than I had dared to make, separated the desired piece. They asked what I wanted it for, and were much amused when I told them that it was for the purpose of making a spoon. This kept me amused for two whole days; hour by hour I perseveringly kept whittling away with a tiny little penknife, one and a quarter inches long, with a most delicate little blade of the best steel I ever saw. Many a day did that precious little knife amuse me, and many a time did I refuse to lend it for fear it should come to grief. Sometimes I was obliged to do so, but then I never rested till it was again safe in my possession.

It was very cold at night, and the ground being very wet on account of the constant storms and rain, I always tried to dry my *capote* as much as I could; but the thick woolen cloth absorbed so much water that I could never do so perfectly, and I always woke in the morning shivering with cold, and with my joints quite stiff. I rubbed my knees for some time, and then tried to get close to the fire, which was always made at daybreak to thaw us, for many of the band were without *capotes,* having lost them on the 16th, when surprised by the **troops.** Some of the men would not let me go near the fire until they were forced to do so by those well-disposed toward me. When warm, or a little less cold, I would try to go to sleep again till about eight o'clock, when we would eat what little was given to us, generally at this time a little piece of very hard stale bread, about three inches square.

May 23. Repetition of yesterday.

May 24. Great rain to-day. Early in the morning we were sent to the cave above, where we had spent the 21st; we got very wet, and had to lie in our wet things all day. In the afternoon there was another frightful storm; all the brigands crossed themselves as peal succeeded peal of thunder. Toward the evening it was fine again, and after sunset the four men who had been out foraging returned with a little bread and cheese.

May 25. To-day was very quiet, Visconti and I talking to each other continually. Through disuse of my own language, I found Italian much more easy than at first, and we got on very well together. I asked him about country life in Italy, and he, in return, of mine in England. He, as well as the brigands, would have it that I was "My lord," and that wretched little Tomasino would come up to me and tell me that, from certain information the brigands had got, I was possessed of 2,000,000 ducats, and that the Italian government was going to pay my ransom, in which case they would not be contented with the 50,000 asked, but would not let me go under 1,000,000. This enraged me immensely, and I am afraid I sometimes was very unkind to the poor little fellow.

To-day Visconti most generously gave me a thick flannel sleeve-waistcoat, as he had two of these articles. It was most acceptable to me, because I was most miserably clothed, my dress being only suited to the hot plains. I do not know how I should have got on without this extra garment. In the middle of the day some of the band arrived with two sheep. I rejoiced to see them, for we had not had any meat for five or six days. The sheep were soon killed, skinned, and in the great camp-kettle; but Visconti and I were horrified at finding we had to eat the meat without bread. I had secured a heart, which I roasted on a stick, and divided with Visconti, as I always did with any thing that I could secure apart from the general division. On searching in my pocket I found a little piece of bread, which I had put away and forgotten; this I ate as dessert, in order to take away the taste of meat. We were told not to eat all, but to reserve some for the evening. But now a difficulty arose with us as regarded carrying it. The cleanest thing we could produce was my white pocket-handkerchief. There was no help for it—I had to sacrifice it; and, wrapping up our joint store, I put it in the left pocket of my coat, which from this time served as my larder. An hour before sunset every thing was packed away, and we were informed that a long march was before us. I was very cold, and a biting wind was blowing, so that I was rather rejoiced than otherwise, for I dreaded sleeping in the open air these damp cold nights. I always dreaded, too, waking up in the morning, on account of the piercing cold—dreaming, perchance, of home, and then suddenly finding myself in the midst of these ruffians.

It was a long up-hill walk through the forest; we rested once for an hour, and then started off again in Indian file. It was very dark, and again I had the greatest difficulty in following. I found the best plan was to grasp with my left hand the shoulder or muzzle of the gun of the man before me. As we approached the summit of the mountain, the force of the wind and cold increased. Several of those in front went on, while we were halted and told to lie down, as the tops of the mountains were always considered dangerous, for the soldiers are often stationed there, and make *baraques*, or round huts, of fresh-cut boughs, in which they pass the nights. With what envy I passed these! I looked on them as palaces, and always asked the brigands why they did not use them, but a shake of the forefinger was the invariable reply. After reconnoitring some way in advance, a low whistle informed us that all was right. We were told to rise, and a few steps took us to the top.

May 26. On looking about, I found that we were on the summit of a very high mountain (Monte Polveracchio). Morning was beginning to dawn, and I could perceive mountains all round us. In the distance, toward the west, I fancied I saw the sea, which proved to be the case. When it grew more light, toward the northwest I perceived the outline of the mountains at the back of Salerno, and stretching out to sea was the part beyond Vietri. I felt too miserable to look longer in that direction, the idea of actually seeing the place where my dear wife probably was being too much for me. Fortunately, the march now required all my attention; it was along the sharp edge of the summit, and in many places a false step on either side would have been attended with great danger, for, on account of the precipices on each side, every step had to be taken with care and judgment, the more so because of the furious wind which threatened often to blow me over the edge. When we had gone some way along this narrow part, I perceived a town below us, on a small and perfectly level plain, one end of which was covered with large chestnut-trees. This, Visconti told me, was Acerno, a place which afterward became of great importance to me, as I was eventually set free when in the immediate neighborhood of it.

We now turned off toward the right down a very steep descent; I slipped and fell, the captain seeing which told one of the band to carry my *capote*, which I was carrying on my back, rolled up and slung with a piece of cord. I was delighted at being eased of my burden, and was able to walk much more easily; my feet were now in capital walking order, and my boots, though by no means new, still in fair condition, and were stout, and fitted me well. This was a great comfort, for it was heart-breaking to see poor Don Francesco, who suffered dreadfully from blisters at his heels, his feet being, as he expressed it, "*Tutti consumati*." Little Tomasino walked capitally for a boy, but he and Visconti were both constantly being urged on by the brigands. I always walked in the front of them, and found no difficulty in keeping up at their pace. After having descended for about three quarters of an hour, we saw a frightful precipice rising perpendicularly on our left, and a deep ravine below us. It was necessary to cross the ravine; but the opposite side was very perpendicular, and the rock very loose and rotten. A halt was called while three or four descended to see whether it was practicable to ascend the other side. When they reached the bottom we watched them in order to know if we should follow, but as soon as they got up a yard or so the rock broke away, and down they slid again; at last, after about an hour, we saw one of them appear on the large rock that jutted out at the top of the precipice on our left, about 500 feet higher than where we were. He called out to us, and we answered. We were horrified with the idea of having to follow to that inaccessible crag. I never saw a place more fitted for an eagle's nest. All those below had found it impossible to follow Luigi in scaling the crumbling rock, his very ascent having made it impracticable for those below him. He sat down contentedly, and watched us below. After a short time, we heard a call from the face of the precipice. We looked round and saw two of the others clinging on to the face of it, and slowly creeping, without their shoes, along its surface. At one spot where they stopped, the little ledge, three or four inches wide, on which they had passed, came to an end, and there was an interval of four or five feet without an atom of support to the foot. Luigi saw the difficulty; he descended to them, and, stretching out his arms, helped the foremost one to pass. This was done successfully, after some minutes' attempt, and when the others saw him safe they all gave a little kind of cheer. I declared it impossible to reach the place, for I saw no fun in risking my neck for these wretches; and poor Visconti kept appealing to heaven. All those with us looked very blue; but, after the second man had passed safely, the captain stepped forward and got over all right. The three now looked like a little flock of goats, feeling as happy at having passed safely as we felt miserable at the prospect of doing so.

I did not like the idea of being outdone by these men, so I volunteered to go next. I found mere little knobs of rock jutting out. Step by step I progressed, without daring to take my eyes off my feet and the inequalities in the surface, to which I clung with my hands. It was a fearful place. I stopped for a moment to survey my position above. The rock was 500 feet high, and below there was a sheer descent of 800 to 1000 feet. I am fortunate enough to possess rather a hard head, not given to dizziness, but I confess my position gave me rather a twist for a moment. However, the thought that the other three had passed gave me courage, and on I crept. At last I arrived at the gap. One of those that had passed came to help me. I stretched my right leg as far as I could, and, with a spring, over I went, and, with a lighter heart, went gayly up the now comparatively easy ascent to the crag. One by one they all came over. Poor Visconti was helped all the way, and when he reached us he was still uttering his pious ejaculations, with his hands raised toward heaven. We now went over the top, and descended among some enormous beeches where the wood-cutters had been at work, leaving innumerable chips covering the ground. A little farther on we halted for the day, and Luigi, an old brigand belonging to Cerino's band, began to cut at a great piece of beechwood with the axe. When he had got it about an inch thick, I asked him what he was going to do with it, and he told me that he was going to make a ramrod for a man called Rocco, who had broken the one belonging to his gun. Thinking it would amuse me for an hour or two to make it, I volunteered to do so, and Luigi handed the stick over to me, my skill at spoon-making having caused me to be considered *talented*, as they expressed it. It amused them much to see my way of going to work. I rested one end against my chest, and the other in a notch which I cut in a tree with the axe, and then, taking one of their murderous knives by the handle and point, I sliced little pieces off till it was about the size required. All the band collected round me, watching me with admiring eyes. After scraping it a little with some glass from a bottle broken on purpose, and greasing it with a little piece of fat bacon, it was pronounced perfect. I was rather proud of my work. It was quite straight and round, and fitted the gun capitally.

When it was done, a bright thought struck me. I asked them what it would cost in a town. "A ducat," was the answer. Then I said, "It was surely worth two ducats in the woods." "*Sicuro*," was the reply all round. "Then give me half a *marengo*," I burst out; "I do not see why you should not pay me as well as a gunmaker." Pepino, the *capo*, said nothing, but all the rest burst out laughing for a quarter of an hour. I kept demanding it, saying "*Da-*

temi il denaro ;" and at last Pepino drew out half a Napoleon and handed it over to me! I told them I should have "*La Banda di Manzo*" cut on it, and that I should wear it on my watch-chain. This delighted them immensely, and they were good-tempered with me all that day, though there was a great lack of food, and we were reduced to eating the crumbs and dirt at the bottom of our pockets, which were always afterward reserved for such occasions.

An hour before sunset we started again, passing through the dense forest, ascending all the time till we reached the summit of the mountain. Here we rested till it grew dark, when we began to descend the open grassy side facing the southwest, leaving the woods behind us on the northern slopes. This was generally the case with all the mountains, the north side getting less of the hot burning sun, and thus retaining more of the moisture, so necessary for forest-trees.

After a descent of 400 or 500 feet, we came to a shallow ravine with a thicket of trees, which was to be a halting-place for the night. They then proceeded to select the sentinels for the night. This was done as follows:

All the band, except the women and those that were ill, stand up and form a circle, and then, at a signal from the captain, throw out their right hands, with various numbers of fingers extended, in the same way as the national game of "*La Morra*" is played. The captain, now inside the circle, walks round and counts the fingers extended, and then, retaking his place, counts from himself all round the circle, and the unlucky man on whom the number falls, together with his neighbors, have to commence the watch. Three hours is the usual time.

I often used to offer to take my turn, especially when only one sentinel was necessary, but I was always refused with laughter and thanks. We went supperless to bed;

that is, we lay down on the damp ground, Don Francesco and I under one *capote*, for his had been taken away by one of the band, they considering that one *capote* was plenty for two. There was always a debate how it was to be arranged, Visconti wanting it to be all above us, but I being firm in having a little piece underneath; so we spread it over, and then tucked in the sides underneath to lie upon; but, if either turned, it reduced the other to grief. Many were the growls this occasioned, for the wet soon made itself felt unless the cloak was well under us, and I always dreamt of rheumatism.

May 27. We all woke up this morning very cold and stiff. Little fires were lighted as usual, but here great caution was requisite because of our exposed position, and many were the ravings directed against those warming themselves, on account of more smoke rising than was considered prudent. They were all particularly savage this morning, as food was wanting, and this always excited their ire against the unfortunate captives, and at the present time against me in particular, for no letters or money had been received from my friends. For a long time they kept surrounding me, pointing guns, revolvers, and knives at me, explaining to me which were the most delicate parts of the body, and how life was the most easily taken.

I always made it a point to appear perfectly unmoved on these occasions. My invariable phrase was "*Se volete*," implying that they were perfectly at liberty to take my life, and that in doing so would save my friends and myself a great deal of trouble and loss of money, and that I was quite sure that they cared more for my money than for taking my life. After a short time I found that my perfect indifference rather amused them, and "*Se volete*" became by-words of the band for every thing whereby indifference was implied. We had very little food the last two days, but to-day there was nothing whatever, and I grumbled immensely, telling them that Englishmen always eat double the amount of food that Italians are satisfied with. Poor Visconti wrung his hands, perpetually saying "*Terribile! terribile!*" Supperless we lay down last night, supperless we did the same to-night, trying to make the best of it, and hoping for better luck the next day.

CHAPTER VII.

Diary of Mr. Moens, May 28.

The second Sunday.—Good News for Visconti.—More Letter-writing. —An Attempt at Sketching.—The Englishman's Appetite.—Alarms. —The Soldiers.—A Tradimento.—Death of Luigi.—Thoughts of Escaping.—The drying Process.—Difficulty of Washing.—A wounded Brigandess.—Assistance given by the Peasants to the Brigands.—Description of the Band.—A regular Feed for once in a way.—Pot-luck. —Unpleasant Sleeping-quarters.—Sheep-stealers.

May 28. SUNDAY, and a lovely day; the air as clear as crystal. I counted seven separate ridges of mountains between our lair and Salerno. Each seemed to stand up clear and distinct by itself. I could distinguish the white houses of the town, and tried to fancy that I could see the Hotel Vittoria. I could distinguish two steamers, which I set down as Florio's boats, coming from or going to Palermo, and I remembered our happy voyage from that city only a little more than a fortnight ago. A trifle to the south I could distinguish the temples of Pæstum, and some ten miles to the north of these a few white houses, representing Battipaglia, where the ruffians who surrounded me had lain in waiting for so many hours. The panorama was superb. I tried to enjoy it, but my heart was too sad; I could only think of all those that were striving to procure my release.

At eleven o'clock I took out my Prayer-book and went through the service, and thought of those many hundred of thousands of our Church who were then doing the same.

As I read I was frequently interrupted by the brigands asking me what I was reading, and wanting to look at the book. After a few days they ceased troubling me in this manner, for they all had great respect for any prayer or other sacred book.

In the afternoon we inquired again when food was coming, but could get no other response than an angry "Who knows?" All at once whistles and other signals were heard, and immediately each grasped his gun and ran forward in a stooping position to face the danger; but the word "*Compagni*" set them all at ease again, and Lorenzo Guerino and four or five others came up. Visconti was in the greatest state of excitement, and asked if there was any more money for him. Joy spread over his countenance as they replied in the affirmative, and seven fingers were held out to represent 7000 ducats. I wanted him to rush forward to receive his letters, but he feared the ravings with which his impatience would be met, for all letters were always read by their lordships before being handed over to us prisoners; but Don Elia's writing was too much for Manzo or Andrea, the secretary of Pepino, and Don Francesco was told to sit down by Manzo's side, and read his father's letters out loud.

More signals were now heard, the same scene of excitement was gone through, and Zacharia, a domestic of Visconti's household, was led forward, bearing bread, wine, and a little chocolate and some sweets from Don Elia and his brother, in order, as the letter to Tomasino expressed it, "to assuage that hunger of which you complain." This, of course, was immediately taken by the band, and divided in equal shares, Sentonio cutting all the cheese, *supersato*, and sausages with scrupulous impartiality. I fortunately fell across the little basket while Francesco Cicco had it. I saw five cakes of chocolate, and appropriated two before I could be stopped for Visconti and myself, but, alas! the women got wind of this, and came to me for some. I had to disgorge at least a third of what I had secured, and the sweets were also divided, but Visconti and I got none. They now came for my **leather drinking-cup, and the** enormous bottle of wine was speedily emptied, the cup being passed round full to **each.** The day of starvation was **turned into** a *festa*, **but at the** expense of the two Viscontis; for **the supply of food, which** was meant to last them till more could be sent, **was eaten** up at one fell swoop by these ruffians. Fifteen thousand ducats had now been paid by the family of Visconti for their two unfortunate members, and Don Elia, in his letter, pleaded great poverty, and desired to know how much more was requisite in order to free them. Many of **the band demanded all** the sum originally asked, viz., 40,000 ducats, equal to £6800; but, after a thoroughly Italian dispute, and many threats toward the unhappy victims, 25,000 ducats, or £4150, was the amount settled upon; and it was intimated that if this sum was not completed and **sent** immediately, **ears and fingers would be dispatched to** Giffoni forthwith. **Poor little Tomasino was made** to write in a **similar strain, only that his head was to be** sent, ears and **all. It was** a touching scene to see the poor little fellow writing his letter in a large round-hand writing.

I was now taken in hand, and told to write to the consul and my wife, but, to my great grief, was forbidden **to write** one word of English. Visconti **was tutored by** Manzo as to the substance **of my** letter, **and, after a short** time, two long letters were **written. I was** very anxious that the insurance on my life **should not be** forgotten to be paid. So, after a great deal **of trouble, I got leave** to insert the names of friends of mine in England, and with them a hint as to the insurance.

I had forgotten the date, and so misdated my letters the 26th instead of the 28th.*

The division of the food, eating it, and the letter-writing had made the time pass so quickly that we had not noticed the shades of evening that had darkened around us, and down we lay again, thanking God for the merciful sending of the food, which had turned our starvation into comparative plenty—the brigands who had brought the money having also brought a large supply of bread.

During the night there was again an alarm, but this turned out to be a false one, or rather of no account; but the next day proved it to be a spy of the troops sniffing round us. Had it been known who it was, his life would have answered for it.

May 29. It was a cold, damp night, and in the morning, when we were awakened by the usual kick and alarm, we found every thing enveloped in a dense fog; the captain told off ten men to go with him in order to receive the answers to our letters, and any money that might be sent.

We were sent off under the charge of Pepino and the rest of the two bands. The Viscontis were the property

---

* After this I took a little piece of paper, and on it endeavored to sketch the superb view before us. All stood round me passing comments on the Inglese that was supposed to be able to do every thing. (My being able to tell them the nationality of their guns and pistols had surprised them.) They did not quite like this new amusement, and in a day or two destroyed my sketch and got hold of my pencil, to the disappointment of both Visconti and myself. He was always making abstruse calculations of francs, ducats, and Napoleons, and, being without a pencil, had always borrowed mine. This sketch was talked about to the peasants, then at Salerno, and then through the Italian journals to the English papers, magnified, of course, and many of my friends were disappointed that I have not a complete set of sketches illustrating my life among the brigands.

of his band, while I belonged to Manzo's, unfortunately for me; for Pepino and his men had no interest in my expected ransom, and all the time I was under his charge I was miserably treated: unfair shares of food, blows, threats, and constant bullying, were what I had to put up with.

We retraced our steps of Saturday evening and ascended the steep hill. How I groaned mentally as I dragged my legs, so stiff from the effects of the damp ground, up the ascent! When we reached the top we did not descend the other side, but turned to the left and went along the narrow ridge. We experienced the same difficulties as before on account of the sharpness of the ridge causing our passing along it to be so exceedingly dangerous. At one place an enormous precipitous rock barred the way, its flat sides overhanging on each side. After examining it all round, we found a place at one corner where, by being pulled up from above and being pushed up from below, we succeeded one by one in ascending a few yards, and then, passing round the corner, went some way along a narrow ledge, and found at last a more practicable path. A little farther on we found two *baraque;* the boughs with which they were made looked as if they had been built only two days before, and the leaves were quite fresh, and not at all withered. "*La forza!*" was the sudden cry of all, and at once all eyes were on the ground looking for the footmarks of the soldiers, and they were immediately estimated at fifty in number.

After walking for about an hour and a half, we came to what was considered a proper place for concealing ourselves; the narrow ridge ceased suddenly, forming a precipice of some hundreds of feet, making our lair quite secure on the side facing the north, while on the west there was another precipice. On the south of the ridge and eastward

there was a narrow ascent covered with brushwood and
large trees; there were two enormous beech-trees in the
two northern corners, and another in the southwestern.
We were told to lie down while Pavone and Justi cut down
small trees and branches, which were placed between these
trees in order to make the place more secure. In the centre there was a large stone, weighing about a ton; this was
attacked next, but it was more than they could manage, as
it was three parts sunk in the ground; but Sentonio and
Pavone persevered, and by undermining it, and cutting a
huge branch to use as a lever, it was moved out of the way
to one side, and the place made level.

These operations took some time, and they were only just
completed, when a sudden grasping of guns, and a movement of all in the direction from which we had come, made
the hearts of us prisoners jump into our throats. I had not
yet got accustomed, as I did very soon, to these sudden
alarms. The brigands' senses of hearing and seeing were
extraordinarily acute; their very lives depended on them;
they could always detect the approach of any one many
hundred yards off; I soon acquired the same habit, and often told them of the approach of those who were fetching
food and water. On this occasion the blue clothing of the
comer soon told them that it was one of their companions,
and he rushed into the centre of the group, saying, in hurried accents, that there had been a *tradimento*, and that two
companies of soldiers surrounded the place where we had
passed Saturday night and Sunday only a few minutes after
we had left it, and that we must immediately leave the
neighborhood. Many were the imprecations uttered against
the troops. I can not admit that we prisoners looked on
them as likely to be our deliverers — the chances seemed
one hundred to one against our being rescued by them; for

the soldiers blaze away at any thing moving, and the prisoners always stood the same chance of being hit as the brigands. Besides, **Manzo** had given strict orders to all his followers to shoot us immediately there appeared the slightest chance of our escaping; and the band were always the most savage against me because I was an Englishman, and they feared that I would give information, when native prisoners dared not, for fear of the vengeance of the band.*
Fortunately Ferdinando brought with him a *maccatore* full of bread, which served for our breakfast; but no time was allowed us to eat it now, as all the *robe* were collected, and off we went again toward the east, walking for three or four hours down hill before we pulled up. The scenery was most monotonous, the whole way being through one interminable forest of beech-trees. The path was exceedingly steep, and we often had to cling on by the branches of one tree, not leaving hold till we could stop our impetus against the stem of another.

About the middle of the day a furious thunder-storm came on as usual, and we all took refuge under trees from the terrific shower of rain that fell. Don Francesco and I sat crouched up under the *capote* that had been given to me. We were under a large beech, but very soon the rain came pouring down from the branches on us, but we could not move because every where the ground was running with water. Below us was a plain with two villages in sight. I told Visconti that I thought it was his country, but he did not seem to know it, and laughed at me for attempting to know a place I had never seen. I told him

---

* How many are now living in terror in consequence of having given evidence against atrocious villains, whose lives have been spared some day, perhaps, to commit new atrocities! Read the history of the brothers La Gala, in Mr. Hilton's "Brigandage in Southern Italy," vol. ii.

that Giffoni was a little more to our left, shut out from our sight by a mountain. (I was quite right, as it turned out; and he recalled the circumstance to my mind when I was at Giffoni after my release, and he pointed out to me the mountain where we had been on that day.)

Well do I remember that day and place, for a terrible judgment fell on Luigi, one of Cerino's band. I was all the more impressed with it on account of an occurrence that took place two days before. Seeing a little cross and beads in the hands of the man, and being always on the look-out for little reminiscences, I asked him for it; but his reply was, "What! give you my life?" He explained to me that, if he lost or parted with it, he would soon lose his life. Luigi was sitting on a mass of rock a few yards from me, with Pepino, Doniella, and two or three others close to him. Between them and me, on the right-hand side, there was a little gap, and below the mountain was rather steep. On our left it was level for a short distance, and then rose to a great height. All at once the cry of "*La Forza*" was raised, and off they all ran, those sitting by us driving us on. Most of them ran up hill. I darted through the gap on my right; for I thought that, if the troops came on, when I got below I could double back toward them; but that wretch Andrea, the executioner, came after me, and told me to stop. It was a false alarm, and Visconti and I returned back to the place we had kept dry under the beech, and sat down in our old position, but in two or three minutes some one said, "Where is Luigi?" He was not to be seen, but one of them found his *capote* where he had been sitting. Three paces from it was a precipice of about 2000 feet, and the poor fellow had in his fright gone clean over it, not having noticed the danger when he sat down. A cry of horror was raised at the discovery, and tears rose in the eyes of all his companions. I could not but feel much affected at his awful death, though at the same time I confess I counted four on my fingers, that being the number now disposed of since I had been taken by the band, and I thought to myself that the more that were killed the better chance I should have of escaping. Luigi feared the hand of man, but little thought that, by his own act, he was rushing, with all the sins of four years' brigandage on his head, into the presence of his Maker!

The women were most affected, shedding tears; and "*povero Luigi!*" was the exclamation of all. He was a tall, thin man, about forty years of age, very reserved, and with far more forethought than most Italians. He was very careful and saving; his clothing was old and full of repairs. He always mended a rent immediately. He carried on his back a wallet of sheepskin, in which were stowed away many useful articles, such as scissors, an awl for mending boots, etc., etc. His trowsers fitted close to the leg, and he wore large, thick woolen gaiters.

After a few minutes' lamentation they went down the mountain in order to find his body, for there was but little doubt as to his fate. After about three quarters of an hour's descent we were halted, while the band went a little way up the ravine on our left to search for him. They soon found him lying on the snow with which the ravine was filled. He was quite dead, with his back broken and his head smashed in. While the search for the body was going on we had been halted in the midst of some tall broom, under the charge of Pavone, and after a few minutes we went on along the narrow footpath. I was in front, and, instead of turning to the left, went straight on, Visconti, Tomasino, and Pavone following me. When the rest of the band, who had returned from their sad task, perceived us, they gave a signal cry to tell us where they were — about 300 yards on our left, on the other side of a little stream.

I now thought of attempting to escape by running along the path; but it was at least two miles to the village I had seen in the morning, and it was getting dark, and I should have had to cross two small mountains, and the odds were too heavy against me; so that when Pavone found out he had mistaken the path, he called out to me, and I turned back with the rest. He was in an awful rage, danced in the air with passion, and cocked his gun ready for use, had any one of us attempted to escape. Had the path been well defined and level, and the time earlier in the day, I think I should have attempted it, for I was at least fifty yards ahead, and before he could have fired at me I should have been a hundred yards off; and I knew that he had only a musket, and before he could have loaded again I should have been at a safe distance; but the two miles to the town and the difficulties of the way determined me to wait for a more favorable opportunity. I was always on the look-out to escape, and constantly bore in mind which direction would take me to the town; but Pavone and Scope never let me go out of their sight, and I could never move my position, either day or night, without the exclamation of "*Che fate?*" or "*Dove andate?*" I could not even sit up without being told to lie down directly. (I never had but one chance, which I will relate hereafter.) When we joined the rest of the band, I found them all plunged in grief; they had stripped poor Luigi of all that might prove useful, but his clothes, being old and ragged, were left upon him.

Poor fellow! He was left on the snow just as he lay when they found him, and in a few days the vultures that abound in this district would no doubt leave nothing but his bones to bleach in the mountain air, probably never again to be seen by human eye. I asked for some little memento of him, and they gave me the little bag full of pictures of saints, which Italians of the lower class always carry on their persons. In it were also three little leaves and some pieces of the gum used for incense in the churches.

After a short time, on we went; it was now dark, and we left the path, and directed our course through a thick wood along the bottom of the mountain. The trees were very wet, and as we pushed the branches on one side in order to pass, we were soaked through by the falling drops; our feet, too, and trowsers, were thoroughly drenched, and I groaned inwardly at the prospect of our night's rest, or rather the want of it.

After two hours' more walking, when we were nearly dead beat, a low whisper of "*fuoco*" was raised by those ahead, and we were told to walk "*cete a cete*"—that is, as silently as possible; and in five minutes we were halted, while two went on to see the cause of the fire in the wood, as the soldiers were known to be all round, and it was feared that this might be one of their encampments. It proved, however, to be only the fire of some wood-cutters, so we were moved on at a signal from the advanced guard, and in three minutes we were warming ourselves round the welcome blaze. Two peasants were there when we came up, but in a few minutes, two more, who had retired on our approach, advanced from the darkness round. These were old friends, if one could judge from the kisses and warm embraces with which they were greeted by several of the band. To our great delight, on one side of the fire a tall rock overhung a little, and had thus kept the ground under it quite dry; this was strewed with dry moss, and Visconti and I sat down on it, and, to our joy, were allowed to remain there. I was dreadfully hungry, not having had any thing to eat since our meagre breakfast of literally only a mouthful of black bread. My eye fell on a *maccatore* hung on a corner of the rock, in which was a little Indian-corn bread. I asked one of the wood-cutters if he would give it me; but, with curses from the band, I was told not to touch it. It was handed over to one of them, and two more loaves being produced, the whole was divided in equal shares, and I ate my portion with gratitude, thanking God for the unexpected fire and shelter that we had fallen in with.

I took off my boots and socks, and dried them as well as I could, but before they were half dry I was made to put them on for fear of our being surprised, and my not being able to run away barefooted. This fear caused them always to forbid my removing any of my clothing for washing purposes. I stood and dried my capote and garments as long as I was allowed to do so, turning round and round, as though roasting on a jack. It was near midnight before we laid down, curled up on the moss that was to have served as the wood-cutters' couch. They sat round the fire, conversing with the band, who thus heard all the news of the district, and were told of all the movements of the troops. Visconti and I slept soundly, but were woke up as usual at an hour before daybreak.

May 30. We left the wood-cutters, who were presented with a Napoleon as a *complimento*, and we ascended higher up the mountain. An hour's walk brought us to a level space, concealed by trees all round. On one side a gully, where the winter rains ran down, formed a straight path down the mountain side. We had to lie down on the wet grass, but soon forgot these little cares in more sleep. When we awoke again at about seven or eight o'clock, we asked for bread, but were told that we should have none all day, and that there would be no water.

In the middle of the day there was one of the usual alarms, which proved to be caused by four or five more of the band who had come to join us. With them was one of the women—Concetta. Poor girl! she had been shot right through the upper part of the arm through the accidental discharge of one of the guns. The ball had broken the bone in two, and the arm was suspended and wrapped up in numerous pocket-handkerchiefs. She did not utter a groan or murmur. Much concern for her was exhibited by all, and all strove to do what little they could for her. Natural ammoniated water was used to bathe and dress it with, and a shirt was torn up and unraveled to furnish lint. Cicco acted as surgeon, and no one could have been more tender in his treatment of her. No food was given to us all day, but, to my joy, I found in my pocket a morsel of bread that I had forgotten. I shared it with Don Francesco, and then turned out my pockets, and, picking out the dirt, ate the crumbs which I found there. We heard from the newly-arrived brigands to-day that the troops were all round us. Great caution was observed. In the evening two or three ascended the mountain to search for snow, and in about an hour and a half returned with a great mass carried on a stick. We ate a quantity of this to assuage our thirst, not having had any water for twenty-four hours. I found this want of drink very trying at first, but soon had to get accustomed to it, and to fare still worse.

The news was also spread round to-day that the government was going to pay for me, and that, as this was so, they were going to demand a much larger ransom. This disturbed me dreadfully, and kept me awake all night. I talked much to Visconti on the subject. He told me it was very bad news for me, and might be the cause of my being detained a long time. Tomasino, like a boy as he was, took the greatest pleasure in worrying me, declaring to me that the brigauds had told him again that if the government paid they would require 1,000,000 ducats; and that, even if I paid this, I should have plenty left, because of the great riches which they all declared I possessed. He also greatly annoyed his cousin, who declared that he was a *vera musca*, alias *musquito*. He certainly was most tiresome, and I am afraid that at times I quite lost my patience with him, and frequently kept my stick by my side as a reminder for him not to come too near me. To add to our misery, in the evening we had more rain. It seemed of little use drying our clothes, or spreading them on a branch in the sun, for they were no sooner dry than wet again, and when once soaked, the *capote* took two or three days to get moderately dry—perfectly so it never was at this period. To-night I discovered that the muslin turban that I used to wear on my straw-hat, when rolled up and doubled, made a capital comforter to wear round my neck at night. I never omitted to use this afterward until the weather got too warm, when it made a secure shelter for those disgusting little animals from which I suffered so much a little later.

Had all the sufferings I had to endure eventually come upon me during the first days, I do not know how I should have borne them; but they seemed to come on gradually, and what I thought dreadful at first I got to think little of afterward.

May 31. It rained nearly all night, and there was a cold, cutting wind, so we accordingly woke up in the morning, if possible, colder and stiffer than usual, and we had to straighten our knees entirely by rubbing them, as no fire could be made on account of the troops around us. We were not allowed to move or speak all the first part of the day, fifty soldiers having passed along the valley a little after the break of day, and there were two posts not far from us. The wood-cutters, who had been busy felling trees all yesterday, and the sound of whose strokes had enlivened the solitude, were quite silent to-day. I presume they had left the neighborhood, evidently fearing being implicated with the doings of the band, should the troops discover where we were; for the peasants were thrown into prison on the slightest suspicion of providing the band with food; and very properly so too, for without the aid of the peasantry it would be impossible for brigandage to exist. As it is, the peasants can not resist the high price paid for every thing by the brigands, and when they meet, like all the Italians of this class, they can not refrain from gossiping about every thing that goes on in the district, particularly the movements of the troops, and the constant *complimentos* paid to them make them anxious to impart every thing that is of importance to these outlaws. Suddenly, about the middle of the day, soldiers were seen on the top of the mountain opposite to us, through the telescopes which were in constant use. This created great excitement, and we were made to lie flat on the ground, and not allowed to move, while one or two of the men ascended the highest trees near, and, with the glasses, reported every movement. The soldiers, about fifty in number, lay down on the ground and rested for half an hour, and then disappeared over the top of the mountain; we saw nothing more of them; but the band was uneasy all day, some one constantly ascending the trees in order to keep a good look-out. They astonished me with the ease and rapidity with which they climbed, taking hold of a branch and swinging themselves up in an instant. As soon as it was considered safe we went farther up the mountain, to my great annoyance; for, instead of the places that we had kept dry, we had to lie

down just where we were told, for we **were never allowed
to use our** own discretion, but were frequently made to settle **down in a nest** of nettles, thorns, or thistles. When we got here a little bread was produced, but so little that it only served to make us more hungry than before. With the bread came the news that Victor Emmanuel was going to pay my ransom himself. **This** was bad news for me, for, as long as there was a **chance of its** being true, they would keep asking the 50,000 ducats.

I amused myself this afternoon in learning all I could about brigandage in the province of Salerno by asking all at various times. I concluded that there were in all about seventy brigands, under four captains, and this turned out to be very near the mark—Giardullo and his band consisting of about thirty, and the two bands with which I was connected being in number forty-two. Of these, seven were runaway soldiers, viz., Manzo, Ferdinando, **Guange,** Amendolo,* Carini, and two others; Giuseppe, from what I could hear, came from Naples. Cicco had once some little amount of money, on which he lived before being a brigand; Andrea, the executioner, had, by his own account, been a master shoemaker; the others all had been agricultural laborers or shepherds excepting my friend Lorenzo Guerino, who had been a sawyer and carpenter. Nearly all had committed homicide. Manzo, however, and Guange, by the account of all, were free from this crime; the former on one occasion shot a follower for refusing to obey his orders, and they all said he would do it again in a moment, if necessary; but, from my experience, a stick laid over their shoulders was **the** punishment when they would not be silent when told. Guange had not disliked his life as soldier, and said that the allowance of food was good, but he had been absent one

---

* In the Appendix will be found an account of this worthy.

day without leave, and, fearing the consequences, took to the woods.

Three or four of the band had joined only a few days before my capture; these had their *carte di soggiorno* with them, and often looked at them and showed them to me. They were still dressed in their peasant dresses, and it was long ere they were able to obtain their brigand clothing; but, before I left them, they all had gradually picked up the proper uniform. This they obtained from the peasants when getting food, and paid for out of their own share of my ransom.

Malone Zara, a native of Acerno, who was one of these recruits, was only eighteen years old, and used to take the milk round to the houses in the town; but one day a friend tried to cheat him out of five ducats, equal to sixteen shillings and eightpence: this so enraged him that a fatal blow from his knife compelled him to become a brigand. He was not *in giro*, as they call it, when I was taken, and thus he had no share in the money, for those only who are present at the capture divide the spoil. All share equally, the captain having no more than the others, and a certain amount being kept back for general expenses.

At about five o'clock the tinkling of bells below told us that a flock of sheep was passing from one pasture to another. Pepino, who was very impatient under a lack of food, jumped up, and, with Generoso and Andrea, started off to see what they could procure. In about an hour they returned leading a fine fat sheep and a goat, which were soon killed, and in less than an hour there was nothing left but the head and bones. Excepting the paunch, every morsel was eaten. When we had got meat, there was a difficulty in cooking it, on account of our position.

With the troops in the neighborhood a fire was most

dangerous, and many of the men declared it was madness to think of lighting it. But we had had too little the last three days to think of foregoing our promised repast, so two of the old hands cut out an oblong hole in a sloping place, and then another at right angles at the end of it; the fire was made with the greatest caution in this, and the pot put over it; two *capotes* were placed in front, so as to conceal any gleam of light; every piece of wood was dried before it was put on, and the fire very slowly fed, and by these means all smoke was avoided; they certainly did make the most smokeless fires I ever saw. When the internal *bonne-bouche* was pronounced ready, we were invited to dip with them into the pot. I took out my pocket-fork and avoided scalding my fingers; theirs were like horn, and no heat ever seemed to hurt them. This fork was much admired; and when I was told that I had eaten my share, which was always on these occasions about a quarter of what each of them ate, one of them took it from me and used it himself, but returned it when the course was finished. The meat was all divided into shares, and, to Visconti's horror, he had to eat it without bread. For drink we had to eat snow, all the water being drunk by our captors, who refused to give us any.

To-night the place where I was told to sleep was the next but one to poor Concetta, whose arm was getting worse every hour, and now began to emit a most nauseous odor. The wind, unfortunately, blew toward me, and, as I was only about four feet from her, my feelings can more easily be imagined than described. The flesh round the wound had turned quite yellow, and each time it was dressed a quantity of thick matter was removed; this, with the dirty lint, was merely thrown a yard or two off, and there being a plague of flies which immediately covered any animal matter, this made me most nervous, lest they should bite me, and thus communicate the poison to my system. How they worried me, perpetually settling on me! All the care in the world would not keep them off; they always disappeared as it grew dark, but then the musquitoes came out, and their demoniacal drumming nearly drove me distracted; but I soon found out that our simple food prevented that inflammation and pain that their bites occasion in civilized life. Two or three hours after dark, Ferdinando, with three others, returned with one live sheep and one that they had already killed and skinned.

CHAPTER VIII.

Diary of Mr. Moens, June 1 to 7.

Wood-carving.—The wounded Girl.—A tantalizing View.—Victims.—The Captives not introduced.—**A Thunderbolt.**—**Rain,** Rain.—Three under a **Cloak.**—Ill Treatment from Cerino's Band.—Their abject fear of Death.—A Blow from Cerino.—Consolation.—New Arrivals.—**Screwing up.**—**A Scrimmage** with Generoso.—The greedy Cerino.—An Installment of my Ransom arrives.—The Proposal to the Brigands to leave the Country in an English Ship.—The Lesson of the "Aunis."—What became of the 10,000 francs.—Gambling.—Visconti is appointed my Agent.—Pleasant Position of his Family.—I am the only Captive.—Quarrels.—The *Argumentum Baculinum.*—I am invited to Gamble.

June 1. WE spent "the glorious 1st of June" in the same place. How long the day seemed, with nothing to do but to brood over my griefs! For want of any thing better to do, I began whittling the stem of a wild jasmine with my penknife, and amused myself in cutting out a little cross, which I meant to send to my wife at the first opportunity. Much interest was taken by the brigands in seeing me cut what all Roman Catholics, however humble or degraded in position, revere so much; *è molto talento* was the constant remark when they saw me at work with the minute blade, the temper of which astonished them so much. We had no bread either to-day or the next day, but they gorged themselves with meat. I preserved as much as I could save in my pocket, not knowing when we should get more; two or three sausages had been kept back from the last division for

Concetta, whose arm was getting worse and worse. Poor girl! she did not utter a sound of complaint, but merely clenched her teeth together and hissed through them when they were dressing her wound and cutting off the dead flesh with a pair of scissors. I translated a few verses of the Psalms to her, and entreated her to think over her past life and ask forgiveness.

She seemed to attend with great earnestness to what I said, and when I had finished she entreated me to pray for her, and was not satisfied till I had promised to do so. I told her that, unless she could get medical aid, it was impossible to hope for any improvement, and that she must prepare for the worst.

Early in the afternoon I was delighted at seeing all the band rise up from the ground and sling their guns on their shoulders. This was the certain sign of a move. We were soon told to get up. I tied up my *capote* with a little piece of string and a cotton handkerchief that Manzo had given me, and with these managed to sling it on my back; it was rather heavy, and I had found great difficulty in carrying it on my left arm, for I wanted both hands — one to carry my invaluable stick, and with the other I grasped the low branches of the trees in ascending and descending the steep places.

My heart quite bled when I saw the poor dying Concetta walking along in the rear, supported between two men. We were between two or three hours in reaching the top, passing many frightful ravines — some of them, which we had to cross, full of snow; this was not like the freshly-fallen snow, but, being constantly penetrated by the moisture from the thawed surface, had crystallized into grains about the size of hempseed, and these were all frozen together, so that some trouble and force were necessary in cutting out a lump to eat. At one of these places we stopped to rest for some time, while Concetta, and those with her, were toiling up the steep ascent to join us. When they came up the poor girl could hardly stand, and threw herself down on the ground, and asked me if I had any bread, for I always kept, if possible, a tiny piece, and invariably ate a little mouthful after our nauseous meat diet. I had a piece the size of a walnut in my pocket, which I could not refuse her; and it was quite a pleasure to see the expression on her face as I handed it to her, and I felt well rewarded for my self-denial.

The usual precautions were taken at the top, and on all being pronounced safe, we rested again for the stragglers to come up. Here there was another false alarm; they all ran, but I never moved, hoping that, if the soldiers appeared, I should have a chance of escape. I took out my little book and began to read, to the great disgust of several of them, who disliked nothing more than seeing me perfectly indifferent when they all were showing fear.

From this elevated point I again saw the mountains with their jagged peaks close to Salerno, the point stretching out to Amalfi, and the blue Mediterranean. How I longed to be on it, in one of those tiny fishing-boats, with lateen sails, that were speeding their way to Salerno!

As we walked along the top I was constantly asked *Che vedete?* for the idea that I was enjoying the magnificent view was the last thing that entered their heads. We soon came up to a place where a dreadfully steep bank between two high precipices led far away down the mountain, reaching very nearly to the bottom. The greatest care had to be taken, for if I had once slipped it would have been impossible to have stopped rolling down some thousands of feet. There was a rank vegetation which concealed the

G 2

loose stones, which were in great abundance, and this made our descent very difficult. Often these would be set in motion, to the great danger of those below, who had to jump quickly out of the way to avoid them. I think this, more than any thing else, raised the ire and curses of the band, for a stone, once set rolling, generally with a great noise keeps rolling down to the bottom, giving notice to any one below that somebody is above, which might be the means of giving the troops warning of the proximity of the band. As we descended we saw several fires, which marked the spot where the shepherds were stationed for the night, and where they make the cheese and *racotta* from the milk yielded by the flocks of sheep grazing on these southern slopes of the mountains.

We no sooner began to descend than we left behind us the dense forests on the northern side. When we came to the level of the first fire, two of the band went toward it, and soon returned with one of the shepherds, who carried a barrel of water, which shepherds always have with them. This was a great luxury, for I had only eaten snow for the last few days. I got up and stepped forward to it, but was instantly told in a brutal way to go back again; for a captive is never allowed to see or speak to a peasant. They do this (as I said before) on account of the peasant, who fears being recognized and denounced afterward when the ransom is paid. In a short time the barrel was passed to me. I took it by each end, and drank, after their fashion, out of the bung-hole in the centre. A little Indian-corn bread was also divided between us, and Visconti and I enjoyed the remains of our cold goat, which we had tied up together in my pocket-handkerchief, having nothing else to carry it in.

When we approached to the next fire the same precautionary measures were repeated; but as it was in our route, we waited till the usual signal (a lighted brand waved in the air) was made by those who had been sent on in advance. The shepherds always tried to put out their fires on the approach of the brigands. I suppose this was for their own protection, lest any one should see that visitors were with them. More bread was obtained, and a little new cheese. The next fire was treated in the same way, but we were never allowed to join the circle collected round for the usual ten minutes' gossip, to hear the news. Immediately after leaving the last fire we crossed a stream and proceeded along a good path on the other side. Visconti was disappointed in not seeing his shepherd, who he thought was in this neighborhood. After about an hour we left this path and made our way through the brushwood. We soon came to a range of cliffs, on the face of which were many caverns. At last we came to one with a dry stony bottom, about fifteen feet high. We were told to lie down, and with guards on each side of us we were allowed to sleep. We were roused by the kicks of our guardians, and awoke with severe pain in all our limbs from sleeping in the bitter cold. There was not sufficient cover in front of the cave to make it safe during the daytime.

June 2. It had rained in the night, and we had, therefore, the satisfaction of getting wet in proceeding to a place under the rocks, with plenty of brushwood before it, where we were to stop all day. We had to ask several times before we got a portion of the bread procured from the shepherds. Pepino and his consort Doniella kept nearly all for themselves, and would hardly give us any. The rest of the band had plenty in their pockets, which they had secured when at the fires of the shepherds. This evening we went to a large roomy cavern that had evidently been made use of by the flocks of sheep, for the ground was covered with abundant signs of their recent presence. Visconti and I picked out the cleanest and driest place we could find in one corner, but we were made to get up and lie down in a very dirty and wet place, with water dripping on us from above. Andrea, the executioner, and two women guarded us, while the others went off foraging. I sat up for a minute, but our wary guard made me lie down again, fearing a sudden rush on him. On these occasions our guards always stood up at a little distance, and never took their eyes off us. In the night the band came back with some water, but nothing else. We were in the same part for the next three days, moving our sleeping-place each night.

One night we were asked if we liked milk, and were told that we were to have some. It took us half an hour to walk to the appointed place, where we found a great wooden milk-pail, about two feet high, half full. Some was poured out into a smaller pail, and some bread sopped in it. We were then told to fall to. This was the first time that I had used my wooden spoon, that I had spent so many hours in cutting from the root of the beech-tree; it served capitally for eating the bread, but it could not compete with the enormous deep spoons used in these districts for skimming the *racotta* off the remains of the milk. One was lent to me, but I preferred taking up the great pail and having a good draught out of it. I never lost an opportunity of telling them that milk was very good for an Englishman, and I always found that they gave me more than my share of it whenever we were so lucky as to obtain any. Some *racotta* was also broken up in some milk, and this made it taste just like cream. The pails were left to be fetched away by the shepherds. Well do I remember the spot, for the rising ground on three sides brought to my mind some of the theatres cut out of the hill-sides in Greece. The bottom was level, and then the ground sloped away to the river far below. Our halting-place was covered with a low broom in full blossom. The moon was shining brightly on all the surrounding mountains; not a breath of air was stirring, and the only sound to be heard was that of the distant torrent below.

June 6. The night was passed in the caves as before, and before daybreak we went back toward the place where we had found the milk, and spent the day on the hill-side. We were forbidden to speak or move the whole day. The bright sky of last night had left us, and all above us was covered with the blackest clouds, when suddenly, about midday, the storm broke in a thunderbolt, which passed whizzingly close over our heads, apparently only a few feet from us, and went right down and seemed to strike the ground near the stream below us. I never in my life heard any thing to equal the awful crackling and roaring sound of its passage. We were all amazed, and one of the brigands said " it seeks the water." They all crossed themselves, and several hurried off to seek the shelter of the grottoes. I wished to do the same, but was not allowed to move. I had no sooner put on my *capote* than a perfect shower of water fell on us. I took Visconti under the cloak with me; when Lorenzo, who had always treated me well, came close up and made me give him part too. I was in the centre; we put our covering over our heads, drew up our knees to our noses, and there we sat five mortal hours growling at every thing! Poor Visconti was in the most fearful state of despair, although two men, who had joined us in the morning, had brought the joyful news to him that the 10,000 ducats that remained to complete his ransom had been paid. How I envied him! He did not seem to feel sure of his liberty, and told me that he should not feel safe till he arrived in his own house. How miserable I felt—no letters, no money!

Three weeks had now elapsed since my capture, and during the last week especially I had been badly treated. Pepino's band, who were to have no share in my expected ransom, looked on me as a nuisance, and grudged every morsel of food they gave me. Except during the two days when we had meat, I do not think I had, in all, more than enough for one day's consumption. They always made a point of speaking to me in a most brutal manner, without an atom of kindness, and they constantly threatened my life with their guns, revolvers, and knives. One great game was thrusting their knives quickly between my body and arms. I never allowed myself to show the slightest fear, and always told them that it was nothing to die — it was soon over, and that the next world was far better.

They all have the most abject fear of death, and I always tried to impress them with the idea that Englishmen never fear to die; and that, if they wished it, they were perfectly welcome to take my life, as it would save me and my friends so much trouble. I felt sure that in a short time they would discontinue trying to frighten me when they found out that I only laughed at their attempts, and ridiculed them for their fear of death.

But I am forgetting the storm of rain. The cloak, though a good cover for two during an ordinary shower, was not of much use for three with the flood that was pouring down. The water collected when the cloak was stretched between our heads, and then dripped, or rather ran, through in streams, each one pulling it more over himself, and accordingly drenching his neighbor. When I attempted a change, I always said "È melior così," but the reply came "È melior per voi, ma peggior per me." I, being in the centre, came off best, but the best was bad enough. The water also collected in pools under us, and at last ran in a perfect stream. At five o'clock we were soaked through, and so cramped from our position that we could not move. I looked forward to a fearful night, and was as miserable as I could possibly be, and very hungry, for we had had nothing to eat or drink all day.

When the word came to us to get ready to start off to join the rest of the band, I asked how many hours' walking, and eight fingers held up told me what I had to expect. Before we started I asked Pepino whether any money or letters had come for me. I was standing on the edge of a mound, and was unprepared for the blow which I received for an answer. I lost my balance and fell down, hurting myself badly on the inside of my leg from striking it against a large stone. What a rage I felt in! I could have knocked him over on the spot with pleasure, but was obliged to choke it down as best I could. I asked him what harm I had done, and was told to be quiet and not to speak a word. They were very savage that no money had come for me at the same time that it had come for the Viscontis; and Andrea reproached me with having caused the death of four of the band who had died *for love of me!* Justi came up to me and said "*Povero Cristiano*," and told me that Pepino was a brute, and that I was not to care for what he said or did.

We now began to descend toward the river, passing along and over the terraces of earth in which the Italians always cultivate the mountain sides; the ground was sopping from the heavy rain, and therefore very slippery. I more than once fell, on one occasion making a bad wound on my shin, the scar of which I still retain. It was very difficult to pass the torrent, which was three times the size it was when we had crossed a few days before.

They told me to drink if I required it, for we should not pass more water. I used the leather cup which Mr. Aynsley had given me in parting, and which I always lent to Visconti. The favorite way with the brigands was to lie down at full length and lap up the water like dogs. Some of them would pick the leaves of a plant that always seemed to grow near water, and, doubling them up in their left hands, formed extempore drinking-cups. We soon found the mule-track or *scorza* as they call it, and, turning toward the north, walked along in Indian file at the rate of about three and a half miles an hour. After half an hour we were halted while some of the band went to get some milk, and we waited for an hour before they returned empty-handed. During this hour I got permission to walked up and down a little, for it was bitterly cold, and I was wet through and afraid to sit down. While doing this I heard some signals in a low voice from the mountain opposite, and reported them. They were at once answered, and down came six or eight men, who had been sent by Manzo to look for us. They were all wet through and half starved, not having been able to get any bread. They were desperate when they found that we had none to give them, and all drew their belts and bands round their waists an inch tighter. They said that they had taken us for *bersaglieri* from my walking up and down like a sentry.

Soon it began to rain so hard that even these ruffians grumbled, and, turning up a little path to the left, went to a large dry cave. I fortunately found a place that must have served as a bed to some one; it was made of the dry leaves that wrap round the spikes of Indian corn, and it was so soft, after the hard ground I had been used to, that I had no sooner lain down than I dropped off into a sound sleep, though my clothes were wet through. It seemed hardly a minute before I was kicked up and told to take my place in the line.

It had left off raining, but it was very dark, and we had to feel our way up the mountain side. With the intervals of two or three short rests, we kept on walking for four or five hours up the pass, till at last, the great caution which was used, and the freshness of the wind, told me that we were close to the top. After waiting a short time, while scouts were sent out, they began to break out swearing at the rest of the band not being where they expected to find them, and, being very tired, they were more brutal than usual. We were always made to lie down immediately a halt was called, for fear we might give them the slip.

The wolf cry was now made, but there was no response. Again and again was the cry of *wow-wow, wow-wow*, uttered in their peculiar way, but it was useless; when one proposed that they should go farther on to the left, where the mountain rose higher, and, after a quarter of an hour's more walking, the signal-calls were again made, and this time with more success; for in the distance a faint answer was heard, and we went on toward the place where the bark came from. The ascent was exceedingly steep, and Generoso, who was behind me, kept hitting and poking me with the barrel of his gun because I did not ascend as quickly as he wished, though I was close behind the man before me. At last I turned round in a pretended rage, and with my stick in both hands raised it over his head. He shrank back and brought his gun up to his shoulder with an oath. Two or three ran up. I caught hold of him, but at the same time they abused me, and seemed taken quite aback at the idea of a *ricattato* threatening one of themselves. I told them that I walked as well as they did, and I would not be bullied, so it was no use attempting it—that they might kill me if they wished, and the sooner the better.

I found this answer capitally, and I was never touched

again while on the march, and it was from this moment that they began to respect me a little for my apparent disregard of death; and when we arrived at the camp-fire it was immediately narrated how I had threatened to kill a *companion*—this being the term they always use when speaking of one another. How joyful I felt when I saw the cheerful gleam of the enormous wood fire! Manzo and the rest of the band were round it, making in all forty-three in number. When we entered the circle they all seemed very glad to see me, for they had had no news of me since the Sunday when the soldiers were disappointed in surrounding us, and they had feared that some harm might have befallen our division of the band. They gave me a large piece of bread and a lump of wet raw bacon, and I went to the fire, and, pushing in through those round it, began to toast the bacon.

Pepino, who, being very tired, had lagged behind, now came up, but too late for any of the bread, which had all been given away. He saw me with my nice large piece, and suddenly snatched it out of my hands. I immediately complained to Manzo, and told him that his lieutenant was no better than a petty thief to rob me of a piece of bread, and I began to rave against all of them; for we had had no food for twenty-four hours, and after our long walk I was very hungry, and had only just congratulated myself on the piece of bread that had been given me—very different in size to any thing I had been used to under the charge of Pepino Cerino; but, to my joy, one of the band took compassion on me and gave me his own piece, which I accepted with thanks. In a short time all but the sentinels threw themselves down on the wet ground and were fast asleep; but I kept near the glowing embers of the fire, and dried myself as much as I could, and sat up on a little piece of stone, for I was still damp, and my *capote* was wringing wet, and there was a bitterly cold wind blowing, and I thought it was better to forego a little sleep than catch a cold, which means a fever in these woods.*

June 7. In two hours I saw the eastern sky light up; and gradually it grew quite light; we were now removed two or three hundred yards off to a small open part, surrounded by very large beech-trees. There was a large rock covered on one side with moss, standing up in the centre, and I sat down under this to be out of the wind, and basked in the sun, which was now rising higher and higher.

Presently Visconti came to me and told me that a guide had come with letters and money for me: one from Mr. Aynsley and one from the consul, but none from my dear wife. How anxious I was for her! In neither letter was there a line about her health, and her name was only once mentioned. No message to me and nothing to console me; the letter from Mr. Aynsley was in English, but merely details of what had been done. The letter from the consul was in Italian, and meant for the band to read; and its tone gave them confidence in him, and they always expressed a high opinion of their trust in his word and actions.

They asked me if my companion, whom they had let go, was to be trusted, and if he would be faithful to me. I told them that he was an Englishman, and all Englishmen could trust in each other; and that I felt sure that he was doing and would do all possible for me, for I was hostage for him, and suffering for him as well as for myself. Manzo now came up and told me that 500 *marengi* had arrived for me, and he wanted to know what my friends meant by sending such a sum, and said that, if they did not send a

---

* I afterward found that the mountain on which we now were was called *Serra Del Castagno*.

large sum at once, he would send them my head. He was in a great rage, and I told him he had better do so at once, as it would save trouble, for it was impossible for my wife to get much money in Italy, as we were foreigners. He gave me a letter from the consul to him, entreating both him and the band to leave the country in an English ship of war. This, however, they were not inclined to do, for they all feared that they would be thrown into the sea immediately they were on board; and they mentioned the case of the four brigands (meaning Papa, d'Avanzo, and the brothers La Gala) who, as they said, tried to leave Italy in a French* ship, after security had been promised them, and had then been betrayed. They also said that the soldiers would shoot them on their way to the sea. It appeared that the consul's letter, which had been dictated by the prefect of Salerno, and which informed the brigands of the consent of the government having been given to the plan, was delivered to Manzo's brother, but he, although bearing a pass from General Balegno, and carrying letters sealed with H. B. M.'s consular seal, was arrested by a subordinate officer in command of a detachment, and nothing was heard of him for nearly a week. When the matter came to Mr. Bonham's ears, he immediately procured the messenger's release, and another letter was forwarded to the band containing the same proposal. It was now, however, too late, as the brigands had heard how the soldiers had respected the first messenger.

I suggested that three or four should go first to see if it were safe, but I was not able to do any thing with them.

* For a full account of the escape of these villains from the fate they so well deserved, see Count Maffei's book, and also Mr. Hilton's, vol. ii. The case of the passengers of the "Annis" is notorious all over Italy as a signal failure of justice.

The man who had brought up my money and letters now appeared, and Visconti was very excited, for he thought that this would be the guide to take him home to Giffoni, as the news of all his money having been paid proved to be correct, and he was told that both he and his little cousin Tomasino were to be set at liberty during the day. They were in the highest state of glee at the hopes of seeing their friends again. Don Francesco told me all about his wife and two little children. He had not had a line from her all the time he had been in the mountains, but had only heard of her through his father's letters.

How wretched all this made me feel! I thought of all those dear to me, and wondered when I should see them again, the horrible fear being over me of the brigands keeping me while they tried to extort a large sum from the Italian government; for they all told me that, if the country paid for me, they would require a far larger sum than 50,000 ducats.

I now saw the captain sit down and spread out a *capote*, and on this he counted out the 10,000 francs sent up for me. The money was all in half Napoleons, and was sent in this form because my friends thought that it would go farther than if sent in whole Napoleons. Fifteen Napoleons were then handed to each of the thirty men that had aided in the capture, and the balance of fifty Napoleons were kept back by Manzo for general expenses.

No sooner was the money divided than little groups were formed for the purpose of gambling, a similar operation having just taken place with the 10,000 ducats (equal to £1700) paid by Visconti. The captain very soon lost his money, and two or three hundred Napoleons more; so he left off playing, and in a sulky humor came up to me, and made me write a number of letters. Visconti was told to help me, and I was told to write them all in Italian, and not to put one word in English. I wrote one to the consul, one to Mr. Aynsley, and one to my wife, entreating her to write and tell me how she was. I was also made to write one to the prefect of Salerno, requesting him to withdraw the forces, and not to take any steps that would injure the band, for that any injury to them would be retaliated on me, and that it was the prefect's fault I was taken, for he had left the road unguarded on the afternoon of the 15th of May, and that he would have to answer for it. When the letters were finished, Manzo read them carefully over, and made me add the postscripts, one of which was to the effect that the 10,000 francs just sent were not enough to keep me in bread.

The man who had brought up my money and letters (and who was not one of Visconti's servants) had also brought a quantity of jewellery for Pepino's band, consisting of watches, gold chains, and rings; these were all brought for my inspection, and I was asked to value them, which I did to the satisfaction of the brigands. One chain I told them was too light, and was not good gold: this was given back to the guide, who was told that, if he tried to cheat them, they would kill him. He declared that it was good gold, but they would have nothing to do with it.

Visconti and I now had a long talk together. He told me that he would do all he could for me; that Manzo had ordered him to receive my letters and send them to and fro, and that he was to find guides in order to transmit my money to the band; and that, if his father did not do so in a satisfactory manner, his family would be all killed, his house burned down, all the olive and chestnut trees belonging to the family destroyed, and the sheep and cattle slaughtered.* He entreated me to keep up my spirits, but not to

* See Appendix B.

expect to get away without paying a large sum of money, for they had good information that I was very rich, and could pay the amount demanded easily. I requested him to go as soon as he could to Naples, in order to see my wife, and tell her that I was quite well, and that it was necessary to send money, and to advise my friends what was best to be done under the circumstances. I also gave him the little cross I had cut to take to her, and a list of warm clothing and other little things that I required. He would not take any thing written in English, or even a private note, because he said the captain would kill him if he found it out.

All at once he gave a little scream of joy at the sight of his old family servant, Fortunato Tedesco, who had come up to act as guide to take him to Giffoni. The old shepherd looked delighted to see his masters, kissed them both, and took off his hat to me. He brought up some food for them, and some cherries, but this was all taken at once by the band and divided into equal shares. How I enjoyed the cherries! I had had no vegetable food for so long that nature seemed to rejoice at such a change of diet.

Three or four men now appeared, each with a sack of bread on his shoulders, and a quantity of cheese. This was hailed with joy, and a present of half a Napoleon given to each man. It was about five o'clock when Visconti was told to get ready to go. He kissed me in the Italian fashion, and then kissed the band all round; two of them gave Tomasino little rings as keepsakes, for he was a great favorite with all of them, and Manzo gave them a Napoleon between them; and taking Don Francesco on one side, cautioned him about revealing any thing concerning the band; for, if he did so, they would come and kill him. Tomasino was told to say that the band was only twelve in number, and not to talk about them much. Fortunato gave Visconti his shepherd's crook as a walking-stick, and in a few minutes they were out of sight.

I then gave myself up to grief; I felt so desolate and miserable at the sight of their going away free, and leaving me behind alone, that I could not control myself; I threw myself on the ground in despair. Justi and Lorenzo came up to me and tried to console me, telling me to cheer up, for when my money was paid I should be free too. I thought it better to put a good face on it, and so got up and walked about two hundred yards to where the sentinels were placed. I found we were on a platform about ten yards wide and two hundred yards long. On three sides the ground sloped down steeply, so that they could run down hill on three sides, while the soldiers would have to ascend the other side; they could run into the dense forest, and soon would have been lost to sight. This was the favorite form of lair with the brigands, and they generally halted when they found a spot like this. From the end where the sentinels were, there was a splendid view right over the plain of Salerno.

It was beautifully clear, and I could see far out to sea. I was only allowed to be here two or three minutes, and I was told to go back to where I had been all the morning. I tried to persuade them to let me remain, but with no avail. As I went back, I passed where all the women were sitting: they were hard at work hemming silk and cotton pocket-handkerchiefs; they had different colored silks to hem, with scissors, thimbles, and all that was requisite. I noticed that their needles were much shorter than those of English make. The gambling was still going on, and many were the furious quarrels that this gave rise to; the captain had to interfere constantly, and would often have to belabor two or three with a stick before he could reduce them to silence. They wanted me to play with them, but I was not sure whether they would pay their losses; so I tried them first with *confetti*, letting two or three be seen, and then clenching my fist. They guessed four, but I had over fifty in my hand. They laughed when I asked them to pay, so I took the hint, and declined all gambling with them.*

A loaf of bread was now given to each, and preparations made for departure. I learnt that Manzo and about twenty-five men were going down into the plain to take a "companion for me," as they expressed it, of whose approach they had had notice.

* At this time they had formed the habit of calling me Don Guglielmo, and by this name they continued to address me until I left them.

CHAHTER IX.

MRS. MOENS'S LETTERS, MAY 17 TO JUNE 18.

Return to Naples.—Hôtel de Genève.—The Coppersmiths.—Telegrams to England.—Letters to the Brigand.—Milords or Photographers.—First **Letter from the Hostage.**—A noble Reply to a Telegram.—The second Letter.—Imprisonment of the Brigand's Relatives.—Arrival of H. M. S. "Magicienne."—Omniscience of the Italian Government.—Sunday in Naples.—Our **Message** stopped.—The Brigandess's News.—Another Letter from the Hostage.—A second Installment prepared.—Letter to the *Times*.—A **Visit from** a supposed *Manutengulo*.—I hear of a Friend coming from England.—His Arrival.

Hôtel de Genève, Naples, May 19. As soon as Mr. Aynsley rejoined **us, he advised our immediate return** to Naples, as he had, as I understood (in order to carry out the idea of the captive being merely a poor artist), told the brigands that he should go thither to try and raise a ransom among the English residents in that city. Our boxes were packed, and we were just ready to start, when young Mr. Bonham, the vice consul, and Mr. Edward Holme,* an English resident at Naples, arrived to offer us assistance and **advice.**

I had the **greatest** disinclination **to leave** Salerno, as I felt that there, at all events, I was nearer to my husband, but I considered it my duty to follow Mr. Aynsley's advice, as my husband had, on parting with him, placed me under his care. On arriving at the station, Mrs. Aynsley and I got into a

* I can not thank this gentleman and his family too much for their kindness to my wife.—W. J. C. M.

first-class carriage, and our kind friends Mr. and Mrs. S——
joined us; but Mr. Aynsley thought that, as we should
probably be followed by spies of the brigands, and our mi-
nutest actions commented on, it would be better for us to go
into a second-class carriage, in order that we might not appear wives of "Milords." He thought that if they could by
any means be persuaded that we were poor, they would
lower their exorbitant demands. The train was on the
point of starting, when the guard came up and told us that
a telegram had just been received to the effect that my husband was free, and that the guard at Eboli had seen him.
We made farther inquiries, but the additional details thrown
in made us doubt the news, so we decided not to change
our plans, and went on direct to Naples.

Oh, how wretched I felt when I first found myself alone
at the Hôtel de Genève, in the noisiest part of noisy Naples!
We had been advised to go to that hotel when we came
over from Sicily, as it was built on high ground, and was
considered far healthier than the hotels along the Chiaja,
where there had been recently many cases of fever. It is a
large building in the centre of the Strada Medina, one of
the great thoroughfares of Naples, and free from all the
bad smells which make some parts of the town quite unen-
durable; but the noise is distracting. Nearly all the shops
around it belong to coppersmiths, whose incessant hammer-
ing is added to the ceaseless roll of carriages and cracking
of whips. Often I can scarcely hear myself speak; my only
quiet hour is at twelve o'clock, when the inhabitants take
their siesta. I find myself constantly repeating a text which
a friend quoted to me: "Alexander, the coppersmith, did
me much harm."

But my great misery makes me forget all these minor
worries, which I must endure patiently, for to take larger

or more fashionable apartments would be inconsistent with the character which Mr. Aynsley still thinks we may be able to keep up. I was very ill when we arrived, and went directly to my room. Telegrams were immediately dispatched in my name, but without my knowledge, to Lord Palmerston, to members of my family, and to personal friends of my husband's in London.

This is a copy of one or two of the telegrams:

"My husband, Mr. Moens, captured by brigands near Pæstum; £8500 demanded for ransom, or life threatened. —May 18th."

"Don't be alarmed about me; am with friends. Husband taken by brigands near Pæstum: 8500 pounds ransom asked; life threatened. Can collect no money here. Urge English government. Italian police and authorities might obtain husband's release if properly pressed. Military useless.

The soldiers will never effect the release of my husband. You can not imagine the difficulties of the country; 6000 troops are out, but the brigands laugh at them. To give you an idea of the audacity of the band, they positively came down from the mountains close to Pæstum yesterday, and took away all the clothes of the ferrymen of the River Sele. Mr. Aynsley has sent a letter to the brigands, offering a small ransom, and telling them that that is all the money he can raise. The brigands are not yet certain whether their captives are rich "milords" or photographers. The Italian papers say two poor artists have been mistaken by the brigands for rich English lords.

May 20. It is now five days since I saw my husband. I can not realize my situation: I feel as if I were in some horrible dream, or rather in the Inferno. I am sure they may well say of us, when we return to England, what the

Florentines said of Dante: "That's the man who has been with the brigands, and that's the wife who has been in the Inferno!" My mind is harassed with perpetual false reports; but we can hear nothing certain of poor W——'s actual position. Mr. Aynsley has sent a letter for the brigands by post to a landed proprietor living at Battipaglia, whose brother was captured the same day as my husband by another band of brigands.* I believe the brigands arranged with Mr. Aynsley that all letters should be sent to this house, and that they would send messengers there for them.

In his letter Mr. Aynsley writes as a poor man who has got up a small subscription among the English at Naples. He thinks the brigands will believe this letter, as when he was with them they certainly had begun to doubt whether they had got the rich prize they expected. Fortunately, when captured, Mr. Aynsley had on a very old coat of yellow silk, which he was wearing for the sake of coolness; and W——'s fingers were all stained with the chemicals he had been using when photographing. One of the brigands asked Mr. Aynsley whether his coat had been torn in the night, and was told that it had been reduced to that state from constant wear.

I have but one consolation, that we have not brought this misfortune on ourselves by any want of caution. We made every possible inquiry as to the safety of the road, and all informed us that it was quite safe, and well guarded by soldiers; in fact, numerous parties had visited the ruins every day during the past week and throughout the season. I hear a rumor that our party was mistaken for Lord Pem-

* After waiting nearly a week in the greatest anxiety, we discovered that the person to whose house the letter was directed refused to take it in; his brother having escaped, he declined holding any communication with the brigands.

broke's; it is even said that the brigands had received a telegram from Rome to be on the watch for him, as he was expected at Pæstum the very day that my husband was taken.* I feel that this would never have occurred if the prefect had been doing his duty. Italians are constantly being carried off to the mountains by the brigands, and the government leaves them quietly to their fate. I am convinced that if a different plan were pursued, and the ransom levied on the province where the outrage took place, brigandage would soon be at an end.

May 21. I was just retiring last night at eleven o'clock when the consul's servant arrived with a letter to me from my husband—the letter I had been so anxiously expecting, but which, when it came, made me feel that all indeed was real, and that I was cruelly separated from him, with a terrible uncertainty as to when we should meet again. A paragraph is going the round of the papers that I am out of my mind with grief and anxiety. I think I should be were it not for my sure belief in God's promise to help the weak. I keep repeating to myself that it is "He who looseth the prisoner out of captivity." The letter was dated the 19th of May, and ran as follows:

"I am pretty well, only tired by night marches over a frightful country, and nearly starved, because the force follows the band. Don't be alarmed, dearest, but trust, as I do, in God, that I shall be restored safe to you. Telegraph to England for money, and make as good a bargain as you can. Pray for me, as I do for your peace of mind. I am still pretty well. *Pray send all the money you can get.* The new address—' Care of Signor Elia Visconti, Commune di Giffoni, Valle Piano, near Salerno.' Write immediately. One of the family of Visconti is my unfortunate companion.

* We heard that his party visited Pæstum on the 13th.

They are jealous of what I write. **I do feel for you so**, dearest; **but** trust in **God**. Telegraph for money, for I cannot stand this awful life, and long night marches. *Do not say any thing* to any one except *Mr. Aynsley*. They think the government will pay for me, so I shall not get off cheap. Remember me to Mr. Aynsley, and tell him that I feel thankful that he has escaped what I have gone through."*

You will observe that he says, "Say nothing to any one but Mr. Aynsley." But this caution came too late, the telegrams having already been sent; and the whole affair became too notorious for us to carry out the private method of arrangement which the Italians take care to adopt when any of their relatives are captured.

A member of the banking firm of Cumming, Wood, and Co. has just been to tell me that he has a credit for me for the full amount of the ransom demanded, viz., £8500. This is the doing of W. S——, who has replied to Mr. Aynsley's telegram by making himself responsible for the whole sum, advancing it at once at his own sole risk, lest delay might prove fatal to my husband. How few do we meet who are capable of such noble and generous actions as this! I have written to those who know about my husband's affairs, in hopes that some of his investments may be realized, and the proceeds handed over to my kind and generous relative, to relieve him at once **from** our half of the burden.

Hôtel de Genève, May 30. The heat is now intense. I never go out until the evening, and then some kind friends come and take me for a walk. We pass down the Toledo and Chiaja to the Villa Reale. The streets are crowded with people, and stiflingly close and hot. I weep as I walk, and think over past happiness. "*Nessum maggior dolore di che ricordarsi del tempo felice nella miseria.*" How few

---

* These first letters were written in English.—W. J. **C. M.**

in that gay scene imagined there was one among them suffering as I was!

The last letter I received from my husband was dated the 26th of May, and was all written in Italian:

"I have already written to you to implore you to send the money at once. The captain of the band says he will have 50,000 ducats immediately (£8500). He says that if that sum is not sent directly, my life is lost. He will cut off my head, and send it to you without pity. I am pretty well at present; but this life in the mountains is truly insupportable and terrible, particularly now, because we are followed by the troops in great numbers, and this places my life in great danger. I am dying of hunger and fatigue, despair and continual anguish: thinking of you is my greatest grief. The captain will make me write in Italian, in which language you must reply to me, so that he may read our letters. Send the money in an iron box—as quickly as possible, and as much as possible at once. Write to England immediately to obtain money: write to me directly, I entreat you. The place where the money and letters are to be sent is to the house of my unfortunate fellow-prisoner's father. Address, 'To the Band, care of Signor Elia Visconti, Giffoni, Valle Piano, near Salerno.' The letter must be sent by hand, *not by the post.*

"I entreat you to send the money directly. Try all the means possible. Go to all my country-people, to the English consul, and the Italian government, if possible, and also entreat that the troops be withdrawn at once. It is impossible to live in these horrible forests, amid perpetual rain. I am always wet, and my clothes are not half warm enough. Write to ——. [Here followed the names of three of his friends.] Send to all these. Make every effort to get me out of this horrible prison. Have faith in God, as I have. I do not know where to direct this letter to you. It is impossible to free me without money. Send the money in gold. Adieu, my dearest wife. Arrange so that the money is sent out without the knowledge of the authorities, or it will be very hard for me. The captain will kill me. Send the money secretly, and let me know the sum you send. Once more, adieu, my dearest Annie. Up to this time I have had no letter from you; this makes me truly unhappy.

"Your unhappy husband, W. J. C. M."*

June 3. My husband's letters make me distracted when I think of them. God help us both! I cry day and night unto Him.

May 31. Mr. Aynsley has sent a letter to the brigands to say £400 would be sent to them, but has received no answer. Two or three messengers have been sent, one of them brother to the captain of the band. He is considered an honest character, and is employed on the railway. He has a safe-conduct and pass from the general, which had been procured with great difficulty; but up to this time no messenger has returned. Martial law has been established all over the province, and the families of the brigands have been thrown into prison, in all, nearly 800 persons.

The brigands now have an idea that my husband is a relation of Lord Palmerston, on account of the telegram. They are about twelve miles from Salerno. Unfortunately, there is a report all over Naples that the consul may draw for any sum of money, and we are in fear now the brigands will demand even more than £8000. The prefect, too, has just been removed to another district, which is unfortunate for us, for, although his successor has an excel-

* The greater part of this was dictated by the captain.

lent reputation, a change at such a crisis might be disastrous to us.

The *Magicienne* steam frigate has arrived in the Bay of Salerno. It seems at first sight rather ridiculous to send a man-of-war to Salerno to liberate a prisoner in the mountains, but from something Manzo said about being tired of his perilous way of life, Mr. Aynsley fancied that he might be induced to accept a small sum of money, and then, with his prisoner, take refuge on board the English ship, to be conveyed in safety out of the kingdom. I hear that years ago a young lady was captured by a band, and, after every conceivable plan had been tried in vain, a similar one to this was adopted for her liberation, and an English man-of-war brought both her and her captors away in safety. So Mr. Aynsley mentioned the matter to the consul general, who, after communicating with the civil authorities at Florence and receiving their assent, obtained the permission of the English government to request the English admiral at Malta to send up a ship.

The troops are scouring the country and acting with unwonted energy, so that it is extremely difficult to communicate with the band, and the laws are very stringent against paying money to the brigands, the punishment for so doing being twenty years at the galleys; besides, the money found on a messenger may be confiscated by the soldiers. You see, therefore, how this increases our difficulties. Every road to the mountains is guarded, and it is difficult to find any one who will run the risk of taking the money. The most insignificant individual is well known to the government, and no one can go from one province to another without a pass. The birthplace, name, and parentage of every one of the brigands are fully known to the government officials here.

June 4. A great feast-day—the anniversary of Garibaldi's entrance into Naples. All the people are out in the streets in gala costume. My enemies, the tinmen, are quiet, but the church bells ring every ten minutes, and, unfortunately, the parish church is close to the hotel, and its bells are very numerous and large, and particularly loud. I was so glad when it was time for our English service, and I drove through the crowded streets, swarming with men and soldiers, to the English church, an extremely pretty building, but very badly ventilated. In the middle of the service the heat made me feel so faint that I left Mrs. Aynsley, and went out and got into a carriage. On my way to the hotel my carriage was stopped by the procession of soldiers. I had to wait in the burning sun while regiment after regiment of cavalry and infantry passed me. General Türr was in a carriage with his aids-de-camp. I did not enjoy the scene. The music, the gay dresses, the military pomp, only made me feel sad. I thought how differently I should have felt had my husband been with me. The sight of the soldiers to me was fearful. I always felt as if my husband was in battle, and who could tell how it might terminate? I reached my hotel at last, and shut the windows to keep out all sound. How desolate and wretched I was! What gnawing anxiety at my heart! How I longed for one of my sisters to be with me, it is so very hard to bear grief alone! St. Paul knew well this craving of the human heart when he said, "Bear ye one another's burdens."

(There is one lesson I hope I have learned through this heavy trial, and that is, to seek out the wretched—not to wait for the wretched to seek me—and to try and comfort them by cheerful and consoling words—to give them a little of my time. Many want that more than money, which can never make up for want of sympathy.)

In the evening there were splendid illuminations in honor of Garibaldi.

I was so wretched at this hotel that I longed to go elsewhere, but Mr. and Mrs. Aynsley persuaded me to try the fourth story, as they still thought of keeping up the character which they hoped the brigands believed to belong to Mr. Aynsley and my husband. I always felt convinced that it would be impossible to deceive the brigands, still I thought it better to acquiesce; and, in accordance with their suggestions, I received no visits from my countrywomen. Those who know how ready English people are to sympathize with their compatriots in trouble in a foreign land can easily imagine of how much comfort and sympathy I was thus depriving myself!

I accordingly went up higher, where I had a large room, and my experience of Italian hotels teaches me always to choose either the third or fourth stories, where one avoids the bad smells, and the air is fresher. I had a fine view of Vesuvius from my room. The volcano was somewhat active during the whole of my stay. I am anxiously expecting news from Salerno, as Manzo's brother has not yet returned.

June 6. After a week of the utmost anxiety, expecting every hour the return of the messenger (Manzo's brother), his mother has come to us in great distress, to tell us that he is in prison, heavily ironed. He was provided with a pass signed by General Balegno, the head of the forces in the province of Salerno, and countersigned by our consul general, Mr. Bonham; but, notwithstanding, he was stopped by a captain of Carbineers, who, on his own responsibility, arrested him, and without informing us of what had happened, has kept him prisoner, until he had farther instructions from his commanding officer; of course Mr. Bonham will soon procure his release, but this delay is terrible: what must it be to my poor husband!

The consul is acting with great care: both he and all his advisers are afraid that if they were to give the whole amount at once, the brigands would not be satisfied, but require just as much again: this is the idea and fear of every one.

A brigandess has given herself up to the authorities. She was shot in the arm through some carelessness on the part of one of the band. For seven days she remained with the brigands. Though the arm was fractured, the brigands would not let her leave them. At last she was so ill, she got away and came to Salerno, and presented herself to the authorities; her arm was then amputated. She had so much nerve that she refused chloroform, and neither groaned nor complained. The only sign she gave of suffering was clenching her teeth. When the surgeons left her she said, "Remember, I had eighteen Napoleons about me when I came here; I must have them again when I am well!" She says my husband is well, and a favorite with the band, because he walks well, and gives no trouble, and amuses himself with sketching. This news is better than nothing, but still I can not help feeling intensely anxious for him, as the troops are still in pursuit. In his letter to me, he wrote that the captain of the band says he will never give him up to the troops alive. The brigands have refused to go on board the frigate; they send word the English climate would not agree with their health; it is too cold.

The last report in Naples is that my husband and the brigands have joined together to get as much money as they possibly can, and that he intends to join the band.

June 8. The first installment of money has at last been successfully conveyed to the mountains; and to-day I received the following letter written (in Italian) on the 6th of June:

"Write to me, I pray you. I think of you continually. I am indeed unhappy; the horrors of the life I am leading are indescribable. I am exposed to all the inclemency of the weather; I am dying of hunger, cold, wet, and anguish. I believe that you would do every thing to see me again. Borrow money directly, and send it immediately to the mountains to ransom me. The captain has received the 10,000 francs that you sent me, and he sends you word that to free me, 50,000 ducats are required. This sum, therefore, must be collected if you wish to see me again. I entreat you to borrow of ———, or of ———, the remainder to make up the 50,000 ducats, and send the money to Visconti's house. Do not hope to liberate me for a less sum. Here I am in constant peril. I can not possibly remain much longer in good health. I send you, by Signor Visconti, a little gift, cut by my own hand: prize it, and think often of me. Send the things that I have written for, and send immediately. Adieu, dearest; pray write to me, and believe in my sufferings and in my affection. Have faith in God.

"Your affectionate husband, W. J. C. M.

"The band treats me very badly: I can not endure it.

"P.S.—I pray you to get the troops withdrawn, if you love me. The captain says that I may be liberated by the troops, but I shall not be alive. He also says that the money, 10,000 francs, is not enough to buy bread for me."

This letter was sent to Signor Visconti, at Giffoni, and by him forwarded to me through the consul general.

Immediately on receipt of it we took measures for forwarding a farther sum to the brigands; and we have determined on limiting the next installment to 17,000 francs, in the hope that the robbers will let my husband go on receipt of that sum, without demanding more.

Signor Visconti, whose son was for three weeks my husband's companion in captivity, has paid me a visit of condolence, accompanied by his son. The interview was a trying one for me.

June 13. I sent my letter to the *Times*, although I have not seen Mr. Aynsley's letter, because every one keeps writing to me from England that life with the brigands can not be so very unpleasant after all, and this, too, at the time when I am receiving such dreadful letters from my husband. I was determined that the real state of the case should be known, and yet I was frightened at my own boldness in "writing to the *Times*," and actually carried the letter to and fro between the hotel and the post-office several times before I could summon up courage to post it.

I am still in fearful suspense and anxiety. We are now negotiating through Signor Visconti, who is a rich landed proprietor at Giffoni, fourteen miles from Salerno. He has been forced by the brigands themselves to receive our money and letters. His son and nephew have been with the brigands two months, and he has had to pay £4150 ransom for the two.

A gentleman who is believed to be connected with the brigands* came yesterday to see me, on purpose to find out if we were very rich people. I was warned of his coming, and prepared accordingly. I had many lectures given me to appear bold and indifferent, so that the brigands might not extort much through my fears. I fortunately wore my hat, which concealed the tears which constantly came into my eyes. He told us he had heard there was an enormous sum waiting to be used as ransom, and that the brigands believed my husband to be a nobleman, and that the government would pay. So you see the difficulties we have

---

* I need scarcely say that we do not now believe in this connection.

to contend with, not to mention the distance the brigands are off. It takes such a very long time to do any thing. It is indeed trying; I feel it sometimes unbearable.

If the troops do not prevent us, the consul general sends to-morrow some more money, some flannels, a water-proof coat, and a Bible. My husband has written to me for these things. He seems to suffer so from cold — very different from us at Naples, who are melting with the heat. He sent me a little wooden cross, which he had amused himself in carving. His letters are all in Italian, as before. The life must be terrible for him. I only hope and pray some one is coming to me from England, for I am in a very lonely position.

June 17. There was a very fearful storm last night. It began in the evening, and lasted until one or two o'clock in the morning. I could not rest, thinking of my husband being exposed to its violence, with no shelter.

At this time H. C——, one of my brothers-in-law, was on his way to Naples to see what he could do for us. I afterward heard that he went to Florence *en route*, and was very kindly received there by the British envoy, who introduced him to some of the ministers, and procured from them for him letters of introduction and recommendation to the prinpal local authorities (civil and military) at Salerno. These letters were of the greatest possible use in furthering the requests which he afterward preferred to these important officials personally on the spot, accompanied by the consul general or Mr. Richard Holme.

On the 17th of June, a gentleman who had traveled with H. C—— from Genoa to Leghorn called on me at his request, to let me know that my friend was close at hand. It was a great satisfaction to me to hear that I should so soon have the assistance of one whom I knew well.

On the 18th of June my friend appeared at the Hôtel de Genève at breakfast. I was so delighted to see him. Only those who have been so long in trouble among strangers, and separated from their own kith and kin, can understand the pleasure with which I now found that I had an old friend at my side. We talked of my old home, and of the kind hearts that felt for me there. Really sometimes it seemed almost worth while to be placed in my present unhappy position just to learn what truly good, and kind, and loving hearts there are in the world. And in the fresh wonder and excitement of hearing what my friends at home had done and said about me, I for a moment forgot my great sorrow. But time was precious, and my newly-arrived friend lost not a moment in seeking out the consul general, and deliberating with him and Mr. Aynsley on what was to be done for my husband.

CHAPTER X.

DIARY OF MR. MOENS, JUNE 7 TO 28.

Thieving Propensities of Cerino.—Generoso's Conduct worthy of his Name.—I am again left with five Guardians.—The *Magicienne*.—A Three Days' Rest.—New and very unpleasant Companions.—Small Amount of Washing done in the Mountains.—A long Rest.—Bread Diet.—Its Effect.—A Peasant Visitor.—Wood-carving.—A Message with Letters.—A second Installment and warm Clothing.—I write again.—My new Treasures.—The Luxury of a Comb.

DURING the afternoon the rain came on again, and I took shelter under the large rock. While there, Pepino came up and asked me for the *capuce* that had been given me. He said it was his, and he wanted it. I told him that I could not possibly do without it; the weather was much too wet and cold, and that a wide-awake was no protection at night, and that it was of no use asking me for it, for I did not mean to give it to him. I always wore it tied round my neck by the string, with the hood hanging on my back; so I looked to see if it was secure, so that they could not snatch it off, for I knew that Manzo would not let it be taken away if I stoutly resisted. But Pepino was too clever for me, and by artifice got the better of me. He went away, and sent one of his band to tell me that he did not care whether he had the *capuce* or my wide-awake. I thought it better to make a compromise, and said I would rather be without the wide-awake, and gave it to him, and I then had to put the *capuce* on my head. I was then called by two or three who were a little way off, and when advancing toward them the crafty ruffian, who was lying in wait behind a corner of the rock, made a snatch at the coveted *capuce*, and pulled it off my head, throwing me back the wide-awake.* He immediately started off with his men, as it had been arranged the two bands were to separate.

I was in a great rage, and complained bitterly to the collected band of the conduct of Pepino, telling them I was sure to catch cold the first night I slept without a covering to my head, and that then I should have an attack of some dangerous fever, which might carry me off and spoil their chance of farther ransom. I thought that there was no chance of my getting another *capuce*, for they were very scarce, only two having them, and one of these was sewed on to the jacket; but I kept on grumbling at their treatment of the poor prisoner, whom they had taken away from his friends in order to rob, like petty thieves and pickpockets, not being contented with the prospect of a large ransom.

They seemed rather ashamed of this; and in a short time, to my astonishment, Generoso, the man whom I had threatened to knock down last night for bullying me while walking, took off his hood and gave it to me. This was the only one they had, and of course I did not in the least expect to get it, though I had tried for it. It was not quite so new as Pepino's, but was equally large and very warm. I was amazed at Generoso forgetting the occurrence of the pre-

* He had before this enraged me much during the morning. I had lent my leathern drinking-cup to Visconti, and as he was passing it back to me, Doniella seized hold of it and gave it to Pepino, who quietly put it into his pocket. I asked for it, but he took no notice of my request, and went away, while I was not allowed to move. I asked several to go to him for it, but they said it was only a joke, and he would be sure to give it me back; but it shared the same fate as the *capuce*, and so I was robbed of both these useful articles.

vious night, for it is seldom that an Italian ever forgets an insult or an injury, and last night he had been most indignant at the captive turning round against the captor. Instructions were now given by Manzo to Lorenzo and Pavone (who, with Antonio, Scope, and Malone, were to take charge of me during the absence of the captain and the rest of the band) never to lose sight of me day or night—that I was never to be allowed to move from the hiding-place chosen—that a *factione*, alias sentinel, was always to be posted close to me; and that, as regarded food, I was to be treated like a companion, share and share alike. This, I presume, was added specially, because, when Pepino stole my portion of bread, I had told Manzo that they had always given us a smaller share of food than they had taken for themselves.

They were also told that if I escaped their lives were to answer for it; that I was to be shot down without mercy should I attempt to run away, and that they were to collect all the bread that they could possibly obtain.

We were then left to ourselves, and Manzo, with about twenty-five men, went down to try their luck upon the plains. We rekindled the fire, and spent the hour that we remained in this place warming ourselves over it. Visconti and his guide had gone away to the south; Manzo had also gone in the same direction; Pepino had taken a northwest direction, while we went to the southeast down the mountain, retracing the path by which we had ascended last night. Scope and Malone each carried a sack of bread on their shoulders, and Lorenzo carried a quantity of cheese in the wallet which had belonged to poor Luigi, who had been killed, as I have related, by falling over a precipice. It was considered too light for us to walk on the *scorza*, for fear of meeting the troops, or being seen by peasants, who might give information to them; so we waited in the *frasche* for another hour, Lorenzo telling me the while that we were now going to have a good time of it, with plenty to eat, and that I was to fear nothing, but that the slightest attempt to escape would prove fatal to me. I felt very wretched; I had seen my fellow-captives go joyfully away, with the certainty of soon being united to all dear to them, while for me all was uncertainty and misery. I could not understand from the letters I had received what my friends were doing, for I saw that none of the band would trust themselves in the power of any one, and the idea of going on board any man-of-war was laughed at and refused, after the way in which the captain's brother had been treated by the soldiers when bringing the consul's letter, and armed with a pass from the general. It was most fortunate for me that they would not hear of it, for my life would certainly have been sacrificed in revenge for the bad faith on the part of the Italian government.

(The civil authorities at Florence had agreed to the plan at the request of our minister there, and on this agreement the consul general had telegraphed to the Foreign Office for a vessel, and they had sent to Malta ordering the *Magicienne*, sixteen guns, Captain Armytage, to go to Salerno with sealed orders. But the military authorities had determined not to allow the proposed scheme to be carried out, and intended to have seized the brigands while on their way to the sea-shore. I learned this after my release, and I am surely justified in thinking that *non tali auxilio, nec defensoribus istis*, would my release ever have been brought about.)

As soon as it grew dusk we ventured on the roadway, but this time it was all down hill, and the descent occupied only half the time of the ascent. We crossed the stream nearly opposite a long low store-house, situated some way up the mountain, on the western side of the stream. How well I got to know that house! for the next three weeks it was always in sight, and I was constantly watching it for the chance of seeing an honest man, a sight which — though I could never approach him — seemed to comfort me. We had ascended along a dark and gloomy ravine, where the ground was very wet from the heavy rain. Our boots and legs were as wet as they could be, as well as our *capotes*, and in this state we lay down on the ground to sleep. I was off in a moment, for I had had no sleep the night before, and had done a great deal of walking during the last two days.

June 8. We woke very wet and cold, and went higher up, where we found a little grotto just large enough for our party; the rock rose above it covered with ivy, and a narrow space at the bottom of this served as a path for us when the brigands wished to go either to the right or left; immediately below us was the ravine, and with a sentinel on the watch, no one could approach without our having plenty of time to escape before they could get near enough to do us any harm, unless the troops were to come from above and below simultaneously, in which case we should have been caught in a trap. It was a most gloomy place, and nothing was to be seen but the trees close at hand.

We stopped here for the next three days, spending a most quiet time — a great contrast to the hard time I had had while with Cerino and his band, who had always ill-treated me; here they left me pretty well to myself, and interfered but little with me. Lorenzo and Antonio went out every night foraging, and always returned with a quantity of bread; once with a large lump of freshly-made cheese, a little meat that had been cooked by shepherds, and some cherries. Another time they brought up a *fiasco* of wine, of all of which they gave me a fair share, telling me they wished to keep me well. They also had some *pasta*, which was always cooked at mid-day; the fire was made against the rock, and if any smoke arose it was lost amid the ivy. I always watched the process of boiling the macaroni with interest, having nothing else to do to while away a weary hour. The great pot was half filled with water, and put on to boil, with a lump of bacon fat that had been well chopped with their knives; pepper and salt was added, and by the time the water boiled the fat was nearly melted. The *pasta*, which they had well picked over, was now put in, and boiled till it was soft enough; the caldron was then taken off the fire and put on one side to cool. They did it with so much nicety that the *pasta* just soaked up the water, and they very seldom had to pour any off. When cool enough we used to collect round, and some with fingers, and some with spoons, soon made the bottom of the pot appear. The quantity they would stow away was surprising. Pavone always went on eating at least five minutes longer than any of the rest. The bread was all taken out of the sacks and stowed away in the holes in the caves; all the new bread that was got, having been twice baked, would last any time, but it was as hard as a brick.

Seeing Antonio writing a letter with great difficulty, I offered to assist him, and composed a letter to his mother in prison, which was read out loud, to the great satisfaction of all the band. Manzo's cousin then asked me to write one for him, which was rather more difficult, as it was to his beloved, who, contrary to the wishes of her parents, had been engaged to this bandit. After many vows of eternal love, she was entreated not to forget her disconsolate lover in the wild woods and mountains, who "trusted to the Almighty to enable him to escape his now desperate course of life." He implored her not to think of any one else. I put it all in pretty language, as endearing as I could manage in Italian. It was (like the other) read out loud, and met with unqualified approbation. I was not allowed to address it, for fear of compromising the beloved one.

One afternoon they were very angry with me, who had offended in the most innocent way. While they were taking their usual afternoon *siesta* I was put in my usual place, lying down (for the cave was too low to allow of any other position) with them all in front of me, so that I could not possibly leave the cave without waking them. They thought I was asleep, and all dropped off fast. I got very tired of being in the same position, and besides this, my hips were quite sore from the hard ground; I tried to sit up, and in doing so my hat touched the top of the cave, and rolled down past where they were lying asleep. I managed to rest my back against the side and sit up. (I always took advantage of their sleeping to read through our Church Service, which I now did daily.) At last they woke up, and when Lorenzo saw me sitting up, and my hat two yards off, he was very angry, and said that I had been trying to escape. All joined with him, and raved at me for the rest of the day. I told them how it had happened, but they would not be convinced but that it was as they imagined.

It was here that I first became sensible that I had become the dwelling-place of dozens of those disgusting little insects whose very name makes one shudder in my own cleanly land, where a very, very small proportion only of the population know more of them than their name; the brigands are always full of them, on account of their filthy habit of not washing, and the difficulty of obtaining clean clothing. Every thing belonging to them is infested with these insects, and if only one gets a footing on a man, it is impossible to escape the plague; and a plague it truly is, as I soon found out. I had worn the same clothes day and night for nearly a month, and had never been allowed to wash myself. If I attempted to remove any garment, I was immediately told to put it on again, for fear of the troops coming, and our having to run for our lives, and water being generally very scarce in our hiding-places. I was not even ever allowed to take off my boots, except for the purpose of shaking out the dust and dirt, and so I was deprived of the comfort of removing them after a long march.

I had never even seen one of my new persecutors before, and I was truly horrified when I discovered that I was covered with them. I had been without a comb, and I was afraid of using theirs for this very reason, and this filthy state their combs were always in. I was not able to touch my hair till the 19th of June, when I received the comb sent me by my friends. In a very short time my whole body was covered with bites, and my skin presented the same appearance as if I had the scarlet fever. Fearful was the irritation occasioned, and my body was very soon one mass of sores. As time went on, instead of getting better, it grew worse and worse till the day of my release. The brigands suffer much themselves; but their skin being harder, and thoroughly inoculated with the poison, it never shows the bites.

Lorenzo offered me a clean shirt, but I was still afraid of leaving off flannel. Next day, however, I gladly accepted it, and for a few days I was better. He had previously got a collar and white pocket-handkerchief washed for me, and now I intrusted this precious garment to his care; but, alas! I never saw it again; and probably it is now worn by the peasant who charged a ducat (or 3s. 4d.) for washing it. One day, when Lorenzo returned from foraging, he reported a better and safer grotto higher up, to which we removed

I

on the 11th of June. It was exactly opposite the storehouse, at the end of the spur of the mountains, between the two valleys. When we unstored the bread, a great deal was found to be mouldy, the weather had been so wet. We had to eat this first; a great quantity had been accumulated, but more was got every second night. We remained here a week, passing a very quiet and secure time, only worried by the musquitoes, which came out by swarms at sunset and in the early morning. I found a pair of kid gloves in my pocket, which I wore to protect my hands; but, notwithstanding all my care, I got dreadfully bitten. House-flies and blue-bottles also were most annoying; they would keep settling on our faces, and nothing would drive them off.

Afterward I often looked back to this quiet fortnight. I grew quite stout from the bread diet and want of exercise. I was always lying down, but could not get into the habit of sleeping in the daytime. How long the day seemed! but I was well treated, Scope being the only one who was not kind to me. The other four were the best disposed of all the band toward me, except the captain. They too, afterward, often alluded to this quiet time, when food was so abundant, and when wine came up to us three or four times. Meat was the only rarity; once only did it appear.

One day we heard a rustle in the wood below us, and Pavone crept down to see what it was, and in a short time returned with a peasant, whom he told to sit down; but, seeing that I was looking at him, he called him aside so that I could not see him. He left his jacket, hatchet, and a large roll of the bark of a sycamore-tree, which is used for the soles of women's shoes, where he had been sitting. Scope overhauled the pockets, and finding some tinder, quietly appropriated it. The cuffs of the coat were tied up, and thus the sleeves were made into bags. This, I suspect, is a favorite way of carrying articles that are meant to be concealed; the jacket is then thrown over the shoulder, which is the usual way of carrying it in warm weather. I had seen a half Napoleon given to him as a *complimento* while he was sitting near me, but I could not find out what for. After Pavone had been talking half an hour with him, he came back and told me to lie down with my face to the ground; my *capote* was then thrown over me, and I was told that the peasant was *infame*, and that they were going to kill him. The peasant was then taken past me, and I drew the cloak on one side and looked out, which drew down on me the anger of all. In a few minutes those of my guardians who went with him came back and told me they had killed him. I asked them what was the use of lying to me so; that if they had been going to kill him they would not have given him a present, and that dead men did not carry their bark away with them. In two days' time I saw the same peasant again, so I asked them if he had risen from the grave; they laughed, and said I was too wide awake to what was going on.

Andrea, the executioner, came up here and joined us with two or three others. He was suffering from fever, and took advantage of this to appropriate to himself any delicacies, such as cheese, etc., that we had by us. They brought up with them a quantity of onions and garlic, which they had stolen when in the plain of Salerno, where they had been with Manzo to look after another victim, but happily without success. They had been close to Salerno, and had been discovered four times by the troops, but had got back without losing any of their number. They grumbled very much at the vigilance of the general, and told me that if the troops were not withdrawn my head was to be cut off. My answer to this was as usual, "*Bene se volete.*"

I had been so long without vegetable food that I was delighted with onions, and ate them like apples; the cloves of garlic also were roasted and eaten, and also put into the *pasta*, so I was forced to get used to the flavor, and after the first two attempts I even got to like it, though previously I would have gone any distance to avoid the proximity of any one who had been partaking of it. The greediness of Scope always disgusted me; not contented with his share, he always took advantage of every opportunity to steal any bacon or cheese that had been put away for the next day, and he was never satisfied unless he was always eating. While in this place I amused myself with carving on my stick — "XV Maggio, 1865. W. J. C. M. J. C. M. A. Presi dalla banda di Manzo." This delighted them immensely, and they were continually making me read to them what I had written.

Early in the morning on the 19th of June I was thrown into a great state of excitement by seeing Zacharia come up. He had two letters for me — one from the consul general at Naples, Mr. Bonham, and the other from my wife — the first that I had received. He also had brought up 17,000 francs, and had left a bundle of the warm clothing that I had sent for by Visconti. But I had to practice patience. The captain had to read the letters before I was allowed to have them. Visconti's man told me that Don Francesco and Tomasino had recovered their fatigues and were quite well. I asked him if the former had been to Naples to see Mrs. Moens. This I was told he had done the second day after getting home. He was given a loaf of bread, and then went away; and the letters and money were sent to Manzo, who was in the neighborhood. In the afternoon the letters were sent down to me, the captain having read them, and also a letter which I had requested Visconti to get his father to write, in order to disabuse the brigands' mind as to my being a "Milord."

This letter was entirely about myself, and did not refer to any other matter. I mention this particularly, because many have wished to implicate this unfortunate family as being *manutengoli*—i. e., "hand-extenders," or supporters of the brigands. Nothing could be more absurd than this, for they had just paid more than £4000 for the ransom of two members of their family, the greater part of which money I saw received by and divided among the band.

When I received my wife's letter I kissed it before them all, and eagerly devoured the contents; but the sight of the well-known characters produced a reaction also, and I felt dreadfully miserable and low-spirited. Among other things that were sent to me was a New Testament.

I was now made to write more letters. How my heart sank at the phrases I was forced to use, the captain standing over me dictating, and threatening the most awful things should the troops not be withdrawn and the money sent at once. I explained to him that my friends had written to England for money, and that it took a long time to receive an answer. I also told him that a letter in English would be far more effective than one in Italian dictated by him, and that the English were not like Italians, and it was of no use to ask so much money, for my friends would never send it. The most they could expect to raise would be 5000 or 10,000 ducats, and even that was very improbable, for I knew the consul would not pay any thing for me. They told me that one of my ships was at Salerno, and five more at Naples; and they wanted to know, if I did not make war on Victor Emmanuel myself, whether the English nation would send soldiers out to do so. I assured them that I did not even possess a little boat, and that the ships were not mine, but belonged to the Queen of England. They would not believe my statements that I was not the rich man they took me for, and the captain would not hear of writing for less than the original sum. He said that the Italian government was going to pay, and that they had a letter from the secretary of the prefect at Salerno stating that all the money was there; but the government were sending only a little at a time, in order to get off cheaper. At last the letter was written. It was rather difficult for me to write without help in Italian; before this I always had the assistance of Visconti.

The captain now went away, leaving with me only five of the men, and giving orders that we were to leave the place where we had spent the last twelve days, and to go to the mountain opposite; so in the evening we descended, crossed the river, and then went up to the place fixed upon. Soon after leaving the river Lorenzo went a few yards from the path, and from the corner of a bank brought forth my things, tied up in a red silk pocket-handkerchief. I was delighted to see a thin water-proof coat, which would serve to keep me from the ill effects of the wet ground at night. I could not examine my treasures then, as I had to devote myself to the steep path before us.

All this side of the valley was cultivated to a considerable height with wheat, potatoes, and Indian corn. We observed great caution in passing the magazine to which I have referred before. We soon came to a deep and most difficult ravine. The rocky and precipitous sides of the narrow chasm were covered with tremendous brambles, the stems of which were an inch thick, and bore a purple bloom. There were also a quantity of nettles, which stung me terribly. At last, after climbing up some way, we found a place where we could manage to lie down. In winter this ravine served for a succession of waterfalls, and the bottom of it was covered with huge pieces of rock jumbled one on another. My place was in a bed of nettles; but there was no denying my orders, so down I went, taking care to keep my *capote* well under me. I could not sleep for thinking of all those that were striving so to obtain my release.

June 20. Toward the morning weariness caused me to fall asleep, and I did not wake till eight or nine o'clock. It was a lovely morning, and there were myriads of large butterflies flying up and over the ravine, apparently attracted by the blossoms of the enormous brambles growing all around us. After I had satisfied my hunger with mouldy bread without any thing to drink (for no water had been brought up last night), I examined the bundle of clothing sent to me, and immediately took off the cotton shirt lent to me by Lorenzo, and put on a flannel one; the warm under-clothing I reserved till we ascended higher up the mountains, for now we were low down and close to the cultivated land. I found, to my great delight, a New Testament in Italian, and a copy of Fénélon's *Conseils*, with various parts marked by my wife for my especial perusal.

How dear these books, together with my little Prayer-book, became to me during all the weeks I was in the mountains! They were my only companions, and many weary hours did I escape in reading them. I often read the Italian Bible to the men, who would listen and make remarks with the greatest interest; I also became the proud possessor of a comb, or rather half of one, for Mr. Aynsley thought that if a whole one were sent it would give the idea that I was too well off. I spent some time to-day combing out my hair and beard, which had been guiltless of any thing of the kind for nearly five weeks, I having been afraid to use the filthy comb belonging to the brigands. I borrowed a little round looking-glass, and found that the bread diet of the last fortnight had filled out my face and made me look much stouter. I determined to make the most of my new acquisitions, and so I put on a clean collar and cravat; my scarf-pin I had great trouble in saving, for it was coveted by many, and nothing but the statement that it had been a present from my wife enabled me to keep it. The brigands did not know what to make of the collars of the period, and all kept asking me what the white thing round my neck was.

Another pair of good strong boots, with extra soles (put on at Naples), were also among my treasures; but these also I reserved till the ones I was wearing were good for nothing. The five weeks' work had already greatly injured them, but they were still equal to two more nights' walking. I enjoyed the sensation of a clean pair of socks, and I reserved the pair I had worn all the time for the chance of getting them washed; but in a day or two I was made to give them up, and I afterward found out that they had passed to my persecutor Pepino. I then put all my newly-acquired wealth in a blue checked bag, in which some *pasta* had come up, and then tied it up in a *maccatore*. This served ever after as my pillow, and saved me always looking for a large stone or piece of a rock, which hitherto I had used for this purpose.

I had searched all the pockets of the water-proof coat for news from Naples, but nowhere could I find a line, my friends being afraid of the consequences, should the brigands have found it out. I was delighted in finding that several pieces of newspaper, in which my things had been wrapped, had not been taken away, as afterward they invariably did, paper being scarce in the woods, and eagerly sought for the purpose of making cartridges, if stiff enough, or else for lighting fires. In one fragment I discovered that affairs in Mexico were in a very bad state, and in a piece of the *Times* I was able to see the present value of various stocks and shares that I possessed. My guardians did not much like my reading these papers, for none of them were able to understand what they were about, and it is contrary to the practices of brigandage to allow captives to read the events of the day.

(These were the first and last things I received through my whole captivity; for, though I wrote for various articles —particularly shirts—which were always sent by my friends, who exerted themselves to the utmost, I never received them, my captors intercepting them and wearing them themselves; and the shirt which I put on clean on the 20th of June I took off on the 25th of August, having worn it day and night all this time!)

The two next days passed very quietly, but I suffered very much from exposure to the sun, which was now fearfully hot at midday; and no one who has not experienced it on these mountains can imagine the torture I underwent in being without protection from the sun's burning rays. The books which I now had by me helped somewhat to while away the afternoons. We were very scantily supplied with water, which was only brought up once a day—about two hours after sunset.

CHAPTER XI.

Diary of Mrs. Moens, June 18 to July 31.

The second Installment received.—Scheme to ascertain the Hostage's own Views.—Journey from Salerno to Giffoni.—The Fire-eating Corporal.—Kindness of the Authorities.—An English Letter from the Hostage.—An Attempt to reduce the Ransom.—A third Installment sent to Giffoni.—The Palazzo Serracapriola.—Signora Q.—Her History.—Political Persecution.—The Questor.—His Kindness.—The Press.—The Rigors of the Troops.—The Neapolitan Detective.—Result of the Ladies' secret Scheme.—Life in Ischia.—The Vendetta.

June 25. Shortly before the arrival of H. C—— at Naples, the second installment of 17,000 francs (the amount fixed upon after anxious deliberation) had been sent on to Salerno, and carried thence to Giffoni by Signor D——, whose name I forbear to mention for fear of compromising him with his countrymen,* but whose services to my husband can never be forgotten.

There was now no possibility of doing more till the receipt of this sum was acknowledged, and an appointment made by the brigands for a farther payment. All parties were, however, on the *qui vive*, and prepared to act at a moment's notice, according to any contingency that might arise.

---

* I may here mention that, if the account given of the manner in which my friends negotiated with the band should appear at all vague or meagre, it must be understood that the same reason applies as is given for withholding this gentleman's name. I am naturally unwilling to say very much on so delicate a matter, when the interests of those who befriended me might suffer.—W. J. C. M.

At last, on the 22d, a letter arrived from my husband acknowledging the receipt of the second installment of 17,000 francs—one addressed to Mr. Bonham, and another to me, giving a most distressing account of his situation. My husband's friends were all still in great doubt as to whether the brigands would keep their word and let him go, even if they should get all the money they demanded. It was, therefore, very desirable that we should hear from my husband himself what he thought of this matter. This, of course, could not be done as long as he was compelled to write in Italian to the brigands' dictation, and therefore an epistle to Manzo was composed, intimating that as my husband's friends knew that he could not write Italian, they did not believe that the letters had been written by him; but that, on the contrary, they had heard he was dead; and that if Manzo did not allow his prisoner to write in English, the friends would neither send money nor hold any farther communication with the band. Mr. Holme started for Salerno on the 23d of June (followed on the 24th by Messrs. Bonham and C——), and, in the hope of reopening the communication with the brigands on a more satisfactory footing, and of inducing Signor Visconti to continue his invaluable assistance to us, proceeded on the 24th to the house of that gentleman at Giffoni with the letter.

(Mr. Holme has, in compliance with our request, kindly written an account of this, his first journey to Giffoni, and I have his permission to insert it here:

"Furnished with letters to the authorities at Giffoni, and with an escort of six troopers of the Cavalleggieri di Caserta (through the kindness of General Balegno, commandant of the province of Salerno), I started early in the morning, accompanied by Signor Michele di Majo (the brother of the landlord of the Hotel Vittoria), whose services in behalf of the English captive were throughout of the greatest possible value. We were armed with rifle and revolver, and we felt that if Manzo or any of his confrères had any inclination to add our names to the list of *ricattati*, we, with our escort, should have been able to give them a warm reception.

"For the first three miles we followed the road to Pæstum, which, like all Italian roads in summer, was thickly covered with dust, and we soon experienced the disadvantage of having a cavalry escort, for, before we had gone a mile along the road, we were well-nigh smothered; and if Manzo or his *compagni* had been on any of the adjacent hills, they might have traced us to Giffoni by the cloud our protectors raised about us. After we left the high road, we turned off inland toward the range of mountains lying to the eastward. The scenery now rapidly improved, and the wonderful difference made by an abundant supply of running water in these fertile regions during the summer months became every moment more apparent. The Indian corn, which, with the tomato, formed the principal articles of cultivation, was in splendid condition; but what would have warmed the heart of many a hungry peasant had a very opposite effect on my companion (who belonged to the Bersaglieri corps of the Salernitan National Guard) and on our escort. They began to look anxiously around: the crops were so high that a man could easily walk upright through the fields without being seen. To them, the luxuriant vegetation and the ripening corn were sources of ill-concealed misery, indicating a secure hiding-place for the brigands. 'How can we hope to starve them out,' said the corporal, 'when the whole country is teeming with food? Would that it were autumn! we should then be certain of capturing the band, and of releasing your unfortunate countryman.' On one or two occasions, our gallant corporal, alarmed at the appearance of several people among the Indian corn, stopped the carriage and galloped forward to reconnoitre; but, being satisfied of their pacific intention, he allowed us to proceed. These little incidents, together with the narration of all kinds of adventures and hair-breadth escapes with the brigands, recounted with great zest by di Majo and the corporal, served to while away the time; and as the events recounted extended over a space of five years, there was no danger of the supply failing; a lively imagination, too often, I fancy, supplying what memory denied. Like old people, who are licensed to grumble at the degeneracy of the present age, so my informants bitterly complained that, in the short space of five years, even the brigands had greatly degenerated: formerly they fought like brave men, and often were the first to attack the troops; but now they always ran away, and never gave the troops a chance of shooting them—a proceeding on their part which, if it shows degeneracy of spirit, certainly shows increase of wisdom, strikingly exemplified in the manner in which Manzo at the present moment holds his own against the troops.

"But to return to our journey. The corporal was so engrossed in his narrative that he forgot to keep his usual good look-out, and it made our hearts leap into our mouths when he suddenly shouted 'Halt!' and unslung his carbine, pointing to several heads peering above the Indian corn. Our coachman nearly brought his horses down by the sudden jerk with which he attempted to pull up; and, not knowing exactly what to do, we all looked anxiously in the direction the corporal was pointing. 'It is nothing,' he said at last, as, looking most crestfallen, he dug his spurs into his horse's flanks; 'I took those countrymen in the Indian corn to be brigands.' As they stared at us with that stolid look which these country people generally put on whenever they see troops, he gave vent to his disappointed feelings in language which, if pure Italian, was certainly not elegant—giving it as his opinion that if they were not brigands by profession, they would have no objection to try their hands at it when occasion offered.

"After this occurrence, our valiant corporal subsided into a sulky silence; and what with the reaction which followed the excitement attending these little incidents, the dust, and the heat, we all felt tired and anxious to reach our journey's end.

"In about two and a half hours from the time we had left Salerno we reached Giffoni. Our entrance created quite a sensation among the villagers, who rushed out to see the 'Inglese' who had come to ransom his countryman. I had hardly been an hour in the place before it was positively affirmed by the knowing ones that they had seen the money I had brought, and that it was at least 30,000 ducats! The authorities received me most kindly, and gave me all the information they could. The military were at that time very sanguine of success; and the commanding officer, Captain Salsa (whose kindness throughout I shall ever gratefully remember), confided to me that, from information received, he fully expected the band would be taken that night, and that I should, in every probability, take Mr. Moens back in triumph to Salerno next morning. Continued subsequent failures soon made me skeptical whenever similar expectations were expressed; but on this occasion, participating in the hopes of the worthy captain, I felt sorely disappointed when, the next morning, I saw the troops returning wearied and disheartened, after a hard night's march; and it did not require to hear the officer's report to know that they had been unsuccessful. I arrived at Salerno on the afternoon of the 25th.")

I should here mention that the letters which H. C—— obtained at Florence were without delay delivered to the authorities at Salerno, and that these important officials invariably treated all my husband's countrymen, who were acting for him, with the greatest kindness; the general constantly placing an escort at the disposal of any of them who wished to leave Salerno for Giffoni, and the prefect also doing every thing in his power to assist them.

July 4. After this we had again to go through a period of harassing anxiety and suspense, until the brigands' answer was received, every one chafing with vexation at the enforced inactivity from which there was no escape. The general, too, who had, at the request of Messrs. C—— and Holme, renewed the pass for a limited time only, was evidently disinclined to extend the privilege farther, and we were therefore exceedingly anxious that the messenger from Giffoni should obtain an answer before it was too late.

At last, on June 30th, arrived a letter from my husband, dated the 29th, in which he had been allowed to write a few lines in English, thus showing that the plan had succeeded.

The bulk of this letter was, like his former letters, written in Italian, with a statement that the captain had allowed him to add a few words in English, which were as follows: "When I write like this (upright), it is from me; when slanting, it is dictated. Where are my friends? Am I deserted? Send money every week, if you can. I have been very ill with diarrhœa and— The food is so bad—nothing but scraps of bread and cheese. *I am free the moment the money is paid.* God bless you, dearest. He sends this trial for our good. *They think this country pays* the money, and so will have all. I have not told them I can pay."

The value of these few lines in English can not be overestimated. They not only gave us the clew to the real meaning of all future letters, but also relieved my advisers here from a great amount of responsibility.

After the receipt of this letter, Messrs. Bonham, Aynsley, and C—— thought that they could no longer hesitate to pay as large a sum as could be safely sent up into the mountains at one time.

The brigands, having intimated that they would be at a certain spot on Tuesday, the 4th of July, prepared to receive money, Messrs. Holme and C—— proceeded to Salerno on the 1st, with 26,400 francs, being 10,000 in addition to the sum which had been brought back from Salerno on the 25th of June.

The brigands' letters had all along shown that they believed the Italian government were going to pay eventually, and had refused to reduce their demand, on the ground that this being so, the captive's means were out of the question altogether. My husband in his last letter also alluded to this, and expressed a wish that some steps should be taken by the authorities to eradicate this notion from the minds of his captors.

On arriving at Salerno, the two gentlemen, bearing this in mind, and with the view of making another effort to reduce the demand of the brigands, visited the general and the prefect at Salerno, asking the latter whether his government would pay, and requesting him to answer the question by letter. This the prefect did, giving them an official letter* addressed to me, not only repudiating, on the part of the Italian government, all intention of paying any of the ransom, but also intimating that the government would do all in its power to prevent money or provisions being sent by me or any one else to the brigands.

* Which will be found in the Appendix, C.

Mr. Holme returned to Naples on the 2d, leaving the 24,600 francs in charge of Mr. C—— and Signor D——, who carried it on to Giffoni on the 3d, with the prefect's letter to me, and one from Mr. Bonham to my husband to the same effect.

(Now came another period of suspense, destined, alas! to be of far longer duration than any which we had undergone hitherto, for, as it turned out afterward, the troops kept such a vigilant watch on the brigands after this that the third installment of money lay at Signor Visconti's house for many weeks, and we did not hear of its receipt, or of the effect of the letters on the brigands, till the 9th of August. What effect the letter of the prefect had will appear hereafter in the course of my husband's narrative.)

July 15. About this time I wrote to Signor Visconti, thanking him for his exertions in my husband's behalf, and I have since received a very kind reply from him.*

Mr. and Mrs. Aynsley left Naples on the 28th of June to spend a few days in Rome, and my brother-in-law advised me to leave the Hôtel de Genève for a *pension*, as he thought it would be more cheerful for me, the life I was leading at the hotel before his arrival having been so extremely solitary, and having affected my health very seriously, for my friends had thought it advisable, for the reasons I have mentioned before, that English residents should not be encouraged to come and see me. I therefore moved from the hotel to the Palazzo Serracapriola, in the Riviera di Chiaja, a short time before my brother-in-law left for England, which he was compelled to do, after waiting as long as he possibly could to see the effect of the last letters and payment.

* I have ventured to give a translation of Signor Visconti's reply in the Appendix, D, to show how considerately and courteously he behaved to my wife at this time of trial.—W. J. C. M.

I well remember accompanying him to the steamer to see the last of him. I could not but wonder whether I should ever again be starting with my husband for dear old England! Alas! I had but too much reason then to fear that this happy time would never come for me.

How I vowed mentally never to leave home again, if we but once got safe back!*

The Bay of Naples looked its very best as the vessel steamed away, but I was too sad to enjoy its beauties while the ship remained in sight.

I watched it with a heavy heart, and when it at last disappeared from my view, I felt the loneliness of my position, which seemed to be more desolate than ever. H. C—— had tried hard to comfort me at the last with the hope that the letters sent from Salerno on the 3d of July, with the £1000, would produce the desired effect; but I had met with so many disappointments that I could not bring myself to think that any thing good would come of the schemes of my friends.

I have now really felt what "hope deferred" means, and

---

* In March I copied into my diary the following paragraph from "Geoffrey Crayon:" "A prosperous life passed at home has little incident for narrative; it is only the poor devils who are tossed about the world that are the true heroes of story. It is difficult to determine between lots in life, where each is attended with its peculiar discontents. He who never leaves his home repines at his monotonous existence, and envies the traveler, whose life is a constant tissue of wondrous adventure; while he who is tossed about the world looks back with many a sigh to the safe and quiet shore which he has abandoned. I can not help thinking, however, that the man that stays at home, and cultivates the comforts and pleasures daily springing up around him, stands the best chance of happiness." To me, *then*, these observations appeared to be true; and, *now* that I am at the end of my travels, I see no reason to change my opinion.
—A. M.

how it "maketh the heart sick." I try my best to cast all my care on God, but real grief is very different to imaginary sorrow.

I like my new home infinitely better than the hotel. I have had the good fortune to make the acquaintance of a Roman lady, the Signora Q——, who has been obliged to leave Rome on account of her political opinions. Her father, a well-known *avvocato*, was in prison there for five years because he was rather too liberal in his ideas. This lady also had been imprisoned herself for five months in one of the dark prisons in Rome, and was liberated eventually without a trial, through her own presence of mind. She one day received a visit from a gentleman, who brought her a letter of introduction from a great friend, with a request that she would receive the bearer for a few days as her guest. The bearer was a great friend of Garibaldi, and had come to Rome to find out whether the people were ready for a revolution. He staid at her house some days, but was at last arrested and thrown into prison by the Papal authorities. His friends wrote to her to inquire what had become of him, and she sent them a letter by the driver of a diligence informing them of his arrest. The letter happened to contain a remark to the effect that "the worst enemy Rome had was the emperor." One morning, shortly after this, she was in bed, when the police came into her room, and obliged her to rise and dress in their presence, and then carried her off to prison. Day after day a priest of high rank came to examine her, to try and find out from her answers something to criminate her. He once asked her a question, an answer to which might have injured her guest, who had been thrown into prison, but she had the presence of mind to evade answering by pleading extreme illness, and saying that the pain in her head was too violent for her to think much. The doctor was sent for, and, happily for her, he told her questioner that the signora was in a burning fever, and must be left in tranquillity for some days to come. The excitement and fear had really brought on a severe attack of fever. During the week in which she was freed from these inquisitorial visits, she succeeded in getting information of her guest's escape. This information was conveyed to her in a packet of tea by means of one word written on a tiny piece of paper. She now knew that he was safe, and on the next examination she felt no hesitation in answering the question freely, and she was liberated. It is said that the words in her letter saved her—"the worst enemy Rome has is the emperor," for the priests are no longer partial to the emperor. The police, however, did not leave her in peace; they paid constant visits to her house, looked into every room and closet, and even ripped open the cushions and pillows in search of letters. This state of constant espionage was so unpleasant to her, that she and her husband left Rome and settled in Naples.

The signora was extremely kind to me, and was always ready to accompany me in my visits to the questor, which about this time became rather frequent. She thought that this officer might be of great assistance in procuring the liberation of my husband, and she introduced me to him accordingly. He was a personal friend of hers.

We have requested the editors of the different Italian papers* to insert paragraphs in their papers in furtherance of the plan set on foot by H. C—— and Mr. Holme at Salerno, to the effect that *the brigands may believe that* the Italian

---

* A letter having appeared in the London *Times* stating that my husband was a "member of the Stock Exchange," one of the Neapolitan papers put him down as a "large shareholder in the Bank of England!"—A. M.

and **English** governments have both positively **refused** to pay any of the ransom. We hope this **will reach** the brigands, and that they will reduce their exorbitant claims.

The 24,600 francs (*i.e.*, about £1000) taken to Salerno by Messrs. Holme and C—— on the 1st of July, and carried on thence to Giffoni on the 3d, is still lying with the letters at Signor Visconti's house, the vigilance of the troops having hitherto prevented **the brigands from** coming to fetch it away. The peasants **are** suffering more than ever from the severe measures **employed by the authorities** to starve out the brigands. **The officers** complain that their want of success is caused by our messengers carrying information to **the band** with regard to the disposition of the various detachments; consequently, the strictest orders have been **sent** from Florence that no messenger is to be allowed a pass, and any peasant found carrying **a** letter or food is ordered to be shot immediately, without trial.

July 16. **No news of my husband; it is now nearly two** months, and I seem to have **made very little progress toward** his liberation; affairs have come to a dead lock. The only answer I get from the general is that it is an affair of police. I am determined to go to the questor and ask his advice. A messenger *must* be found, and as I hear the questor is an **extremely clever, kind** man, he may perhaps find some means of helping **me**.

July 17. **I went to the questor, who advised me to** go myself to Salerno, and try and **find out the brother of Manzo, and bribe him to go again. The questor will send a** detective with me; but, for better security, the man is **to hold no communication with me. I am not even to know who he is.** I am simply to let the questor know by what train I go. The detective is never to lose sight of me; and if I prevail on Manzo's **brother to take my letter, I am** to drop a handkerchief from my window at a certain hour. The detective will then attach himself to the messenger, and follow him every where, and thus find out the channel of communication.

On the 18th I started accordingly for Salerno, accompanied by a kind friend, Mrs. T——, an English lady, whose acquaintance I made at the *pension*. We left Naples in the evening, to avoid the extreme heat.

Mrs. T——'s quick eyes soon found out our detective, a man dressed as an Italian peasant. We noticed the same man lounging at the door of the hotel at Salerno; and when we took a walk the next day, he followed us. In fact, the "secret" scheme was carried out in so open and transparent a manner, that one evening, in the dark, we called the man behind a cart, and told him every one would certainly suspect him if he thus dogged our footsteps, and we arranged that he should only take his station before the hotel at certain hours after sunset, when we would communicate with him, if we wished it.

I sent for Manzo's brother, who is an *employé* on the railway, and bears a fair character. He is a young man with a plain countenance. I felt very much on seeing the brother of the man who had caused all my grief, and I implored him with tears to take a letter to my husband, offering him fifty pounds if he would do so; but neither tears, entreaties, nor bribes could prevail on him to go. It certainly would have been risking his life, for, if discovered taking a message to the band, he would, as I have already said, have been shot on the spot. We could find no one willing to risk his life; and all that came of our magnificent plan was the imprisonment of the poor detective by his brother police-officers, who arrested him as a suspicious character!

Finding I could do nothing at Salerno, I returned to Naples, and had another interview with the questor, who always treated me with the utmost kindness, and put aside all other business to listen to mine, though both his large ante-rooms were crowded with people of all ranks waiting to see him; police emissaries and telegrams arriving and departing at every moment, and a continuous stream of applicants pouring up and down the broad staircase of his *palazzo*. Whenever I sent in my card I was admitted, and listened to with the greatest patience. He now suggested sending emissaries to Rome, to do all that was possible there. They were sent, but this plan failed, like the rest.

I forgot to say that before I left Salerno I was told that a rich proprietor had offered to show the place where the brigands passed through his grounds, and to allow the troops to lie in ambush for them there; but, unfortunately, this gentleman's servant having quarreled with the troops, he refused to assist the latter in any way. Afterward the troops, when searching at the spot, found scraps of paper with English upon them, torn up by my husband but a short time before.

When at Salerno, on the 19th of July, I was summoned to Naples by telegraph, and started off, hoping and praying for good news; but when I arrived, overcome by the intense heat and excitement, it was a cruel disappointment to find that it was only to write another of the many useless letters I had already sent to the captain of the band. During the next week I suffered terribly from constant anxiety, till at last, on the 22d, I became so ill that my friends advised immediate change of air, and I accepted the invitation of my kind friend, Mrs. T——, to stay with her at Ischia. So we embarked together on the little wretched steamer that runs once a day between Naples and Ischia, across the bay. It was crowded with people, nearly all of them peasants; the sea was very rough, and every one was ill. The manner of

Italian peasants under these circumstances is sufficient of itself to cause illness in an Englishwoman; and when I made complaint to the captain, he gave me a very vague answer, remarking that the Neapolitans were a dirty people, because they never traveled, whereas the English, on the contrary, were always traveling, and that thus their manners were improved!

After three hours on the sea, we arrived at the lovely little island of Ischia. The fishermen's wives and children ran out of their cottages to welcome my friend Mrs. T—— back to her island; we were escorted to her house by them, all their faces beaming welcome. The house was beautifully situated on rising ground, with a magnificent view of the sea and the Bay of Lacco. I was never tired of walking on the roof of the house, to look at the beautiful panorama before me; I could see the Bay of Naples, Mount Vesuvius, the coast beyond the island of Procida, with its large white castle, and the Isle of Capri.

No words can describe the beauties of Ischia; it is such a lovely little island, and contains no brigands! I could enjoy long rambles in the country, without the unpleasant feeling that men were watching me to carry me off for ransom. In the centre of the island is a very finely-shaped mountain —Monte Epomeo—whose sides are covered with chestnut groves, vineyards, and tomato fields. I had a long walk with Mrs. T——'s children through vineyards reminding me of our hop-gardens. We were allowed to pick the bunches of grapes, as the owner of the fields was with us. They hung temptingly over our heads, and it was a curious sight to an English eye to see the immense profusion of a fruit which in England is rare enough to be considered a luxury. If any one wishes to enjoy fruit, and scenery, and climate, he should visit Ischia in September or October. October is the time of the vintage, and the weather then is not too hot for walking expeditions. Even in the hottest season, however, the air is constantly refreshed by the cool sea-breezes.

On the 28th I was summoned again to Naples by telegram; I had first to embark from Lacco in a little boat to catch the steamer which starts from Casamicciola. My kind friends put me under the care of a poor woman going to Naples to see her husband, who had been in prison there for seven months, waiting to be tried for an offense of which every one considered him innocent.

The poor woman told me her husband's story. Each fisherman is obliged to have a document from government authorizing him to carry on his trade. When the new government was established, the old documents or "books," as they are called, were called in, and new ones given out. Singi, my companion's husband, applied to the syndic of his village for his book. This syndic, a very bad man, obtained it easily from the maritime consul, with a clause in it stating that as Singi was a married man with children, he was exempt from military service; but before he would give the book to Singi, he demanded an exorbitant sum, which the poor man was unable to pay. The syndic then sold the book for 150 lire; and Singi, having no book, was thrown into prison on the charge of selling it, and had been there for seven months, leaving his family without any means of support. The poor woman was taking some little present for her husband, and had in her arms a dying babe, yet she was happier than I was, for she knew that her husband was living, and where he was, and was permitted to visit him, whereas I did not know whether my husband was alive or dead, and I was beginning to lose all hope of ever seeing him again. She cried bitterly as she told her sad story, and I could not help mingling my tears with hers.

My visit to Naples was a fruitless one; there was no

news of my husband, nothing could be done, and I returned to Ischia. I was strongly impressed with the fact, which I was assured of on all sides, that the great reason why no one will betray the brigands is fear of the consequences to the informer.

All over Southern Italy thus the *vendetta* holds sway, and fear of suffering from the revenge of the malefactors' relatives completely paralyzes the hands of justice. I heard a story in the island which strongly illustrates this. A poor woman living alone, with only a little dog as a companion, one day cut some grass for her goat from a neighbor's field. The man was angry; they quarreled at last; he stabbed, but did not kill her. Fearful of the consequences, he dragged her shrieking through three or four fields to a precipice, down which he threw her; he then took a circuitous route of two or three miles to the foot of the precipice, and finding her still breathing, he literally crushed her with an enormous stone; he then dug a hole and buried her, and covered the place with branches of trees. The poor creature was missed; two or three women had heard her shrieks, and had seen her dragged through the fields, but no one tried to save her — no one would breathe a word as to what they had seen, and her relatives sought for her in vain. One day her brother, with her little dog, was walking near her grave, when the animal whined, howled, and refused to go on. The brother tried to force him to follow, but in vain; the dog stood howling at a particular spot. This excited the man's curiosity; he pulled aside the branches, saw that the earth had been newly turned, dug it up, and discovered the dead body of his sister. No one would give evidence against the murderer for fear of the vengeance of his relatives, and he still walks about unpunished in Ischia! This murder was committed only a few weeks before I visited the island.

CHAPTER XII.
DIARY OF MR. MOENS, JUNE 21 TO 30.

On the Move again.—Without excess of Luggage.—The dépôt of Provisions.—We join Cerino's Band again.—Effect of the Arrival of H. M. S. *Magicienne* on the Amount of the Ransom.—A new Hat.—"Brigands supplied" by London Hatters. — The Charcoal-burners. — The Troops again in Sight.—Sheep-stealing.—Meat once a Fortnight.—Scope's Treatment of me.—Pavone's History.—Generoso at Death's Door.—Cold.—I have to Write more terrible Letters.—I am left with Eight or Ten of the Band.—Harsh Treatment.—Tantalizing View.—Wine and Rosolio.—I become very Ill.—Andrea's Heart softens.—Letters from my Friends, but no more Money.—My Ears in Danger.—I am made to Write again.—Cerino's Band go off with the Letters.

ON the evening of the 21st of June we were startled by hearing signals from the mountains above, and we immediately got ready to join the new-comers; they proved to be three of the band from Manzo, who had been sent to tell us that there was a large increase of troops in the neighborhood, and that we were to join him without a moment's delay: this was very provoking, for a supply of bacon, fruit, and wine, together with several shirts, and among them my only change, which had been "sent to the wash," were to arrive this very night; but there was no disobeying the orders, and I never saw my garment again.

After the long rest of a fortnight, without the slightest exercise, and always lying on the ground, I found the greatest difficulty for the first half hour in keeping up with my companions. The road lay up hill, through the thickest underwood, and at times I was perfectly unable to go on from utter want of breath. Lorenzo, who usually treated me well, was very savage from the loss of the expected clean shirts and the provisions; for when a peasant is commissioned to get any thing, he always insists on being paid first at exorbitant prices, a ducat for two *rotoli* of bread—about sixpennyworth—and every thing else in proportion. Twenty Napoleons had been left with him for our expenses; these and fifteen more had been spent for the expenses of about six men in a fortnight; this will give an idea of the rate at which these men live. At least four fifths of all the money that is extorted from their captives goes to the peasants, and the other fifth is spent in the shops in the towns. No wonder all the peasants encourage brigandage and cry up the cause of Francis II., imagining that the brigands fight for him, because they are pursued and hunted down by the soldiers of Victor Emmanuel. Nothing will stop the system but levying the ransoms on the districts where the captures take place.

When we came to the store-house, we found several more of the band, who immediately attacked the two sacks of bread we had collected. Justi told me to put some in my pocket, for I had a very long walk before me, and the band we were to join would have nothing with them. Scope was in a great rage at my pocketing any thing, but some of the others took my part, and I was able to retain my spoil.

I had now regained my powers of walking; after some hours we gained the top of the hill, walking in the moonlight by the side of the noisy stream, with waterfalls in many places. On our left rose high mountains clothed with wood, and on the right there were two ridges of unequal height, covered with the same bright green, while in front rose towering mountains, with tops of all conceivable shapes. I felt well and strong, and if I ever enjoyed any walk while under restraint, it certainly was this night's tramp.

When we arrived at the top of the pass, instead of turning to the left as we did before, we went straight on, descending the mountain through dense forests, till at last we came to an open space where the charcoal-burners were hard at work, the ground being strewed with chips of wood. All at once we fell in with Pepino and his band, who looked most miserable, having met with a *disgrazia*, as they termed it. The very day after they had left the mountain, where Visconti had been set free, the soldiers had discovered their resting-place, and they had to take to their heels, leaving behind them all their belongings—two new camp-kettles, the leathern flasks that I had so often drunk out of, and all their *capotes*, among them the two splendid ones of fine blue cloth belonging to Pepino and Doniella, while on Pepino's was buttoned the *capuce* that he had snatched off my head. I told him that it was a judgment on him for having robbed me, at which all round laughed most heartily. They had fared most miserably ever since; they greeted me, however, in a cheerful way, being glad to see me well, for all expected that somehow or other the Inglese would find the money that they demanded.

The coming of the man-of-war to Salerno, and the number of troops that were looking after us, made them naturally think that Mr. Aynsley and I were of importance, and nothing that was said or written to them could upset their idea that we were the joyful possessors of two million ducats. One of them was sent off to Manzo, who, with some of the others, were sitting near a fire in a hollow where it could not be seen. Immediately after this Manzo came up and took my wide-awake off my head, replacing it by the one that was on his head; this rather disturbed my peace of mind, for I thought of the new family that would in all probability be introduced to the one that had already taken possession of me. He told me he did not consider the hat I had been wearing suitable to a person of my distinction, and that he had got one of the best that could be found in Naples specially for me, at the cost of a Napoleon. It certainly was a very good one, of a brown color, with a tall crown and wide brim; one of the band doubled in the crown, pressing in each side with his hands, and then gave it me back, telling me that that was the way *signori* always wore them. I looked at the label inside, and, to my astonishment, found that it had been made by Christy, the celebrated hatter in Gracechurch Street, London, whose establishment I always visit when in want of a covering for my head at home. I told the brigands that it was *un cappello Inglese del mio proprio cappellaio:* this amused them immensely, and they all came one by one to compliment me on my improved appearance. One of them lent me his little looking-glass, in order that I might "admire myself," as he expressed it.

It was now about nine o'clock; but when I inquired where we were to stop for the night, I was told that *molto cammino* was in store for me, and that we were to walk all night. A short time after starting again we came to where the charcoal-burners were engaged in their occupation. There were several enormous round piles of wood, covered with damp earth firmly beaten down. From fissures in the piles a suffocating smoke was issuing, and the ground on the lower side was quite soppy with the wood spirit and tarry matter that was running from them. A little way off were the wood huts of the *carbonari*, which are constructed of straight pieces of wood stuck in the ground and then bent to a point at the top, a span being left for an entrance. There seemed to be two or three men in each hut, which were all visited in succession, in order that all provisions that could be spared might be taken. We finished all their water, the wooden barrels being passed from one to the other, and the water drunk through the bung-holes. I was always obliged to get as much down my throat as I could in as short a space of time as possible, for they always took the barrel away from me in a moment.

In the entrance of each hut was a large wood fire, in the embers of which the inmates were just about making *pizza*, that is, a mixture of Indian-corn meal and water, baked for about a quarter of an hour. Manzo bargained for this and one of the water-barrels, giving for them half a Napoleon. I was taken to a little distance off while the *pizza* was being made, and managed to get a little sleep; but we were soon marching along again in single file, the line extending a considerable distance. We kept ascending all night in a northerly direction, and toward the morning arrived at a large tract of level land near the top of the mountain. It was a great treat, walking on the smooth turf, after having had to force our way through the lower branches of the trees, in the dense woods with which nearly all these mountains are covered. The brigands were all very tired, for we had been walking since seven o'clock, up hill nearly all the time. I always found that I could keep it up for a number of hours with less fatigue than they could, while they, on the other hand, were quicker and more agile for a short time, especially on the rough ground. Our halting-place was in the midst of some high heather, a *factione* was called, sentinels set, and we were all asleep in a short time.

About midday the troops were seen on the top of a mountain not more than a mile off, and we had to hide close in some clumps of trees. To my disgust, I discovered on the ground, in a place where Manzo had been sitting, several scraps of paper that had been torn up, that had formed part of a letter from Mr. Aynsley; but I could not make any thing of it. They had been busy making cartridges, and his letter had gone in this way; it was most provoking to think that the wretches had received letters for me which they had not given me, but I suppose that it having been written in English was the cause.

We could not remain here because of the troops, so two hours before sunset we descended the mountain through the woods, and when it was dark, crossed over the cultivated valley to the mountains opposite. We walked through the growing crops till we came to a stream, where we all slaked our thirst. Here, to the amusement of all, old Sentonio fell down into the water. We now passed along a good mule-road, and then began to ascend the terraces of earth to higher ground, without having seen a house or human being. Great caution was exercised; notwithstanding some of the band being always in advance, I was kept in the rear, as usual, with only three or four behind me. At last, toward twelve o'clock, we got into the woods again, and at about two came to a suitable place, where we stopped till the next morning. Some of the band had been left in the plain to look after food, and in the middle of the day two peasants came up with bread and a quantity of cherries. During the day we heard the tingling of the sheep-bells, but could not at first see the flock. At last I pointed it out to them, on the other side of the valley, near the place we had come from, and it was determined to send over to get two sheep in the evening. Justi and four others started off, and returned toward the morning with the carcasses of the sheep hanging on their backs; they reported that they had had great difficulty in getting them, there having been no less than twelve persons at the place where the sheep were collected for the night, and these had stoutly refused to let the brigands have any; but Justi and the others pointed their guns at them, and threatened to shoot them all unless two were killed immediately, and of course they got their way. They were cooked at once, and I enjoyed the change of diet very much, for I had not tasted meat for more than a fortnight. A hatchet was also obtained from the shepherds, but during the day there was a dispute about the price paid for it, and Rocco, in a rage, took it up, and, after trying to break it against a stone, which he struck several times as hard as he could, threw it some distance into the thick underwood, where they were unable to find it.

It was a noisy day, for gambling produced the usual quarrels, and toward the afternoon one of the band let his gun off by accident; the captain was always in a great rage at this, and no wonder, for it was nearly sure to bring the troops.

In the morning we started again, spending several hours in ascending the mountain, and at last came to a terrace near the top, with several caves; we halted here for some time, I enjoying the view toward the west, being able to see the whole province with the sea behind it. All at once I was amazed at seeing all the band go mad, as I thought; their game seemed to be that all should vie, one with the other, who could roll the largest piece of rock over the edge, so that they might go crashing down the mountain side. This was done as a signal to those left foraging in the plain; we could hear the rocks rolling down far below us, making a great noise; it had the desired effect, for in an hour or two the party below came up, but with their pockets empty. We slept here half the night, and then continued our course, passing along the narrowest ledges round the shoulder of the mountain; we now came to a large level tract of grass-land studded with clumps of trees.

It was quite light enough to enjoy the English park-like scenery, with the bare rocks at the top of the mountain rising in front. The glades were of the finest short grass, with a quantity of a pretty yellow flower growing abundantly. We passed some *baraque* recently made, which much annoyed the captain, and a halt was called while a council was held, and the ground examined for the footprints of the soldiers. We were on Monte Marano, the highest mountain of the province, and had expected to find it quite safe and free from the soldiers. I told them that it was now all the safer, for if the forces had passed them recently it would be some time before they came again. They rather agreed with me, but I was told to be silent, and not to listen to their talk. I told them it amused me; but as they talked such bad Italian, I could not make much of it. On we went again, and at about seven o'clock arrived at a place surrounded by very high trees, and the ground was very wet, but down I was made to lie all the same. A fire was soon blazing, for it was intensely cold at the great height at which we were. Two were sent off at once to get some water from a fountain higher up the mountain, and sentinels set in every direction.

June 23. In about two hours the captain ordered a change of place, and we retraced our steps, crossing the tracks made by dragging the timber along through the woods; we then passed over another dry "nullah," and retired to a corner of a glade from whence the track was visible. Sentinels were set, one being sent a quarter of a mile off where he could view the country in another direction. I was sent off (under the charge of Pavone and that demon

Scope, who always ill-treated me) to some rising ground about two hundred yards off, so that, should there be any danger, I might be hurried off while the main part of the band covered our retreat. I had not been here long before the tinkling of bells told us that a flock of sheep was approaching, and a detachment was sent off in order to secure some mutton. They returned in about half an hour, bringing the shepherds with them, who were very unwilling to part with their sheep, because there was a report that several shepherds had been put into prison for having let the brigands take their sheep. But what can these men do? If they will not sell their sheep, they are soon taken from them; and should the shepherds give any information, their unprotected position makes them to be easy victims to the vengeance of the brigands.

Manzo was unwilling to make these men enemies, for it was a new part of the country, and he intended stopping here some time. He said he was willing to pay a fair price, but all grumbled when they found that thirty-five ducats was demanded for three sheep. This was very nearly £2 a-head, but the shepherds would not let them go for less, for they were of a peculiar large breed, and much valued. The flock passed close to where I was lying, but the shepherds were made to go round, so that I could not see them. Two of the sheep were immediately killed and put into the pot, and within an hour the meat was turned out cooked. It was very tantalizing to see them all eating the best parts, while we were left without any. At last Scope went to get some, and he returned, carrying in his hands what was supposed to be our share—that was, for me, Pavone, and himself; but when it came, Pavone and I became indignant, there being hardly a mouthful apiece. I had seen the greedy wretch eating as fast as he could on his way to us. Pavone would not stand this, and when the second sheep was ready, he told me to come with him to the fire; but Manzo in an angry tone told him to take me back; he remained, and two others marched me back to my old place. The same trick was repeated when food was brought again to us; experience had, however, taught me by this time that there was no use in grumbling, so I ate what I could get with thankfulness.

I was very ill all this day, and, to improve matters, it turned out a pouring wet day. As soon as it began to rain Pavone came up for half of my *capote*. Scope wanted to come under it too, but I was very firm on this point, and told him that Pavone was one too many, and that the captain had given me the cloak for myself. While sitting together, Pavone told me that as soon as my money was paid he meant to present himself—that is, to give himself up to justice—and asked me not to recognize him should I see him in prison. He did not seem to know that the government knew all of them better than I did. He told me that his wife and children had been in prison all the time he had been a brigand, this being the custom, and a very good one too, of the Italian authorities, and that they would be released directly he gave himself up.

He also told me his history. He had been an agricultural laborer, and having committed murder (or homicide as he called it) during the reign of Francis II., he had been put in prison for three years. Soon after being released he repeated the same crime and took to the woods. He showed me the weapon which he had used on both occasions—a stiletto, the blade of which was about six inches long; he had a superstitious reverence for it, and was quite uneasy whenever it was out of his hands. I used all my persunsive powers to induce him to aid my escape, in which case I promised to give him 2000 ducats, and to get a free pardon for him; but he was afraid of Manzo's vengeance against members of his family, all of whom would be murdered on the first opportunity. I tried to work on his feelings as a husband and father, but was as unsuccessful with him as I afterward was with many others.

As night came on, we returned to where we had stopped in the morning, and an enormous fire, made in the most skillful way, was lighted. The pile was at least ten feet high, and as many in diameter, and round this we laid ourselves on the wet ground, those who had not capotes picking branches of leaves, and after drying them by the fire, spreading them on the ground. A dreadful scene took place in the middle of the night. Suddenly waking (for I now slept as lightly as any brigand), I saw Generoso, who was sleeping next to me, writhing in agony; his hands were clenched and lips drawn up, and he was deadly cold; Antonina, who was always with him, was in the greatest distress, appealing every moment to the Madonna. I soon saw he was seized with convulsions of some kind, and recommended that hot pads should be applied to his person. He was foaming at the mouth, and in a short time struggled so that it took five men to keep him down. At last he was quiet, but by this time his pulse was hardly perceptible, and he grew colder and colder. There was great concern exhibited for him, as he was a great favorite, and all thought he was dying. I told them to keep rubbing his limbs, and, not wishing to see his last moments, turned away. I had been standing over him for two or three hours, and, exhausted by fatigue, fell asleep. When I awoke in the morning, to my great astonishment, he was all right again. I asked him how he was, and he told me that his legs were rather painful at the knee-joints, but he did not seem to have any recollection of the fit.

A little more to the north than where we crossed the valley yesterday, I observed an old mediæval castle, partly in ruins; the walls had inclosed some extent of land, all of which was now cultivated; many of the walls were covered with ivy, and close by was a modern small farm-house. Near this place I noticed several peasants haymaking: this seemed managed in a different manner to what we do in England. When dry, the grass is all twisted up into tight wisps—in fact, made up into short lengths of thick cable and then stacked away. It struck me that it was a sad waste of time.

June 24. To-day the captain ordered the band to go higher up the mountain to the fountain, because the shepherds had reported that the troops had passed where we now were only two days before, but had not ascended higher up; so he considered that a change would be safer for us. I was very unwell, and the climb up much tired me; but it was no use showing any disinclination to go on, so I said nothing, hoping that we should not have to go far. This proved to be the case, fortunately for me; and when I was told to lie down, I sat on a large block of wood, and the brigands set about collecting firewood, for all complained of the great cold. To my dismay, Manzo did not allow me to come near the fire when it was made, but sent me off again to some little distance under the charge off two or three of his men. I had the advantage of a magnificent view, with the sea in the extreme distance, but this did not make up for the want of the fire which all the others were enjoying. At last Manzo sent for me to write horrible letters to my wife and the consul, which he dictated; he would not allow me to insert a single word of English, and still persisted in asking for the same sum as at first. How my heart always sank when, after my entreaties to diminish the sum, he would say, "Write as I say, 50,000 ducats!"*

Provisions now began to flow in, two peasants having brought up a number of round loaves with a large hole in the centre. I saw them through the trees sitting on the bank by the fountain; but as soon as the brigands saw that I had noticed the strangers, they were removed to a place out of my sight. I must now describe this fountain.

It was in a lovely spot, quite level, about thirty yards long and ten wide, surrounded by beech-trees; on one side there was a sloping bank on which the members of the band were extremely fond of lying basking in the sun. The water issued from the ground on the eastern end, and ran in a little stream which formed pools every two or three yards, and finally ran down the incline of the mountain. "Forget-me-nots" grew most luxuriantly; also violets and many other wild flowers were mingled with the short grass that covered the ground. In the afternoon I was allowed to go and sit on the bank in order to enjoy the sun; and a share of some delicious cheese, only just made, was given to me, and also a tiny piece of old cheese, which I reserved for a time of want. The bread varied in every district, and what we had here was far superior to the dark and coarse loaves of oval form which we got when near Giffoni.

When the peasants wished to go away, I was made to cover my head with a *capote*, so that I might not be able to recognize them afterward, and then they passed by me and were soon lost to sight in the woods. About two hours before sunset Manzo selected eight or ten of the band to stop with me while he went back to Giffoni to take my letters and get some more money (but many a weary journey had he to perform before any more was received, on account of the number and vigilance of the soldiers).

* See also Manzo's Letter to Visconti, Appendix E.

Though already very high, we went still higher up the mountain, having to pass many most difficult places. At one of these the men ahead got separated from us, through my being unable to climb up quick enough. Those behind were in a great rage with me when they found their signals unanswered; but Manzo soon sent two or three of those with him to look for us. In about half an hour we arrived at another of those curious ledges about one thousand feet from the extreme summit of the mountain, with about eighteen inches of space to walk along, the mountain rising perpendicularly on one side, and the precipice being on the other. I fortunately had rather strong nerves, for if I had been in the least dizzy, I must have fallen over. If I hesitated for a moment a harsh cry of "*Camminate*" would be raised by the man behind me. Manzo now repeated his orders, which were very precise, and provided for every emergency, and then left us, saying that he would return in six days.

I must now describe my position: we were on the top of the highest mountain* in the province of Avellino, to the extreme northeast of that portion of the Apennines which traverses the greater part of that province and that of Salerno. The side we were on faced the northwest, and looking that way Vesuvius appeared a moderate-sized isolated mountain, with a long line of smoke drifting away from the summit. Naples was not visible, Mount Vesuvius just shutting it out from view; but behind, the island of Nisida, and the coast-line of the Bay of Naples near Baiæ, ending at the Point of Misenum, were very clearly marked, and farther on the lofty island of Ischia. The coast to the north gradually became indistinct, till at last it was lost in the extreme distance. How this view brought to mind a happy day we

---

* This mountain, I think, must have been Monte Marano.

had spent exploring the remains of antiquity at Baiæ, and our little voyage by boat to Misenum only three days before my capture! Nocera and the other towns between Vesuvius and Castellamare were exceedingly distinct, every house being visible.

I remembered that I had seen nearly the same view from the top of Mount Vesuvius about five years before; but going up a mountain for one's own amusement, as I did then, and being taken up forcibly against one's will, are very different things, especially when, in the latter case, instead of stopping a short hour, one knows for a certainty that one will have to stop there six days, and perhaps longer, being all that time exposed to the cruelly cold wind which generally blows at this elevation. This evening it blew from the north, and seemed to pierce right through me. I complained of the cruelty of exposing me in this manner; but, though suffering bitterly themselves, my captors had the impudence to tell me that it was my own fault, and that when the money was paid I might go back to my friends and enjoy the comforts of a house! I told them that they would never get the 50,000 ducats they were always talking about; and to that they would call out, in a mocking tone, "*impossibile, impossibile,*" those being the words generally uttered by an unfortunate prisoner when they demand unconscionable sums.

To-day was Sunday: but

"The sound of a church-going bell
These valleys and rocks never heard;
Never sighed at the sound of a knell,
Nor smiled when a Sabbath appeared."

Though we were all feeling the cold so much, we had no fire to-night, being in too exposed a position, and my sufferings in the morning were most severe. The fine weather of last night had gone, and with it that lovely view; in its place was nothing but the mist and clouds with which we were enveloped, the wind driving them along the side of the mountain. Pepino and several others who had slept by the fountain joined us, bringing a good supply of bread, some *confetti*, two terracotta jars and two *caraffe* of wine, and two or three bottles of rosolio, a kind of strong liqueur, and a large handkerchief full of cherries, which had got wet the day before, and were now in a fermented state; but I had been so long without vegetable food that I ate all my share; they then drank a bottle of rosolio, each taking a little out of my leathern cup.

I suffered terribly after this. I do not know whether the severe cold had any thing to do with it or not, but for the next four days I had a most violent attack of diarrhœa, and I fully expected that the brigands would have had to scoop out a shallow hole to put my body in. The wine and spirit made them rather merry to-day, and they played a noisy game, thus: All stood in a circle, one being chosen by lot in the same manner as the sentinels were selected; he took a bottle of rosolio and drank a little, and the bottle was then passed round from one to the other, and if the starter made the noise one does with the tongue when driving, the holder of the bottle was not to drink, but to pass it on; but if he said "*esso*," the lucky holder at that moment was allowed a draught. Of course the expectant is often tantalized by a pause, and after all is disappointed. When the bottle gets low, it passes round and round again without any one being allowed to drink, and the merriment is great. Of course the one who has been allowed to drink then gives the word to the others. I was asked to join, but I was too ill to enjoy the fun.

I thought of trying to escape to-day. I was left alone a

few moments, and immediately went quietly along the ledge away from the band, but very leisurely, as if escaping was the last thing I was thinking of; and very fortunately too, as Giuseppe and his consort were some little way off in the direction I was going. They saw me, and immediately wanted to know where I was going, and I had to make some excuse, and those in charge of me had a good blowing up for not looking better after me. In the evening I was delighted to hear that they would not sleep again in such an exposed position, for all had suffered severely from the cold and wet, and we went back to the fountain, and a large fire was made, round which we all slept, with our feet toward the glowing embers. As soon as the sun was up we all went to a retired place to sun ourselves, as it was dangerous to keep up a fire during the day.

June 27. A new companion came to-day; he was a nice-looking peasant lad; his crime, as usual, was murder, but he was as merry as possible, and remorse did not seem to trouble him in the least. The captain is expected on Thursday; and, to my horror, I heard that he has written to the Prefect of Salerno to say that if the money is not sent up by the 5th of July, my ears are to be cut off and sent to my friends. I was also told that they had received a letter from the secretary of the prefect. I felt too ill to care about any thing, and told them that every thing was as God willed, and that they might do what they liked with me.

June 28. I suffered agony all day, and some *pasta* which I ate made me worse. I felt so miserable that at times I longed to die. I had not heard from my friends for nine days, but I still hoped that to-morrow the captain would come with money and letters. Money! money! if I had known that none would come for nearly two months, I do not think I could have lived. I found a comfortable soft place between the trunks of two enormous beeches, a few yards from the rest of the band, so that I escaped hearing the frightful language they constantly made use of. To my joy, I was allowed to remain in this place; but two or three never took their eyes off me.

To amuse myself, I cut names in the back of the tree, and also a large cross. I also tried to cheer myself up with the idea of the captain coming to-morrow with sufficient money to induce them to come down in their demands, for I felt sure that until at least 15,000 ducats came they would continue asking 50,000. The reason I had for this idea was that the original sum asked for the two Viscontis was demanded again and again until they had paid 15,000, and then the 40,000 ducats was reduced to 25,000, and I thought it would be much the same in my case. I could not sleep a wink all this night; I felt so ill and wretched, and the horrible idea of the 5th of July approaching would come into my head. I did not believe what they had told me; but still it might be the case, for they have no regard for any one's feelings: they only think of the most ready way of forcing money from the relatives of their captive.

It was a fearful night, blowing a perfect hurricane, and the trees were all lashed into a perfect state of fury. It did not rain, but the clouds with which we were enveloped kept driving by, drenching every thing. Pavone slept and snored under the half of my *capote*, and his odor was very "loud" and unpleasant. The feeling of being obliged to lie in such close proximity to a double-dyed murderer was almost more than I could endure, and I am afraid that he must have found me a most uncomfortable bedfellow. I kept hitting him to stop his snoring—rolling myself round and so dragging the covering from him, and groaning from the pain I suffered; but I must say that for all that he was most forbearing. He could see that I was very ill, and I kept impressing on him that I should be dead in a few hours unless a change for the better took place. He told me that there was a chance of some cheese made from cows' milk coming up to-morrow, and that it would be very good for me. It seemed to me a most curious remedy, and the last thing in the world I should have chosen, but in the end it certainly did me good.

June 29. In the morning I discovered that they had half a bottle of absinthe: this was given to me by Andrea the executioner, to my great astonishment, for he always grudged me every mouthful; but just now he was suffering from an attack of fever, and I suppose this made him feel a little for me; he told me to keep the bottle in my pocket, so that the others might not take it from me. I put a little into all the water I drank, and from this time I gradually recovered, but I was not well for several days. I am thankful to say that this was the only serious attack of illness I suffered from all the weary days of my detention; at a later date I nearly died from starvation, but I soon recovered when I obtained a fair supply of food.

To-day it was very clear, all the clouds of last night having blown away, and from the place where I was lying, all that well-known view of the plain of Salerno, bounded on the south by the mountains below Pæstum, was visible. I could see the white houses forming the village of Battipaglia where I was taken, but the old temples, yellow from age, were not to be distinguished. I had, however, no taste for scenery just now, for I could think of nothing but the coming of Manzo, hoping that a good sum of money had been sent to him. Minute by minute, hour by hour, the day passed by: how long it appeared! at last darkness set in, and we retired to the place where it was possible to make a fire in security; then another sleepless night was passed, though I did not suffer as I had done the night before.

June 30. About the middle of the day I was thrown into the greatest state of excitement by seeing Manzo and Lorenzo quietly walking toward us. The captain said nothing to me, but handed me an Italian-English Dictionary I had written for, and in it were two letters from my wife, and one in English from Mr. Richard Holme. (This was the first I had heard of this gentleman, who so nobly stepped forward on behalf of Mr. Aynsley and myself, and who, at the risk of his life and liberty, went backward and forward between Giffoni and Salerno, carrying letters and money to Signor Visconti's house, to be forwarded to the brigands for my liberation. Manzo and the others had often told me that the secretary of the English consul was at Giffoni or Salerno, having no doubt heard of Mr. C—— and Mr. Holme being there at different times, and they might have made an attempt to pounce upon the money *en route*. I afterward heard that the general in command at Salerno invariably offered my friends an escort of soldiers when they wished to leave Salerno, an offer which was, of course, thankfully accepted. In Italy it is highly dangerous to carry large sums of money; life is held in such little esteem that hundreds would have thought nothing of taking any life that stood between them and the coveted gold.)

I was delighted at the sight of the letters, but my heart sank when I asked Manzo how much money, and the answer was returned of *niente*. The horrid talk about my ears came to my mind again, but I was relieved when I was told that no money was sent because my friends thought I was dead, and would send no more unless they received a letter in English from me to prove I was alive. I directly saw that this was a clever device to induce the brigands to let me write in English, and enable me to give hints regarding the course they should pursue at Naples.*

As soon as I received the letters (and how those from my wife made me grieve!), Manzo came to me and told me to write to the consul and my wife, and that I might write two lines of English in each. I told him that it was impossible to say any thing in two lines, and got with difficulty permission to write *five* lines, but not a word more. Into these few lines I contrived to squeeze as much information for my friends as possible, telling them of my real state, and of my great desire to be liberated; also how they were to distinguish in future between what was really written by me and what was dictated; and I mentioned that the band would never reduce their demand as long as they believed that the government would pay. These letters were sent off by Pepino Cerino and his band. Manzo remained with us, and told me that the messenger would return in four days.

* I afterward heard that this letter was concocted by Messrs. Holme and C—— at Salerno with the view I supposed.

CHAPTER XIII.

Diary of Mr. Moens, July 1 to 17.

Waiting for an Answer.—The Soldiers again.—We Retreat.—How they encouraged me to move on.—A narrow Escape.—News of Giardullo's Capture.—How it was effected.—Gambling again.—I lend my Comb.—Place aux Dames.—Orchard Robbing.—A Meal of Onions.—Pavone steals my Socks.—The Fame of Crocco and Borjès.—Telescopes.—Sheep-stealing.—Another Night Walk.—I write more Letters.—Guange offends Manzo.—Manzo enforces Discipline.—Feeling of the Band toward him.—Scarcity of Water.—Sentonio's Water-bottle.—Mysterious Disappearance of the Contents.—Lorenzo physics himself.—I am threatened by all.—I think seriously of cutting my Ears myself.—Proposal to Emigrate under my Leadership.

The next day, Manzo, after his usual custom, sent me off under the charge of Sentonio and Lorenzo higher up the mountain. It was bitterly cold, and where we were sent there was no chance of getting any sun. Lorenzo here again confided to me his intention of giving himself up to justice as soon as my money was paid. I tried the plan of bribing him, but got the same answer that Pavone gave me —that he feared the vengeance of Manzo on his relatives. What a horrid place we were now in! It was very damp, and the ground covered with large pieces of rotten wood, crumbling to dust at the least touch.

In the evening the band came up to sleep in this place, Manzo considering that it was hardly safe close to the fountain, for fear of the soldiers coming there for water. Ferdinando, who had been a soldier in the Italian army, with four others, was sent down to the plain to forage for bread. Manzo was far more cautious than the others, and would allow no fire in the morning.

Every morning my joints grew stiffer and stiffer from the effects of the cold and damp, and I dreaded much the rheumatism that I felt sure I should suffer from afterward. About nine o'clock there was an idea that some people were at the fountain, and Manzo went a little way down to reconnoitre, but returned, saying there was nothing; in five minutes more, the sentinel who had been sent farther down came running up in a great state of alarm, saying that fifty soldiers were at the fountain. I was immediately told to run up the mountain, and they would hardly let me pick up my little bundle of things and my *capote*. The bread was taken, but the water-barrel and *caldaja* were left behind, and I was driven before them.

I was exceedingly weak from the effects of my late illness, and soon slackened, but they immediately stimulated my pace with the muzzles of their guns, and they used all their exertions to put at least a mile of thick wood between them and their foes. (From a conversation I had after my freedom with the officers at Giffoni, I found that the troops had had no idea that those they were looking so eagerly for were so close to them.) And when the brigands found that they were not followed, they took it more leisurely, and after another mile they halted on a high mound, sloping down on three sides, the other side being in the opposite direction to the soldiers.

Here we waited for the men who were expected with bread, great fears being expressed for their safety, lest they should have fallen in the way of the troops, who were just where they would pass in making their way to join the

L

band. In about two hours some stones were heard falling from the extreme top of the mountain, and scouts were sent immediately to go and see whether it was occasioned by their companions or by the soldiers, when it was found to be the former; and in the course of another hour they rejoined us, reporting that they had seen the force at the fountain. They had not been able to get any bread on account of the force in the plain. The soldiers had caught some women who were bringing up bread, *confetti*, *rosolio*, and bacon on the back of a donkey, just as the things were about to be given to Ferdinando and his party, who actually saw the soldiers seize every thing, being only a few yards off. Had they come up a few minutes later, the brigands would have been captured with the food.

This all shows the difficulty the troops have in finding the brigands; they had no idea where they were, and yet the brigands saw the soldiers, and escaped without the latter even knowing that they were near. We heard that about a week before, the band got information that in the southern part of the province of Salerno, the *Capo* Giardullo, another brigand captain and his band, consisting of about thirty men, had been surprised, and four killed and three wounded. Giardullo, and eventually all but four old hands, gave themselves up to justice, and are now safely lodged in prison at Salerno. Great commiseration was expressed for them. "Oh, dear companions!" being the phrase continually uttered. In Giardullo's case information was gained that a peasant had just taken food to the band; he was met by the troops, and with a pistol at his head was made to retrace his steps, and show where the hiding-place of Giardullo was; the sentinels were all asleep, and the brigands were pinned in the cave where they were passing the night. They immediately fired at the soldiers, who returned their

GIARDULLO DI PESTO.

fire with the result mentioned above. The rest all escaped, but gave themselves up afterward. I presume that they had realized sufficient plunder to enable them to live comfortably in prison, for their friends, under certain regulations, are allowed to send them food and any thing they may require.

The band remained here all day, and for a wonder gambling went on quietly for some time. I felt very miserable, for the messenger was to have returned on Sunday to the fountain, but now this fresh *disgrazia* would make a fresh delay. Early in the afternoon we crept silently through the woods, descending the mountain, and at last struck a path which led us over some hills covered with broom. We arrived at last at a spring of excellent water, where we rested half an hour, and then went on again for an hour, halting on some open ground surrounded by low hills. Here the captain and three men went on some distance in order to see whether the country was clear from the dreaded force. The ground was a soft marl, to which the heavy rains so prevalent in this part of the country had cut deep courses. There were many boulders of white limestone scattered about, some of them supported on pillars of earth, the surrounding ground having been washed away.

I was told here that we were to go on walking till daylight, so I took the opportunity of getting all the rest I could; but the inveterate gamblers were hard at work again. It was here that some of the band insisted on borrowing my comb, and it was returned to me full of filth. I felt very disgusted, but had to make up my mind to this, as well as to giving up to one of the women, Maria by name, a piece of bread I had saved, who exercised the privilege of her sex in changing her mind, having refused to eat in the morning when she was offered her own share. While here I was delighted at hearing a number of linnets singing most sweetly. In about three quarters of an hour, a whistle from the direction the captain had taken told the band all was safe, and in a few minutes we were on our way again.

We soon came to an excellent mule-road passing through plantations of enormous chestnut-trees, the fields being all well cultivated. It now grew quite dark, and we began to descend, the road being on the verge of a precipice for some miles; the valley was deep below us, and the site of a town was clearly marked out by a grand illumination, which speedily broke out into a blaze of fire-works, the rockets illuminating all around. I inquired what it was all for, and was told that it was a *festa* in honor of the Madonna. We stopped some time enjoying the spectacle, the good people of the town of Montella little thinking that the dreaded brigands were so near. When we got lower down greater caution was observed, and we walked through the cultivated ground a little way from the road. We passed some large heaps of firewood, and at a hut near a dog barked most violently at us; at last we reached the bottom of the mountain, and an excellent level road crossed our path at right angles, evidently leading to the town.

I felt a great inclination to dash along it and make an attempt to escape, but I was too closely surrounded by my guardians, who had had fresh orders to look carefully after me. I heard some of them tell the others that it was here that the provisions had fallen into the hands of the soldiers at ten o'clock last night. I could now see the high mountains on the other side of the plain, and I was told that we had to go right over the highest, which was a very long way off, and that we must get a long way up before daybreak. We soon came to a river: some walked through without hesitation, the water coming a little higher than their knees. I took the opportunity of drinking some water, for our long walk of seven hours had made me very thirsty. I asked when we should have something to eat, but was met with the cheering answer of "Who knows?" A sturdy fellow now came to carry me over the stream on his back, and he deposited me safely on the other bank.

A very little way farther on we came to a small house standing by itself, and close by were the ruins of another. We were hidden behind these while Manzo, and Andrea, and the secretary of Cerino's band went to the house, and in about half an hour came back to us with a quantity of Indian-corn bread; but this, when divided, was but little for about forty men, and the share of each was very small. Mine was very mouldy, and I was told to keep half for the next day. The moon was shining brightly, and lighted us through a succession of orchards and gardens. At one place we pillaged a patch of onions growing in rows between Indian corn. I secured several, besides those that some of the band gave me. How delicious they seemed to me! Nature craved for vegetable food after a long abstinence from it, and I fancied some of my fastidious friends' expression of face could they have seen me devouring these odoriferous bulbs like apples. Manzo would not allow a repetition of this onion plundering, lest too apparent traces of the band should be left behind. At another place a cherry-tree being discovered, up went one of the band in an instant, and instead of picking the fruit from the boughs, the branches were torn off and thrown down to those below, and in a few minutes little more than two or three bare poles were left. Unripe plums, apples, and pears soon filled our pockets, and after great difficulty all were reassembled in marching order, and climbing up the high walls forming the terraces of earth, and gradually getting on higher ground.

We passed a newly-made road, running from a village that was a little higher up on our right-hand side, and appearing to join the highway, which I was told went to Apulia. Hour after hour passed as we toiled through corn-fields, every now and then having to wait for the stragglers, among whom was Lorenzo, who always had been kind to me: he was suffering from tertiary fever, the result of a cold caught in getting wet through a few days before. At last they all got so tired that they told the captain they would not walk any more; but he told them that when it was light they should rest for a few hours, so on we went till the day broke, and then they threw themselves down under an oak, and in a few minutes all but the sentinels were fast asleep. Here Pavone took advantage of my slumber to extract a new pair of socks from my pockets, which I kept there for a change, and I had the satisfaction, a day or two after, of seeing him wearing my property. I tried to rescue them, but he only laughed at me. I did not wake up much before ten o'clock, and found the brigands in a great state of excitement, the sentinels having seen four carriages passing along the road to Apulia. I was told that Apulia was the head-quarters of brigandage, and that they had a general there named Crocco,* who they said was in communication with Rome. I asked how many he had under him. "A thousand men and many captains," was the reply, "as well as six hundred in the Basilicata."† They also told me that in 1861 Spanish generals came to lead those fighting for Francis II. against Victor Emmanuel, and that one of them, named Borjès, had an enormous black beard, which they said he always held in his left hand when he drank milk, of which he was very fond.

At midday we went to the top of the mountain, and waited there till the evening. To-day I had the luxury of a little butter which Andrea had obtained from the house when he went with Manzo to get the bread. In this part of Italy it is very rarely made; but when they do make it, it is put into little bladders. The brigand way of eating it is to spread it half an inch thick on bread, and then to put it out in the sun to melt. It was rather rancid; but by this time I was not overnice as regards the quality of any thing, particularly luxuries.

Telescopes were in full use all day; the captain had got a new one from somewhere or other, and was very pleased with it. In one letter to my wife he made me write for the best English telescope to be obtained in Naples, either from

---

* For an account of this distinguished "general," I must again refer my readers to the works of Count Maffeo and Mr. Hilton. The doings of General Borjès are also there fully described.

† See Appendix F.

a man-of-war or merchant vessel, without any regard to cost; but, fortunately, I had written two words in English, and this had determined him not to send the letter, and thus saved my friends the trouble of looking after a glass.

I was rather amused at seeing one of the men turn out of his pocket a pair of blue cloth trowsers, which Manzo immediately seized and put on; his old ones he gave to Scope, whose attire was in the most deplorable state. We were very thirsty, for we had had no water since last night, and had walked many hours after drinking.

When it grew dark Manzo and all the band (except four or five who remained with me) went away, with orders that I was to be brought on in about an hour. After waiting this time I was taken over the crest of the mountain, along ground level at first, and then slightly descending to some rocks, where we found the rest of the band eagerly watching a large flock of sheep passing along the bottom of the valley. I came up just in time to see how they take the sheep. Manzo, Justi, and two or three more had gone down the hill-side stealthily, and hid behind a rock, and when the flock passed opposite them, they darted out and rushed down to the two shepherds, who of course were powerless in the presence of armed men; two then went with the flock to their resting-place, where the sheep are milked and the cheese made. As soon as they had gone, we went down to join the captain. The brigands raced down the hill with much joking. I tried to do the same, but found that I could not manage it like they did, and so I went down more soberly. When we reached Manzo we heard that the shepherds were going to cook three sheep for us, for the band could not do the cooking because of the loss of their caldron, and that the captain had ordered them to bring up some milk for me. We then ascended the hills on the other side of the valley, and at the top waited for the promised meal. In a short time one of the shepherds and a little boy brought up a barrel of water, which was most welcome, and then I laid my head on my *capote* and slept soundly for about an hour and a half. I was then awoke by the arrival of the milk and some bread, which were very welcome after two days' diet of mouldy Indian corn-bread. A few minutes afterward the meat came up in milk-pails, and was divided into shares. I was unlucky in my share, as it consisted only of large bones with hardly any thing on them; but I felt thankful for the bread and milk I had just had. We could now see the fires of four sheepfolds along the valley, which were all visited on our way, the band waiting at each one while two or three of them went to the shepherds and took or bought their stock of rye bread. The dogs in the valley kept up a tremendous howling, which did not die away till we got some distance from the flocks. The walking to-night was of quite a different kind to any I had experienced before.

The country, instead of being wooded and mountainous, was bare, undulating, and very sandy, and with very little or no water, and we suffered much for want of it for two or three days. Here and there were patches of rye and potatoes; and when passing the cultivated parts, Manzo ordered the band to scatter, so that no distinct trace might be left of their passage. We kept walking all night in a southerly direction, and toward the morning went down a steep hill, and descended into the rocky bed of a winter torrent. Here I was told to sit down, and was left under the charge of the secretary of Cerino's band, who told me that we were going to Calabria. This made me very miserable, for the farther I got from Giffoni the more difficult it would be to get the money, as Signor Visconti very properly would

L 2

not hand over any without an order from me. While I was waiting here, the rest of the band went down the river bed searching for water, and at last they found a little that had been left in a deep hole; but this was putrid and full of sand, and I thought it prudent not to drink any. In a short time I was told to follow Andrea, who, while I was with him, kept me at a little distance, and never took his eyes off me. We followed the river, having to go down most awkward places, which were waterfalls when the river was full. All the stone was polished, which made walking very difficult; and at last we had to climb up a most precipitous rock in the best way we could. The foremost would pull up the next, while the one behind assisted by pushing.

It was now morning, and we entered into a dense wood covering the mountain, which was destined to be our hiding-place for some time. In a few minutes we came to a grassy spot, and orders were given to stop there for the day. The grass was very wet from the heavy dew, and, to make it more comfortable, it soon began to rain heavily. The bread obtained from the shepherds was divided; it was made of rye flour, and was as hard as a stone. In a very short time the blows of an axe were heard close by, and then those of another a little way off. At the sound of these the brigands pricked up their ears, and Manzo, with two or three others, went to see what use could be made of the wood-cutters. We were told to creep noiselessly farther away from where they were at work, and fault was found with me (as always was the case) because I did not make myself sufficiently invisible, my observation that I was a foot and a half taller than some of them only serving to increase their anger. Many a time did I get a thump on the back because of this. When the captain returned, he reported that there were two men and three women, and that they had arranged to bring some bread for us. Our sufferings from thirst were very great again to-day, and I was compelled to drink the muddy water, the flavor of which was not improved by being brought to me in the inside of one of their wide-awakes. At nightfall we went to a gully near the top of the mountain. It was full of dead leaves, with which I made a comfortable bed, and Sentonio built up a level space close to me with the stones he had picked up. Some slept above and some below me, in order to prevent all chance of escape.

The next day, July 5, I was ordered to write more letters, from which I knew that I was going to be left under the charge of a few while the others went for more money. Manzo was rather irate with me to-day, and told me that if money did not come this time, my head would be sent to my friends. I made my usual remark, "Just as you please," and asked him how long he would be, and was told six days.

I had a specimen to-day of the treatment which members of the band received on displeasing their captain. Guange, who had been a soldier in the Italian army, and who had become a brigand merely for having been away from his regiment one day without leave, was having an altercation with one of his comrades, and, like these people, wished to have the last word. Manzo told him to be quiet; and just because he did not obey at once, he rushed at him, knocked him down, and kept hitting him and rubbing his face on to the stones. Still Guange would not be quiet until Manzo had pounded his face into a jelly, it being quite bruised, and bleeding freely. Even his gums were cut badly from the grinding against the ground.

Manzo looked a perfect demon when excited; he curled up his lips and showed all his teeth, and roared at his victim, jerking out his words. The implicit obedience generally shown to him by the members of his band was extraordinary. They loved him on account of his unselfishness as regards food, he being always willing to give away his own share, and they feared him because he had shown on one or two occasions that he did not scruple to shoot any of them on the spot if they refused to obey his orders.

In the afternoon the promised provisions arrived in the shape of bread, a ham, and sausages. Shortly after this **Manzo** went away, leaving six men with me. **The next day (6th** of July) we moved lower down the mountain, and found a small level spot, free from trees or bushes, close to an old hut that **had been used by the** woodcutters in the winter. In this **was found an** earthen jug of a curious shape, which **proved very** useful. **A quantity of** strawberry and **raspberry plants also grew** here; the strawberries were just in season, and were most delicious. I longed to be allowed to search for them. One day, a lover of fruit went on an expedition after them, and brought back his **cap** full; these were divided among us, I getting **my share with** the **rest. We remained on this mountain till the 16th** of **July.**

The weather **was** very **fine** but very hot, and I suffered frightfully from thirst, being supplied, like an animal, only **once a** day, or rather once a night, for the water always **came** up at about ten o'clock, an hour or two after I had gone to sleep; and it was so cold that it always **kept me** from sleeping half the night. **Two or three times** they brought up none for me, **and I had to do** without it for forty-eight hours. **A small wine-bottle** full was the quantity **they gave me, and sometimes one** of them would drink half of that before handing it over to **me.** They abused me terribly if I asked for more; but one night I got the better of them. The old brigand, Sentonio, was sleeping next to me, and he had got an earthen-ware jar full of water, which he (to prevent its being drunk) used as a pillow. I had been done out of my allowance by him the day before; so, when he was asleep, I quietly pulled out the leaves, which always serve the brigands for corks, from the mouth of the jar, and then inserted a tube, and, exhausting the air, I got all I wanted, and before morning nearly emptied the vessel. It was great fun to see his puzzled face when he woke, as he put it to his lips for a draught.

The fountain where they got the water was at least a mile off, and once or twice the soldiers went to it; but information was always given to the brigands beforehand by a peasant who lived in a cottage at the bottom of the mountain, a regular system of signals having been established between him and the band by means of blows of an axe on a tree, a different meaning being conveyed according to the number of blows. They were much put out one day by my telling them that their friend wanted one of them to come down to him, and that he was waiting in a patch of potatoes. I knew that there was a cottage by the constant barking of a dog in one place. I always made a point of telling the brigands all I found out, and the different lies each would tell about the same thing served to confirm me when I was doubtful about any thing. One day we moved our position, and I was sent with Pavone and two others to our old place in the gully at the top of the mountain; they missed the way, going too far to the right. I kept telling them they were going wrong, but they would not listen to me; but at last, after a great deal of bad language, and the poor Madonna being called all sorts of names, they took my advice, and we soon found the desired place. Afterward I heard them telling the others that I knew far too much. It was very tedious lying all day and night in the same position, for many days in succession.

One day they amused themselves by telling me that Manzo had given himself up to justice, and that they were going to increase the sum required for my ransom; then one **by one they came to** me, telling me in a confidential way that this was the worst thing that could happen to me, for Manzo always took my part **when** they **wanted to mu**tilate me. Pasquale, who was always **urging** Manzo **to cut my** ears off, told me that he had been chosen captain; but I told him that they would never choose a man like him, for **he could** neither read nor write. He told me that he had 4000 ducats deposited with his friends, which was afterward confirmed by several of the band; but I told him that money did not make a **man.** Ferdinando told me that they had had news that my **wife was** dead, and though I felt sure **that** they were all telling falsehoods, yet the thought often came over me, and did not tend to cheer me up. The captain was so long away that food began **to run short;** for peasants, after they have provided **a certain** quantity, and secured a **good sum of money, do not like running a** farther **risk of 20 years in prison—their** punishment, should they be discovered in aiding and abetting the brigands.

At first the woodcutter sent up a supply of first-rate bread **every** two days, the loaves weighing seven pounds a piece; and on one occasion, a quantity of cooked macaroni in a sieve, as well as a boiled fowl for Lorenzo, **who still suffered** from fever. He did not fancy it; I offered to cut it up for the whole party. I began in **the** usual way, but this was far too slow for the savages, who took it in one hand, and then tore off the limbs with the other, and it was divided into eleven **shares.** Lorenzo at last got some quinine and castor oil; and as brigands never do any thing by halves, and this rule holds good with medicine, he drank a good-sized bottle of the oil at once, and took every ninety minutes as much quinine as would lie on a franc. This violent treatment seemed to succeed, for it cut short in one day the fever which had been on him a fortnight, and he soon recovered his usual strength. Another man suffered from a dreadful abscess inside his cheek, and for this he used a fomentation of a kind of straw in water. A week after Manzo left us we had to go two days without any thing to eat, so a foray was made into the country near, and three sheep alive brought back. When they were being cut up, I was much disgusted at seeing Generoso and Antonio, who generally acted as butchers, tearing mouthfuls of raw meat, with their teeth, from the carcass, just like wolves. I asked them why they did not wait for it to be cooked, and they said, "Why should we, when we are dying of hunger?"

To make amends for this unpleasant night, I was delighted at seeing a new water-barrel, which would hold a good supply, sufficient for the day, so that my torments from the want of water this hot weather I hoped would be spared me. Few living in our land of comfort know what it is to be without water for forty-eight or even twenty-four hours —the fearful thirst one wakes with, and the throat so parched that it is almost impossible to speak. Just before these arrived, Pavone and four others went down to the cottage to see if they could get any thing, and returned with some small potatoes and some peas, which they call *ciceri*—the word which all were required to say on the night of the Sicilian Vespers; those who were unable to pronounce it properly being set down as French, and killed. It is a curious sort of pea, there being only one large pea in each pod. I was so hungry that I ate a quantity uncooked; an earthen vessel was procured, in which the meat was stewed, in place of the *caldaja*, the loss of which they deplored much.

Day by day I got more desponding at the non-arrival of the captain; the 15th had arrived, and it was about eight o'clock, when an earthen jar was broken in order to make a sort of plate. The noise of this directed Carmine Amendolo to us, and he suddenly appeared in the middle of the party without their having heard his approach; he looked very sulky and half-starved. I asked him where the captain was, to which he only vouchsafed the reply of "Above." I then inquired whether money and letters had arrived, and a jerk of the head upward told me that I was again disappointed, after all the painful hours of anticipation I had gone through.

At this all broke out reviling me, some darting at me with knives, threatening to kill me. Even Pavone, who always had half of my *capote* at night, threatened me, and I spent the most uncomfortable hour possible, expecting every moment that their threat of cutting off my ears would be carried into execution. I had determined, should they approach for that purpose, to cut off the top of one myself, hoping thereby to save the bottom of the ear, as I could conceal the loss of the upper part with my hair; but happily the captain showed himself, and told me that Visconti had not sent his messenger to the place appointed on account of the numerous force round Giffoni.

One night, while in this spot, I was taken with the band to the fountain where the water was procured. A piece of hollow wood had been thrust into the ground, and the water ran along it, pure and sparkling, into a large wooden trough. At a right angle to this trough was another very long one, which I presume had been placed here for the convenience of watering sheep: they had, however, the appearance of not having been used for some time. I took advantage of being here, and washed my face and **hands with a** little **piece of soap** I had begged from Andrea **some time ago**: it **was a** great luxury at the time, but the next **day I** suffered more than ever from the musquitoes, who seemed to enjoy **the clean** flesh. I wished to do more in the washing line, but **my** cautious friends would not hear of it, being afraid lest the soldiers should suddenly **appear.** It was a lovely night, the moon shining **brightly;** and instead of returning to our lair in the **wood, the band ascended the** hills in the opposite direction. **I was delighted with the** exercise, for I had not been allowed **to** move for several **days.** When we arrived on the top signals were made, which were soon **answered** by the half dozen who had left our part of the **band a few** hours ago, and we saw them moving along the sharp **outline** of the rocks, the bright moonlight making the **brigands look like giants.** We made our way up to them, and I was told to go to sleep; **but the** scene was too lovely to lose, and **so I sat wrapped up in my cloak, with** my back against a large stone. In a short time I heard **the tramp, tramp of** men passing over stony ground; it came nearer **and nearer,** and at last I could see four or five of the brigands approaching, carrying a supply of bread, which had been sent from **some town.** Home-made bread is as different from baker's **bread in Italy as it is in** England, **the** latter being not half **so satisfying as that made in the houses of the** peasants. We then went **down to a most inaccessible place on the** side of the mountain **toward the east: it was most breakneck** work, the descent being nearly perpendicular.

We stopped here all the next day. At about midday more bread arrived, and on **my** remarking on it, and giving **my opinion** that it was made in a house, I was told in a **most angry way by** Lorenzo that **I** was to see and know nothing, and never **to ask any questions, but to be** satisfied when provisions came, and not to care where they came from. He added that I knew far too much—in fact, more than was good for me. I laughed, to the disgust of several of them, and told them that I wanted to learn all I could about brigandage, to tell the good people in England, for they had no idea of their manners and customs, and that they need not care about what I knew, for I should go immediately to England, fifteen hundred miles off, when I was free.

I used to have numerous questions about England, and they were astonished to hear that we were governed by a queen, who I told them was good and beloved by all; that there were no brigands there, not even one. They made minute inquiries about the royal family, the army, and prices of provisions, and so forth, and said they all longed to be in a country where labor was so well rewarded. It was most amusing to see their eyes when I told them of California and Australia, where gold was dug out of the earth.

At last they said that they would all go there if I would be their captain! I thanked them much for the honor they showed me, but I told them that both I and my wife loved our country too much to leave it, and that I thought that if she went with us she would be in the way, and that I could not leave her behind in England. Justi then proposed to come with me to England, and offered to work for me for nothing if I would give him food and clothing: up to the last he was harping on this idea, but I always talked of the difficulty of his leaving Italy with a passport. In the evening we returned to the place we had left the night before.

The same day that Manzo arrived soldiers were seen on the mountains opposite, and after a careful survey through the glasses, I was sent off to the top of the mountain, and we waited on the opposite side till the captain and band came to us. It was a very noisy and quarrelsome day, for the men that had just returned with Manzo were half starved, and would eat up the meat that had been kept in reserve; and Manzo was very indignant when he found that two sheep had been eaten in about an hour. This was the first time that I had seen the operation of roasting on a grand scale; the small pieces of meat into which the whole sheep is always cut up were stuck on long skewers, and then these were rested on forked sticks, and the pieces were eaten as fast as done. Sometimes it was rather underdone, and then the piece would be thrown down into the hot ashes, and, when it was done to their fancy, would be eaten, though covered with dirt. The correct way to clean it was to rub it on the first thing handy, generally their trowsers. I came off very badly to-day, only getting a tongue, which I had to cut out of a head that had just been skinned: the operation made me feel rather sick, but I found necessity a hard master, and one whom I was obliged to obey.*

In the early part of the afternoon we had the excitement of hearing a gun go off close by; all began to bolt, when it was discovered that the captain's had gone off by accident. I told him that whoever let his gun off ought to be fined thirty ducats, to be spent in buying rosolio for the band the first opportunity. This rather took their fancy.

* I can not help feeling that my narrative may be open to the remark that it contains a great deal about cooking, eating, and drinking. It must be remembered, however, that these operations not only form the most important features in the domestic life of ruffians living, as brigands do, from hand to mouth, but that, while I was with the band, these operations were of sufficiently rare occurrence to be highly interesting to me.

CHAPTER XIV.

Diary of Mr. Moens, July 17 to 22.

A good View of the Country.—A real live Wolf.—A good Omen.—Striking a Light with a Percussion Cap.—A Brigand Bivouac.—Cooking Scene.—The first Whisper of a Reduction in the Ransom.—Pasquale's kind Advice to the Captain.—Manzo leaves me again.—Scope's Gun goes off.—I venture to chaff him.—A fair Challenge.—His Revenge.—Visitors from Giardullo's Band.—Their Adventures.—Manzo's Return.—A Skirmish with the Soldiers.—The Band is divided.—Awkward Position of my Party.—I am in great Danger.—Thoughts of Escape.—I hesitate to kill two Sleeping Men.

July 17. THE captain now required six men to go with him, the rest having to remain. I could not understand why all were so loth to go with him, but I heard afterward that a supply of food and some clean shirts were to be waited for, and all wanted to get them; but he called the required number by name, and they were obliged to follow us. In a short time we left the woods, and found ourselves on the highest ridge of a mountain; the rock was all limestone, much worn by the action of the rain. Though in such a very elevated spot, it was considered unsafe to continue walking while it was still daylight; so we lay down, and I had an opportunity of enjoying the extraordinary view.

We were on the extreme east of the province of Avellino, and, looking in that direction, a great plain lay stretched out at our feet, extending out to the south. Beyond the plain the mountains of Apulia were very visible, and over these the hazy blue of the Adriatic could be discerned. Turning round in the opposite direction was the Bay of Salerno, and between it and us all these mountains which had been my home for the last two months, and with the outlines of which I was now so familiar. A little to the west of north was Mount Vesuvius, and a little more to the west, and farther off, was Ischia. To the northeast were the rugged heights of the Basilicata, and to the south the lofty mountains of Calabria. The River Sele, near its source, presented the appearance of a little silver thread that ran to the south through the plain, and at last lost itself in a large lake that lay glistening with the reflection of the setting sun; from this ran another river to the westward, which passed to the south of the Salerno Mountains, and, uniting with another branch that runs from the southward, forms the large river which we crossed between Battipaglia and Pæstum. There was a town a little to the southeast, on the other side of the plain, and another some way to the south, near the tremendous precipices in which the mountains of Avellino seemed to terminate toward the east; and to the south of the lake, in the far distance, appeared a very large town.

This view gave me a thorough insight into the topography of all this part of Southern Italy, and I recommend all those who intend to make a new map of Italy to ascend this mountain, and not to take for granted that the old maps are correct. I have not been able to find a single one that gives the least idea of the correct position of these mountains and plains. The brigands were amazed as I pointed out all the places to them, and eagerly inquired how I could know the directions, being a foreigner, and never having been in this part before. I told them that any boy in England could do the same who had been taught at school; that the setting sun gave the points of the compass, and all the rest was a matter of course. "È molto talento" was the remark of all;

but the conversation was suddenly stopped by an apparition a very little way from us. We saw a great gaunt figure, with long ears, looking at us intently. "A wolf! a wolf!" was whispered round; and, without moving, we all looked at our visitor. At last Generoso got too excited, and ran toward it, intending to have a shot at it; but Manzo forbade him; and at the sound of a human voice the beast disappeared. I asked if wolves were common in these parts, and was told that there were several about, especially in winter, and that they carry off many sheep and lambs. We soon saw the wolf again, trotting along the ridge on our left, about half a mile off. He did not go farther, but sat up again on his haunches, and did not take his eyes off us. We looked at him through the telescope, and a savage beast he appeared. At last, after sitting quiet for ten minutes, he jumped from stone to stone, coming toward us; but we soon lost sight of him, and did not see him again. He evidently wished to pass in our direction, probably in search of water.

It was considered a most fortunate omen by the brigands; for who, they said, are greater wolves than we are? and they all determined to call this place *Lup' a Lup*, as they expressed it in their barbarous dialect. I noticed here a pair of ring ouzels, which kept flying from rock to rock; also two jays, which flew screaming past us.

When it grew sufficiently dark, we descended over the loose stones. It was blowing rather hard, and I had to tie my cap on with a handkerchief to prevent it from being blown away. The brigands were most anxious that I should put on my cloak, on account of the cold; but I found it so much in my way going down steep places, that I generously lent it to one of them who was without one. I found it most difficult to keep pace with them, for, as I said, they ran down the mountain sides like goats. At last, after some hours' work, we came to cultivated land, and we ran down full pace. Then I could outstrip them, for I was not afraid of the loose stones. At the bottom we passed over a good deal of land covered with rye which was nearly ripe, and, as I went along, I plucked several ears, which I put in my pockets. At last we came to where the mountain stream had cut a deep course in the solid rock, where, after rain, it ran thirty feet below the level of the adjacent ground. We had some difficulty in getting down to the bottom, and, after walking a little way, found several pools of water which had not yet evaporated. It was not at all good, but we drank it eagerly, for we had been walking some time, and had nothing to drink for over ten hours. We walked on, over the polished stone and dried mud brought down from the mountain sides, and passed down perpendicular places the tops of which were scooped out by the rapid winter torrent.

At last we came to a place by the side of a giant trunk of a tree, which showed the force of the water that had carried it down such a way from where it grew. Here a fire was to be made, to cook two legs of mutton that the provident Lorenzo had hidden from the harpies in the morning. Wood was collected, and, contrary to my usual custom, I assisted in the work, and, sitting on the large stem, broke off pieces from the parts that had become decayed by time. But, when all was ready, it was discovered, to our great dismay, that there were no matches, for they had used the last one in lighting their pipes in the afternoon. But the old hands knew a trick or two, and obtained fire from a percussion cap in the following way: Some tow was rubbed in their hands, and a little gunpowder from a cartridge sprinkled among it. A needle was then passed through this, and the inside of the cap was scratched with the point of it.

After a few minutes the cap exploded, and the ignited tow was carefully blown to spread the smouldering sparks. The tow was then covered with dry leaves, and, after a gentle fanning with small twigs, it was fairly blown upon, and a blaze appeared. In a few minutes the meat was roasting on spits. Some bushes grew by the side of the great log which was at least from three to four feet in diameter, and on each side rose the white rock inclosing the rugged bed of the torrent, while above us was a lovely sky, with the stars shining, as they know how to shine in a southern clime, all the brighter from there being no moon.

Around the fire, illuminated by its blaze, were Manzo and his men, all watching with intense interest the preparation of their meal. When it was ready the others wanted, as usual, to stint me in my allowance; but Manzo interfered, and gave me twice as much as any one else, and reading them a lecture the while for not treating me more kindly. We had no bread; but I had got used to anything or nothing now. The great thing was to get something, however little it might be. The captain now appealed to me to know when the moon would rise, for it was too dark to think of moving without great necessity. I referred to my little six-penny Letts's Diary that I had with me when captured, and in which I wrote my notes, and told him about two hours before day. We then lay down in the river bed on the hard stones, and soon fell asleep. When I was kicked up by Scope, the moon was high and shining brightly. We left the river, and were soon ascending again, and in a couple of hours came to a halt in a thick wood, where we waited all day for the rest of the band.

July 18. I had saved a cubic inch of meat; but, with the exception of this and the ears of rye I had in my pocket, I had nothing to eat or drink all day. I was made to write more letters to-day, and was still compelled to demand 50,000 ducats, notwithstanding all my entreaties and remonstrances. "Write as I tell you," being the only response I could get from the captain. He told me, however, that when the next messengers arrived from Giffoni perhaps he might write for a little less; there had been a grand talk a few days before among the band, and there was a pretty general consent to take 30,000 ducats, but they still had the idea that the government would have to pay for me, and firmly believed that all the money was at Salerno, and they expected it all when the messenger arrived. They little knew what use I had made of the permission to insert a few lines in English in my last letter. If they had only known that I had requested my friends to pay the whole sum! How I longed to write just one line more to tell my friends that perhaps 30,000 ducats would be accepted after all, but not one word would Manzo allow; he carefully read over every line to guard against it.

Early in the morning, when all the men were asleep, I saw Manzo sitting up and writing a letter, and as he clearly did not wish me to know any thing about it, I pretended to be asleep.

About the middle of the day we started off again, and made our way through the thick wood and fern. After about two hours walking we came to a deep gully, down the rocky sides of which we descended with great difficulty, and then climbed up a steep bank covered with the dead leaves of many past autumns. Here I was ordered to lie down, which I did with difficulty, resting my feet against one of the trees growing there. These sloping banks I disliked immensely; many a time I had to sleep on them, and all night I would keep slipping down. I found it impossible to manage the operation as they all did. I firmly believe that any brigand would sleep soundly on a bank at an inclination of 80 degrees, and he would hang on by one elbow, and never move all night.

After being here about an hour, a rustling of the leaves and a snapping of dry twigs told us all (for by this time my hearing had grown quite as sharp as my captors) that some one was near. "*Sono Christiani*" was whispered round (for among the brigands every human being goes by the name of a Christian); their guns were all pointed in the direction from which the noise came, and the captain and Justi crept noiselessly across the gully, and hid themselves in bushes on the other side. The comers proved to be twenty goats accompanied by a boy, who was pounced upon by Manzo and Justi when he reached their place of concealment. The poor little fellow was very frightened at first, but soon recovered, and all three sat down, while the boy was carefully questioned by the two brigands. They were too far off for me to hear what passed, but I could see the little fellow gesticulating with his arms, most probably assuring them that he would do all they required, when they threatened to cut his throat should he attempt to betray them. This scene always takes place when the brigands fall in with peasants whom they do not know, especially in a strange district such as that in which we had been for the last month. The number of troops in their old haunts about Giffoni and Acerno had, as I have said before, rendered it necessary for them to seek new quarters. Two or three times the shepherd boy ran off on an errand to procure bread and meat, and as often was he recalled and rethreatened. I presume the goats would have been missed, and the captain was unwilling to let it be known in the plain below that we were in the neighborhood; for the goats are taken down twice a day to be milked at the houses where milk is required. When the goats and the goatherd had left this part, we went on a little farther to the east, and found a level place, which we made our head-quarters for some time.

Two or three of the men went away, and returned in an hour with a black sheep and a goat: these were taken a little higher up the gully where we had rested, and a fire was speedily made with the aid of a percussion cap, as before. The ground was covered with a very deep coating of leaves, which were all removed before the fire was lighted, for fear of their making a smoke; and before it was dark both these poor animals had disappeared down the throats of the detachment of the band, consisting of eight persons only! It was fearful to see them eat this mass of meat without bread. Manzo was most pressing that I should eat as they did; for, notwithstanding the abundance, some of them grudged every morsel I ate, and he had to lecture them again on the way they treated the poor foreigner. "Is he not a Christian?" said he to Pasquale; "why should he not eat as well as you?" This Pasquale was one of Cerino's band, and did not participate in the ransom money which was paid for Mr. Aynsley and me, and he had not at all approved of the way in which he had been hunted about with the others by the soldiers, half starved for so many weeks. In his answer to the captain, he blamed the latter for not having cut off my ears long ago, as he would have done had I been an Italian. "Send his ears to his friends at once; and if that does not bring the money, send his beard with his chin attached to it." Some of the others agreed with him, and there was an animated debate on the subject, all in my hearing. This, perhaps, was a good way to teach me the Neapolitan dialect, for I could not afford to lose a single word; and every now and then I had to feel my ears, to make sure they were still my own property. I told them that they had better not touch me, for the general would kill all their relatives who were in prison should a hair of my head be hurt; and, to turn the conversation, I asked Manzo what he would do with Victor Emmanuel, should he by chance fall into his hands? They all chuckled at such an idea, and Manzo declared that he would have ten millions of ducats, and *then kill him*. To Francesco II., if they caught him, they said they would give a good dinner, and then release him.

Carmine Amendolo had brought back with him a very curious pipe that he had obtained from the shepherds. It was made by them of wood, quaintly carved, and was brought to me *that I might make several like it*, for they had the idea I could do any thing in that line. I excused myself on account of the smallness of my knife, and the want of the right sort of wood. This pipe ultimately came into my possession after my liberation, being presented to me by Mr. Holme, who obtained it from the officer who captured Amendolo, near Giffoni.*

When it grew dark, Manzo and all but Pavone, Antonio, and one other, went off with the letters to Giffoni, leaving strict orders that, if the rest of the band should arrive, they were to go on at once without stopping, to join him at an appointed place near Acerno. The valley to the south of us ran the whole way between the mountains to that place. I had seen Manzo point this out a day or two before, from

---

* Apropos of pipes, I may mention that I had requested that a smart pipe should be sent to me that I might present it to Manzo. H. C—— accordingly forwarded one from Salerno; but Manzo intercepted it, and appropriated it at once, thus saving me the trouble of making a speech on presenting it to him. He did not, however, let me know that he had taken it.

the top of the high mountain where we had seen the wolf.

After they had gone, we were all four sitting close together, when I noticed Scope with the point of his gun turned in the direction of my head. I objected to this, and told him that it was evident he was not an old brigand, for he did not know how to handle a gun. He could not bear being laughed at, so for fun I told him that I did not believe he could hit a haystack a few yards off, and offered to let him shoot at me a hundred yards off as often as he liked, if he would allow me just one shot at him first at double the distance. I added that he would be firing at me all day for nothing, but that I should kill him the first time. He was speechless with rage, while his companions were roaring with laughter at him; but one of them put his finger on his lips as a sign to me not to chaff him any more. All poor Scope could answer in return was to recommend me to go to sleep, which was the equivalent in their language for a hint to *shut up*.

By-and-by the rest of the band arrived; but, instead of bringing the expected supply of food with them, they had eaten it all up on the road, and they were in a great rage at finding the captain gone without them, and refused to go farther that night. Pavone and Sentonio had a regular quarrel on the subject, but it all ended by our going a little way to the north, and lying down to sleep. They had brought the news that a very large force was concentrated round Giffoni, and that, instead of being, as usual, on the plains, the troops were on all the mountains.

This was important news, for it placed Manzo and those with him in great danger, on account of their knowing nothing about it. I placed my wide-awake, and the stick that had been my friend all the time, against a tree at my feet; but in the morning, when I was roused an hour before sunrise in order to get more into the thick of the wood, I could see nothing of my stick. Pavone looked round for it, but without success, and I was obliged to leave the place without it. I found out afterward that Scope, in revenge for my having turned the laugh against him, had thrown it away; for he, like all the others, knew that I valued it, as I had cut an inscription on it. I generally put it by my side, but to-night I had omitted to do so. It was just like losing an old friend, and I did not get over the loss of it for two or three days. Justi told me all about it, and said he would cut me a better one.

Sentonio, and all except eight, now went to overtake the captain, but that night's delay on their part kept me in the mountains much longer than I should have been had Manzo known the precautions the soldiers were taking to prevent the money, which they knew had been sent to Giffoni, from reaching the brigands; for, although the civil authorities knew every thing my friends were doing, and professed to do all they could for us, allowing Signor Visconti to undertake the task of forwarding the money, the military authorities were still determined that the ransom should not reach the brigands, and I am afraid it gave them infinite vexation to find out that at last it passed through their lines safely into the brigands' hands. During the next two days three more sheep were eaten. The sheep in this district were all very fat, and the brigands' grease-pouches (which they all carried for greasing their boots and shoes) were all filled; and two or three little baskets of *racotta* were brought up from the shepherds. This seemed to me most delicious, having eaten nothing but meat for some days.

Just before daybreak on the morning of the 20th of July there was a great alarm from the noise of several persons coming up the mountain from below, but on their giving the proper signal they were admitted past the sentinels; the rustling of the leaves in the distance awoke me with the rest, and I saw four men, all with guns, approach us; one had a cap on that had belonged to a captain of the national guard, and military trowsers with a red stripe. I could see at once that these were members of another band of brigands, and was much amused at seeing the enthusiastic way in which they were received by my guardians, who kissed them all round. They had brought up with them a kind of candle made by putting a piece of linen rag inside some fat; this was lighted, and they all sat around, discussing the last news. I was introduced to them as the *Inglese* about whom had been so much talk in the country, and which had of course reached their ears.

The remains of the evening's meal of meat was brought to them in the *caldaja* which the shepherds here had been forced to lend to the band, but unfortunately it had been put close to an ants' nest, and the ants had found their way to the meat and covered it by thousands, so that the pieces required much shaking and rubbing before they were eatable.

There was no more sleep that night, and many were the stories told by the hosts and the visitors. These four men turned out to be the remains of Giardullo's band; all the others, after the surrender of their captain, having followed his example.* There was a great deal of talk about me and the two Viscontis, who had paid their ransoms; and the new-comers—by name Carmanocchi, Carmine, Francesco, and another—recounted the exploits of their late band, and how they had been surprised in a grotto. Francesco,

* The troops had shot and wounded seven, as I before related (see p. 242).

who wore the captain's hat, told how they had taken prisoners a captain, lieutenant, and ensign of the national guard all at once, as they were driving along the road; they had carbines with them, which, with their uniforms, etc., were taken possession of at once. They were released after paying a ransom.

They also told how one day they were walking along with three captives, and they had fallen in with the troops, who immediately fired, and killed, not one of the brigands, but one of the *galantuomini!* This anecdote was told to me with great glee. These men were much jollier and kinder to me than the men of Manzo's and Cerino's bands, and always shared with me their portions of food if I had none of my own. From what they told me, I concluded that Giardullo's band was satisfied with much smaller ransoms than Manzo demanded, the figure being generally from 5000 to 8000 ducats. The new-comers were well supplied with powder, caps, and balls, dividing the percussion caps with those who wanted them. I asked them how they knew we were in this part, and ascertained that they had learned it from the shepherds, who communicate the movements of the brigands to one another with astonishing rapidity. They knew this part of the country well, and directed my guardians to go to some shepherds two or three miles from us to the southwest, as our other shepherd-friends had refused to bring any more *racotta*, or even to let us have any more sheep.

All but three went foraging, and, after a good meal of milk and bread at the place where the sheep were, brought back a little pail of milk and a round loaf of bread for us. The bread was sopped in the milk, and I, with the three brigands, sat round the pail and made a good breakfast, though at the early hour of four o'clock in the morning.

July 21. This was the last food I was destined to taste for three days. During the night we were kept awake by a slight noise as of some one walking three or four hundred yards off; this was heard at intervals for two hours, and at last was ascribed to some wild animal. In the afternoon I most fortunately cut another walking-stick of sycamore, Justi not having been able to find a holly-tree for me, which wood makes the lightest and best sticks. Though heavy at first, it soon got lighter as the sap dried up. During the day Manzo and his men returned suddenly, and I saw at once something was wrong—they had not been able to communicate with my friends at Giffoni. They were in a dreadful state, having been walking the last three days and nights incessantly, without having had any thing to eat, and they were of course grievously disappointed at our having no food for them, and vented their feelings accordingly by abusing and threatening me. Their eyes were red and glistening from the feverish state in which they were from over-fatigue and want of food; their clothing, too, was very much torn, and covered with dirt and dust, and the majority of them were very foot-sore. For a long time I was afraid to ask them any questions, going on the principle of "least said the soonest mended," especially as the question of cutting off my ears, etc., was again discussed. At last I learned that there were 4000 soldiers concentrated round Giffoni, and posts on all the mountains, so that the brigands were unable to remain near the town; and besides this, the peasants would not provide any bread. Acerno and Giffoni were described as depopulated.

I farther heard that Lorenzo, Amendolo, Vaccara, and two others, had been left behind to endeavor to get the money, and that they were down in the plain inside the cordon of the military force. My friend Justi told me to cheer up, for he had no doubt they would be able to get the money, as my letters had been sent in safety to Signor Visconti's house. In one of these I had asked my friends to send me some American tobacco, in order to soothe the minds of some of the brigands, who wished to hasten the arrival of the money by depriving me of my cars.

(I presume these letters, with one to Signor Visconti asking him to send on the money deposited in his house for that purpose, were all lost or destroyed by the messenger who carried them, for the five men above-mentioned could produce no authority from me to receive the money from Signor Visconti, and after a few days they were all captured, as is related elsewhere.)

In the afternoon a wood-cutter was commissioned to bring up bread to the shepherd's fire, and thirty ducats given to him for that purpose. At dusk the band went toward the shepherd's station, and when we came to the place where my stick had been thrown away, I was left behind under the charge of Pavone, Sentonio, and Scope. Sentonio grumbled much at being left, for he had been to Giffoni with the captain, and had not eaten any thing for more than three days; he stipulated that a good supply of milk and bread should be brought back. Those who went left their *capotes* with us, and we settled down for two or three hours' sleep; a long march was in store when the band returned from the shepherd's. About a quarter of an hour after they left us, they having descended into a little valley and ascended the opposite hill, we heard the dreaded cry "*A te ch' è la?*" —the challenge of the Italian soldier—and immediately two or three shots were fired, the new-comer in the captain's cap firing first, Manzo coming next in order. After this there was a volley from the troops, and then the firing became general, all their balls coming straight in our direction. After this I distinctly heard the *"Avanti, avanti,"* of the Italian officers, encouraging their men to the attack. We all rose and took shelter behind the trees, for the balls were unpleasantly near our heads. The engagement lasted about a quarter of an hour, and then the firing gradually ceased, a few dropping shots only being heard afterward. Pavone and Sentonio soon made up their minds to be off, talking much about the *tradimento* that had evidently taken place; and, leaving every thing behind them, drove me before them in the opposite direction to that whence I had heard the voices of the Italian officers.

We traveled toward the north at first, then eastward down the mountain side, as my keepers hoped there to fall in with the rest of the band, who were supposed to have run in that direction. We were in a desperate plight and without money, and I now began to be very apprehensive lest we should not fall in with the others, as I knew well the vengeful feeling entertained toward me by the men who had charge of me, now that they were excited by the recent skirmish. Backward and forward we walked for hours, hunting the ground like pointers, but nothing was to be seen of our game, and it was impossible to make signals, because the soldiers might be near. At last Sentonio grew almost mad with despair and hunger, and two or three times ran at me, flinging his arms about in the wildest manner, and tearing his hair out in handfuls. I kept as far from him as I could; but Pavone, who was afraid of losing me, made me keep close between him and his maddened comrade. I fully expected to be murdered every moment; but, after a time, Sentonio calmed down and became almost childish in his manner. After a consultation we directed our course to the south, walking over the roughest rocks; and at last descending to a stream by a most difficult route,

I drank a quantity of water, which had to suffice me for the three next days, during which we could get neither water nor snow.

After crossing the stream, we passed a short way along a mule-path, and then walking through some standing wheat and rye, with which I filled my pockets, soon began to ascend a very steep mountain. Sentonio was speedily so worn out from his three days' walk to and from Giffoni that he could go no farther, and all three of us lay down. I was so tired with ten hours' walking that I did not unroll the heavy *capote*, but, resting my head on it, was instantly asleep. In the morning of the 22d I was so stiff from the exposure to the night air after walking that I could hardly move; but the stiff climbing, at which I was compelled to set to, soon relaxed my muscles. Sentonio was very weak, and could only go a short way, and then he had to rest a while. We passed some great rocks and large caves, and after two or three hours rested in a small grotto for some considerable time.

I was placed inside, while Sentonio and Pavone laid their carcasses across the entrance, side by side, and Scope sat a little on one side, out of our sight, keeping guard. The two former soon fell fast asleep; and Scope took off his shirt for the purpose of freeing it from vermin, having moved two or three yards away from his gun in order to get into the sun. I could not go to sleep, so I amused myself watching the beautiful butterflies of many species that kept flying about the face of the limestone rock, when suddenly a new thought struck me. My eye fell on the guns of the two men sleeping in front of me; one was a double-barreled one and the other single, and both were lying within reach of my arm without my moving. Here was the first time that I had met with any thing like an opportunity of escaping; but, to take advantage of it, I must have shot two men, and then have been ready to shoot the third if he attempted to move. It was easy of execution, and I could not fail, there being no more of the band near, and I knew the way to the path we had crossed not very far off, which led to the town a little to the eastward. It was very tempting, and I set to work deliberately to think it over; but the more I considered, the more my mind revolted from shooting in cold blood two sleeping men, both of whom had always treated me as kindly as their circumstances would permit, and the probability of having to shoot a third —though perhaps I should have had less compunction in his case than in that of the other two. I also thought that, sooner or later, our ransom would be paid, and that my life was not in immediate danger. If it had been, it would have been very different, and probably I should not have hesitated, but should have felt myself fully justified in doing any thing. I also thought of the remorse I should feel afterward if my plan was successful. It is a very different matter to kill a man or two in the excitement of a regular hand-to-hand fight, but I could not bring myself to do this sort of cold-blooded murder.

So, to divert my mind, I took out my Prayer-book and read the Psalms, when—very curiously, and as if to guide me—I came across the passage, "Deliver me from blood-guiltiness, O Lord!" This struck me so forcibly that it appeared to me as if sent for my special guidance, and it confirmed me in the determination to which I had come. What a relief this was to me! The half hour I had been pondering over the matter was, I think, one of my hardest trials, and thankful I am that I did not give way to impulse, and blaze away without reflection.

I next amused myself by picking out the grains of wheat

and rye from the ears I had plucked, and ate them thankfully with the crumbs from the bottom of my pockets, which I had carefully to examine in order to separate the earth and dust there was mixed with them. Some cattle now passed quite close to us: this woke up the sleepers.

CHAPTER XV.

DIARY OF MR. MOENS, JULY 22 TO 31.

My Guardians are without Money.—A bad Look-out.—My Penknife put to a new Use.—Meat and Fuel, but no Fire.—Necessity is the Mother of Invention.—The Attack of the Soldiers explained.—Failure when Success seemed certain.—Scarcity of Water.—An Attempt at Bribery. —A cheerless Spot.—They play me a shabby Trick.—Manzo arrives again.—An Abode assigned to me for the next Fortnight.—Traces of Giardullo's precious Tenancy.—An Attempt at Washing.—No Food for three Days.—A little raw rancid Fat.—A Bone.—I feed in a decidedly canine Manner.—Two more days without Food.—I am at the last Extremity.—Great Hardships.—Manzo joins us again.—I write once more at his Dictation.—Cerino's Discomfiture.

July 22. WE recommenced our weary way. It was only possible to go slowly, on account of the weak state of Sentonio, who required rest every ten minutes; tighter and tighter he drew his belt,* and every time he groaned over the number of holes in the strap outside the buckle. He did not expect to be able to procure any food for the next two days. All hope of finding the band in this part of the country was gone, and his pluck began to give way. Pavone told me that they knew the point for which the band would make, but it was a long way off, and there was no chance of meeting them before Sunday, whereas to-day was only Friday.

* This was their way of *screwing themselves up* when suffering from fatigue or hunger.

They did not like being without any money; so, to cheer up Sentonio, I told him I had a Napoleon and a half, for I did not like the idea of his getting desperate, remembering his frantic state the night before. A complete change came over his face, and he said they would soon get food now that there was money, and, curiously enough, I heard the tinkle of sheep higher up the mountain. My keepers told me there were none there, but in a minute or two they too heard the sound clearly, and determined to have a sheep at all cost. They asked me for the money; I gave it to them, but did not tell them I had another Napoleon in reserve for another occasion. Scope was sent on ahead in the direction of the sheep, and we followed more slowly. At last we came to them, and I was made to sit down while Pavone and Scope bargained for the sheep. Pavone milked a goat into the top of his wide-awake, but he would not give me any of the milk, though I was suffering much from thirst. The shepherd came down with a sheep to us, and my half Napoleon was given to him as a *complimento*, and I got into a scrape because I looked at him. Very few minutes were lost before the poor sheep was killed and skinned, my tiny penknife being borrowed for the latter operation, because it was sharper than the other knife they had.

But, when all was ready, the discovery was made that there were no matches, and no needle to do the percussion cap trick with. Scope was sent back to the shepherd, but he could not help us. We all looked at each other in a most despairing manner, when suddenly the thought struck me that my penknife was of excellent steel, and would do as well as, or better than a needle. They shook their heads at my idea, but I told them to try, and in a few minutes we had a blazing fire; it was an exposed position, but hunger was not to be denied. As a great favor, I helped to collect wood, and we sat round the fire watching the roasting of the meat. Pavone gave me the heart as a treat, and we made a good meal, that is, as good as we could without bread or water. As soon as we were satisfied, the fire put out, and the remainder of the sheep stowed away in their pockets, they hurried from the spot, fearing lest the soldiers might have observed the fire. It was very lucky finding this flock of sheep, for they were on their way down the mountain to go to the water, as they do every other day, and had we been ten minutes later we should have missed our supply of food. We went on much more cheerily now, and in a short time came to a place where we had a good view of the direction we were to take. Up the valley to the west there was a great smoke rising out of a wood, and this was set down as coming from a fire made by the soldiers (this I learned afterward was the case). It was a lovely view facing the west. We saw on the right the mountain of Calabritto, where we had passed the last week, its gentle slope down to the valley clothed in many places with wooded clumps; we saw the place where the fight with the soldiers had taken place the evening before; the shepherd had been questioned about it, and he told the brigands that none of their party had been hurt, but that two of the soldiers had been wounded, and that the last shots came from the soldiers firing at Guange at a distance as he crossed the river, and that he stopped in the middle and returned the compliment with both barrels. The brigands, after the first firing, made their way down the mountain.

The wood-cutter who had received thirty ducats to take up bread thought it better to send up a hundred soldiers instead of the loaves, and these hundred men were stationed in three companies: one at the flock of sheep, and one on each side, so that the brigands could not fail of falling into the ambuscade. After hearing the details from Pavone, which he had heard from the shepherd (and which I found correct on my arrival at Giffoni after my liberation), I was much astonished at the band getting off so easily. This shows the difficulty there is in putting down brigandage with the military force, for all turned out exãctly as had been expected, the band walking right up to the lion's mouth, and yet the lion was obliged to be content with a roar or two, without inflicting any injury on his intended victim.

The valley ran a very long way between the mountains, and in the extreme distance over it I could discern the sea. To the south of the valley there were dense forests clothing all the slope of the mountains.

The brigands pointed out the way we had to go toward the S.W. It did not look at all tempting — forest and uphill work all the way for miles and miles. By midnight we had gone a long way, suffering dreadfully from thirst, and not finding any water or snow in the deep gullies, which were all anxiously examined, and then piously cursed by Sentonio and the two others for not containing any refreshment.

July 23. We slept for four or five hours, and then went on again. Suddenly Scope rushed forward to a hollow rotten log, and began to suck up some fœtid water that had been left by the last rain days before. I was only just allowed to put my lips to it, and was pulled away from it without my being able to get more than a mouthful, but perhaps it was better for me, as the fluid tasted most nauseously of decayed matter.

As we walked on I found two or three ripe strawberries,

which were most grateful to my parched mouth, and by-and-by they appeared in great abundance in a lovely glade through which we passed. We spent an hour picking and eating this delicious fruit. At midday we dined on some of the sheep, but no water or snow was obtainable. I tried again to bribe the three men who had charge of me, offering them 3000 ducats, and to obtain a free pardon for them if they would deliver me up to the authorities. Pavone was inclined to listen to me; but when he consulted Sentonio on the subject, the latter threatened to shoot him if he attempted any thing of the kind.

In the afternoon we arrived at the top of Monte Neve, having been two days and the most of two nights in performing this task, and I was informed that the descent to the south was so steep that two hours were sufficient to gain the plain. To our great delight, snow was found here, and, after satisfying our craving thirst, we set large pieces up on slabs of wood left by the woodcutters, and the water trickling down, gave us a good supply. Scope as usual grudged me even the snow, though there was an abundance. A flock of sheep passed near, and Sentonio obtained from the shepherd a little tobacco and a tiny piece of maize bread, which he carefully divided among all, giving us just two mouthfuls apiece.

The forest at the top of the mountain was composed of most enormous beeches, standing some little distance from each other. Two or three years ago a great number were felled and left to rot on the ground. In one place there was great difficulty in making our way, as we had to clamber over these dead giants. I was not allowed to remain where I could see all the plain below, with the well-known temples at Pæstum, and the two streams which united to form the river. But I now knew our position: on the high mountain to the south of the mountains of the province of Salerno. Just one month ago I was at the north of the province of Avellino, having traversed all the eastern side of this mountainous district in the mean time. Sentonio kept a look-out to the south, and at about five o'clock signaled Pavone to come to him, in order to begin the descent. Here all the trees had been cut down, on account of the facility of bringing down the wood, and the stumps which had been left in the ground were all bleached white. It was one of the wildest scenes I have ever seen. A little lower down, at some time or other, a fire had burnt all the branches and bark, and had left the trunks of the trees standing. There was not a leaf to be seen, and a strong wind driving the clouds along, enveloped us and every thing about us in a dense mist.

It was desperately cold work waiting for a thick cloud to conceal us as we crept from place to place. Great caution was exercised at one place, which several *baraque* showed to be a favorite post of the military force. These *baraque* had evidently been made some time, and had served for a large number of soldiers. I was much astonished at the post being right in the track that led over this mountain. It struck me that if it had been placed a little on one side, out of sight, and with sentries carefully concealed, there would have been a much greater chance of surprising the brigands; but on every occasion that I saw these posts, they were placed in similar positions to this, as if with the view of warning the brigands off.

The soldiers also had evidently made enormous fires, which would alone have betrayed the position of the troops, and had told all the peasants and shepherds in the district where the force was, and these immediately gave information to the brigands. I found a piece of a *Pungolo** published during June, thus announcing when the soldiers had been in this place. We did not descend down the mountain directly, but edged along toward the west.

The night was terribly cold, and early in the morning of the 24th we made our way down to some little hills below. The side of the great mountain was clothed with the most lovely flowers, a large red lily being very prominent, and I recognized many of the flowers that adorn our gardens in summer. Pavone told me that they expected to find the captain and band here to-day, with Lorenzo and the four others who had been left behind near Giffoni to get the money.

While lying on the ground this morning, I was thrown into a great state of excitement by Sentonio telling me that he had agreed with Pavone to escape with me if I would give them 2000 ducats, and that they would give Scope the slip. They told me to write a letter to the consul telling him to send a steamer to embark us on Thursday night opposite the Temples, and that the steamer was to throw up a rocket, and that we would answer by making a fire. I wrote all this in pencil and gave him the letter, which he said he would send to Naples by a priest, who was a friend of Pavone. I did not know what to make of it all: the plan was quite practicable if they would trust me, and they might have told me an untruth about meeting the band. Sentonio now left us for an hour, and all this time I was full of hopes of seeing my wife at Naples in four or five days; but all these sweet illusions were dashed to the ground by my hearing Sentonio making the well-known signal of " Wow-wow, wow-wow," and hearing a response from the side of another mountain some little way off. I now saw

* A newspaper published every evening at Naples.

that they had been making fun of me, and asked Pavone for the letter which I had seen him put in his pocket, but he told me that he had given it to Sentonio, and I did not recover it until three weeks afterward, when I snatched it out of the hands of Antonio and tore it into little pieces, and I found that it had gone the round of the band.

Great was the delight of all three of my guardians, who immediately made me follow them toward the direction of the response, and we hurried down and met Manzo, and all those who had fallen in with the soldiers as they were going to the shepherd's.

Rocco only was missing, and I found out afterward that he had been separated from the rest, and had given himself up to the authorities. They told us that, after firing for a short time, they all ran down the mountain to the river, and that the soldiers had not followed them far. They then went to another flock, and made the shepherds give them four sheep and a quantity of milk. The night we were looking for them I had heard in the distance the dogs barking and the sheep all running together, and told Pavone that I was sure that Manzo was safe, and getting sheep. This is a good hint for the troops, for the dogs always bark at first when the brigands come to the flock; and when the sheep are caught they always run together, and this is easily detected by the peculiar noise the bells make when they do so. Manzo and all were delighted at seeing me safe and well, for they feared that I might have been lost or have escaped during the skirmish with the troops, and many of them shook hands with me. I was glad to see that Manzo was safe, for I trusted to him to secure me against the brutality of many in the band; and I also rejoiced to see the carcasses of two sheep being carried by some of the rascals. They walked boldly along a path by the side of a sparkling

THE BIVOUAC AT NIGHT NEAR CAMPAGNA.

stream, though it was daylight, and, striking up a dark ravine densely wooded, soon came to a safe place, where a fire was made and the meat roasted.

After all was consumed, with the exception of two legs, they gave themselves up to songs and merriment.* I was requested to give them a song, and they were greatly astonished to hear that singing was not one of my accomplishments, for all in Southern Italy are perfect masters in this respect. It was a wild but exceedingly picturesque scene, and would have made an excellent subject for a picture. The next morning early, Manzo, with eight or nine men, took me through some cultivated land, on a little plain between the mountains, to a rugged ridge on the east side of it, one of Giardullo's men acting as guide, for we were in the part of the province they used to infest. We had to cross a stream at the foot of the mountain, and then Manzo pointed out a place where Pavone, Scope, Vicenzio, Malone, and another were to keep me, while Sentonio and Justi were to hide in the mountain, a mile from us on the other side of the plain, to procure what food they could for us. The band was very short of money, and three Napoleons were all that Manzo could leave with them; and he went away to look for the five men near Giffoni, leaving strict injunctions that no fire was to be lighted where I was kept, and that none of those guarding me were to go foraging, for fear any one should find out where we were, and betray us to the troops.

It was very hard work climbing up the almost perpendicular rock, which was of white crumbling limestone, and at last we reached a little flat ledge concealed by the trees some way up. Here we stopped; but after the second day a better place was found a little lower down. While Pa-

* For words and music of a brigand song, see Appendix G.

vone and another were looking about for this place, the others lit a fire to roast some potatoes which they had brought up with them, which they shared with me, to my great amazement. Pavone was in a great rage with them for lighting the fire, for if any one from below had seen the slightest gleam, it would have betrayed the presence of brigands in this part, which the authorities considered free from them, since the destruction of Giardullo's band. I found out that they had given me some of the potatoes *in order that I should not tell* about their lighting the fire; and Pavone, who had seen it from below, would not believe their statement that Scope and Vicenzio had given me any thing until I confirmed it.

This spot had served Giardullo and his band of thirty men for the same purpose last May, and they had left many traces of their visit. It was a level space, about eight yards long and three wide, with the mountain rising at the back covered with fern and trees, while below a gully ran down the mountain side; two or three trees hid us perfectly, though we could see what was going on below. On each side the former occupants had made little paths by constant passing to and fro for the space of a month, the time they had stopped in this place. A tiny little spring, that never ceased running, kept us supplied with excellent water: as soon as we arrived I busied myself with clearing this out, and supporting a piece of bark with stones, so that the water ran as if out of a spout. This Scope constantly used to kick down in order to annoy me. A small *pagliatta* had been made for Giardullo to sleep in during the wet weather in May; on this had been put some goatskins as a farther protection from the weather.

Two or three places had been covered with small branches and fern, on which his men used to lie, in order to keep themselves off the wet ground, and another just wide enough for one person, which I was told served as the **couch of their** prisoner. All **these** arrangements indicated greater refinement than Manzo's band possessed, for never in the wettest weather had they taken the slightest trouble to protect themselves or me from it. **A thick** layer of wood ashes showed where they had their fire, **and** the many bones and skins of goats and sheep **proved they had not** wanted for meat; a broken *terrina*, which they **had** left behind, with a number of squares marked out with the end of a burnt stick on the bottom of it, looked as if they played at draughts, and a very large, long spit was found, on which they roasted **the meat.** One day a pair of *very small* though thick shoes were turned up, and supposed to have belonged to one **of** the women belonging to the band.

The first **week we were** supplied at intervals of two or three days with **a small quantity of meat** half cooked. I came in for the **underdone** portions, for **nothing an Italian** dislikes so much as crudely-cooked meat. No **bread was** procurable, with the exception of a very small piece of rye bread: this tasted to me most delicious, for, with the exception of two mouthfuls of maize bread, we had had none **for a fortnight.** There was great grumbling at the diet, for we **only had enough just to keep us** from **starving. I** thought that here I might manage to wash a little, and began by taking off my boots **in order to commence with my feet.** I had washed one and was doing **the same to** the other, when that wretched Scope rushed at me, and began hitting me with a stick he picked up because I did not immediately put my sock on to my wet foot. I did not pay the slightest attention **to him,** and wiped my foot dry, and then put on my sock and boot, he continuing to strike me all **the** time. I told him that "it did not hurt me, and I supposed it amused him" (remembering an anecdote told once by a noble earl in the House of Lords with excellent effect), and I recommended him to take care what he did, or I should complain to the captain. The others took my part, and, though he did not repeat the offense, he often threatened me, and I really was frequently in fear of my life by reason of his brutal disposition. One blow slightly raised the skin on my forefinger, and I suppose the stick must have been in contact with some decayed matter, for the wound became very troublesome, and did not heal for three weeks, when I had got some bread and made a poultice for it.

The captain did not return at the end of the week, as he had promised; all the money was gone, and no food came for three days. I was so hungry that *I begged for some of the raw fat three weeks old*, that they had kept for the purpose of greasing their boots! This I forced down my throat, after masticating for a quarter of an hour, but at the end of that time it was just as clammy as at first. I three times ate a little of this fearfully rancid stuff. At last, one night, half a sheep was sent up to us, which four of the men took down again to cook, for Pavone, who stopped with me, would not have a fire made where we were. The greedy wretches cooked and ate nearly all of it, putting a quantity away in their pockets, and brought up a little to Pavone, but only gave to me a scraped leg-bone, which Scope threw in my face, hurting me a good deal: it was perfectly raw, and had but very few signs of meat about it. I gnawed at this in the dark like a dog, eating as much of the sinewy appendages as I could manage to find and to bite; I then put it by (also after the manner of dogs) till the morning, being too famished to lose so precious a morsel; but that dear brute Scope, seeing it, took it away to see if he could make any thing of it—though he had plenty of meat in his pocket — and, finding nothing on it, threw it at my head again. Not a morsel would the others give me, and for two more days I had to go without food, or to take to the raw and stinking fat again! Each day I had been getting weaker and weaker, till at last my voice failed me, and I could only speak in the lowest whisper, as at last I lay stretched on the ground, praying for death.*

On the morning of the 30th of July Malone and Vicenzio were sent to get food at all hazards, for they saw I was in a bad state, and they all (particularly Pavone) were getting very queer for want of something to eat, but no one was so ill as I was.

At about ten o'clock we heard a low whistle above us, and I saw Antonio coming down with something in his handkerchief slung on his gun. When he came to where Pavone was sitting, he turned two loaves and a number of pears out of his pocket. I was so excited at the sight of this that I burst into tears at the goodness of God in sending food when I had quite given up hopes of life. I was too weak to go to the bread, and Antonio brought me three pears. I tried to say "*pane*," but I could not manage it, so pointed at the bread, which they gave me immediately; and by eating a small quantity at a time I soon felt better, and by the evening recovered my voice.

When it got dark, the two who had gone for food in the morning returned with a little rye bread which they had procured from some shepherds, with two baskets of *racot-*

---

* But a short time before we had plenty to eat, but no water; now we were safe from thirst, but could get nothing to eat. The brigands have a saying,

"Quando è pane, non c'è aqua:
Quando è aqua, non c'è pane:
Quando è carne, non sono aqua o pane."

ta; but this they had eaten at once, to the great disgust of those left behind, who rated them severely for their greediness, as it was a mere chance, and quite contrary to Manzo's orders, that Antonio came in the daytime; and if he had not supplied us, the two who had gone foraging would have fared well, while all left behind would have hardly had any thing. To-day Scope pointed his gun to the sky, and, to my great astonishment, off it went, to the horror of all! I looked at it, and found that the stock was cracked across, and this made it go off as easily at half-cock as at full-cock. To my delight the nipple blew out, and rendered his gun useless. Vicenzio had lost the lock of his, and thus two guns were rendered good for nothing.

While in this place we had a week of thunder-storms and showers, which greatly added to my misery, and brought on rheumatism in my right arm. It was curious to notice how soon the slightest rain-fall affected our spring, and caused it to run merrily into the earthen vessel that was put under the bark spout.

On the 24th of July the harvest was begun in the plains, and I could see the women carrying away the sheaves of corn and rye as soon as cut. It was supposed that, as soon as the reapers came up from the country below, food would be obtained for us in quantity; but this proved an illusion, and all the peasants were pronounced *infame*, or traitors to the cause of brigandage.

July 31. Early in the morning Antonio appeared again with bread and a quantity of pears, and brought the information that the captain had arrived; but once more I was doomed to disappointment, and my ears began to twitch again at the bad news I had heard — no money, and no letters! And this was not all; they told me that Lorenzo and the four others left to receive the gold from Giffoni had given themselves up after receiving 6000 ducats, equal to £1000.* Hearing this made me very low-spirited, for I knew it would enrage the band, who were without money, and much increase the length of my captivity; and, besides this, I knew that Manzo would consider it my loss, and require the money to be sent up again. Not a moment was lost, and I was hurried over the top of the mountain, behind the place where we had spent the last fortnight, in order to go to the part where we had found the captain before. It was fearfully steep and dangerous, and I was so weak from starvation that I could hardly drag myself along; they had to rest every now and then on my account. I was now so miserable that I did not care what became of me. The last letters from my friends in Naples were dated *seven weeks* ago, and there was no chance of my hearing again for another fortnight; and after my many disappointments, I could hardly count upon that. During the walk I found a plantation of wild raspberries, the fruit of which was quite as large and as well-flavored as those grown in our gardens at home.

At last I was told to sit down, which I did most cheerfully. More pears arrived, but they were very hard and unripe; this, however, was nothing to the cormorants in whose keeping I was, and I got into great disgrace for presuming to pick out a ripe one. I attempted to pare it, but was told not to waste good food, and, whatever might be the custom in England, it was different with them, and that if I pared another I should never have any more. I had to put up with much of this treatment. On one occasion I had thrown away a piece of sinew, and they took the trouble of going to look for it, to see if it were, in their idea, eatable. They often gave me the windpipe of a sheep, and made me eat it

* This was false.

before I was allowed any thing more. I always told them they did this to keep me employed with a bad piece while they were eating all the rest.

In about two hours Manzo came up to us in a very sulky state, and made me write a letter to the consul to request him to inform the prefect of what had occurred, and to demand that all these five men might be immediately shot, unless they gave up the money they had stolen. I had not known whether to believe the story or not; but when Manzo told me all their names at full length to insert in the letter, there was no doubt about the truth. When this letter was written, he took a piece of paper from his pocket-book, on which was written a letter he had composed to my wife, which I was to copy. It took me a long time to decipher the writing, which I could only do with his aid, and I wrote each word afresh over the original. He commenced "O moglia *ingrata*," etc. I told him that I never wrote such a word, and that my wife would not understand it; but my objections were of no avail, and I had to write this dreadful letter as he wished; but I slanted my writing as much as possible, to show it was his dictation, and afterward added some upright of my own composition, and got leave to add two lines in English, taking advantage of a report current among the shepherds that I was dead.* I always took the opportunity of letter-writing to ask Manzo for more bread, telling him it was a great exertion, and that it was impossible for me to write Italian when hungry, and on this occasion I did not forget to adopt the usual plan, though with but little success.

In the evening we joined the rest of the band, when I found that they had reunited with Cerino's party. Many of the men showed much commiseration for me on hearing of the sad state I had been in for want of food.

* This letter is given at length in the Appendix, H.

Cerino himself looked very chapfallen. He had been deposed from the post of captain, I believe, on account of his unfairness in distributing food, and Cicco had been elected in his stead. I also heard that there had been a great quarrel among the members of the two bands, I believe about mutilating me because the money came up so slowly, and those who did not share in the ransom objected to the constant harassing and want of food occasioned by the excessive measures of the Italian government.

Andrea, Cerino's secretary, and Pasquale, would not serve under Cicco, and had joined Manzo. Poor Cerino had also been deserted by Doniella, who had left the mountains for one of the villages, and altogether he looked at this time very like a fighting-cock who had just got the worst of it in an encounter. *Quantum mutatus* from the Cerino I formerly knew! Instead of being made much of by every body, no one now spoke to him, and he skulked about, utterly ashamed of himself.

CHAPTER XVI.

DIARY OF MR. MOENS, JULY 31 TO AUGUST 22.

Illness of Scope, my Bête Noir.—Starvation threatens again.—Scarcity of Water again.—The Brigands observe Fast-days.—Their religious Feelings.—Their Respect for my Talents.—Fearful State to which I was reduced.—The Soldiers once more.—We leave the Cave.—A Meal of Mutton and Potatoes.—I am sent away to meet Manzo.—In sight of Acerno again.—Rigors practiced by the Troops on the Peasantry. —Hard Work of the Women.—I hear that 6000 Ducats have been received.—Prospects of Freedom.—Antonio's new Suit.—More Gambling.—Two Days we live on Apples.—All the Money had at last.— Manzo's Behavior.—Division of the Spoil.

July 31. THERE was some mystery about this time which I never have been able to fathom; all the band had been warned not to give me any information about the receipt of money or letters for me, and I saw signs being made to those whom I questioned about my affairs. All at once I was taken away from the rest of the band by about six men, and made to lie down out of the light of the moon; they, too, concealed themselves, and I heard signals made and answered, and then the noise made by men walking through standing corn. No supply of food came up, or I should have known of it; and, at the time, I could only conjecture that I was being deceived about Lorenzo and his companions, but this afterward proved not to be the case. At last another brigand joined us, and we went along the south side of the valley, that was toward the southwest, in the direction of the town (which proved to be Campagna); after going a short way we struck up the mountain.

I was so tired from walking, and the weight of my *capote* and little bundle of things, that I could hardly stand, and I had to pull myself up with the aid of the small bushes and oaks that covered the side of the mountains; at last we reached some rocks that raised their bare sides from a bed of fern, and behind some bushes we found a capacious cavern: it was about eight yards deep and four wide, the two sides meeting in a point at the top. The bottom was of fine black mould and very sloping; this made it most difficult for me to keep my position when I was told to go to the end and lie down, and I kept slipping down on the man below me all night.

In this cave it was intensely dark, and there was a large bat flying about continually, which did not increase my comfort. It was impossible for me to sleep, and, to add to my grief, my bundle of valuables rolled away from me, and in a moment went bounding down the mountain side; I never expected to see it again, but in the morning it was recovered by Pavone.

Scope caught cold on one side of his head to-night, which made it swell very much. I told him it was the effects of the good living we had been having, which had fattened one side of his head; this raised a great laugh against him, and I repeated "*Povero Scope*" once or twice, which tickled their fancy immensely, for they all knew that there was no love lost between us, and for some time they all pretended to commiserate him in the same way.

I began to fear that the starvation system was to begin again, as the following extract from my notes made at the time will show.

"We arrived here on the 31st of July:

"*Aug.* 1. No water; small piece of bread.
"   2. No water; a little rye bread at night.
"   3. No water till midnight; no bread; Pavone went to get sheep."

Each night the brigands went down for water, but they had nothing in which to bring up any for me, and orders had been given not to allow me to move. It is a fearful thing, in a hot climate, at this time of the year, to go without drinking for three days. Each night I raved at them for their cruelty in not bringing me up water; but they only jeered at me, and told me to do without it. When it did come they did not allow me to drink much, though a large earthen jar had been procured and brought up full. They had also brought up a copper *caldaja*, and they wanted as much water as possible to cook some *pasta* which they had also obtained.

The next day, the 4th of August, was the anniversary of my wedding-day, and I whiled away an hour by going through the wedding service, and all day thought of the gathering of my friends on that occasion, and followed them all, mentally, to their happy homes. I wondered, too, whether the day would be remembered at Naples.

Some *pasta* was cooked, but the want of bacon-fat, salt, or pepper made it very insipid; but hunger forced all to eat it with thankfulness. In the evening there was great rejoicing. Pavone, Antonino, and Antonio returned with three sheep alive, and the carcass of one they had killed, 11 lbs. weight of excellent bread, some cheese, an enormous quantity of pears, and plenty of salt. The next night, five loaves, weighing 7 lbs. each, and more cheese and pears, appeared, and this lasted me and my five jailers the fortnight we stopped in this place.

I have not mentioned that from religious scruples the

brigands never eat meat on Wednesdays and Fridays, unless it is impossible to procure other food. Their religious feeling is also shown by their invariably raising their hats when the Madonna's or our Savior's name is mentioned; also when they hear the church bells ringing for vespers an hour after sunset. While in a place like this, I got rather clever at telling the time from observing the shadows cast by the sun, and they always came to me to set their watches. By some of them I was considered to be possessed by a devil, because I knew too much, and foretold the weather so well. One day I was asked the hour some time after it had got dark. I looked round and said, "One o'clock;" for they always, in this part of the country, count from sunset to sunset, 24 hours. As I spoke, the clock of the town below sounded one, and they said, "We always thought you possessed with a devil, but now we are sure of it;" and afterward, though their watches were pretty correct, they preferred asking me.

With some large stones I built a little wall across the cave, and digging down the part above with the end of my stick, made a level space to lie down on; and one evening I was allowed to pick a quantity of fern, and this made it much softer and more comfortable. My sides had become very sore from rubbing constantly against the hard ground. For a long time my body had been in a fearful state from sores arising from the bites of vermin; not a spot about me had escaped from their attacks, and the wounds were constantly festering from the bad state of my system, induced through inadequate and improper food. After an exclusively meat diet for a week or a fortnight, I invariably grew much worse. These wounds required the greatest care, for the filthy state I was in from not being allowed to wash, and the black, fine dust of the cave, soon caused them to increase much in size. I always applied a small bread and water poultice; I kept a small supply of crumbs tied up in a corner of a handkerchief for the purpose.

The rye bread was curious stuff. After it was two days old it fermented, and was full of a viscid transparent matter. If it did not turn mouldy in this stage, but dried all right, it would last sound for months, though it required soaking before being eaten. A great deal of this fell to my share, for it was despised by the others, who ate the best there was. All day long I heard the constant beating out of the corn, which was going on just below us, and I could often see the women carrying the sheaves on their heads from the fields for this purpose. There was a dog at this place, which constantly kept barking. I do not think these peasants supplied the brigands with food, for they went at least an hour's walk for it, going out at dusk, and not returning till ten or eleven o'clock, and often not till the next night.

One day, while they were cooking at the end of the cave, a flock of goats came close to the cave, and there was great fear lest the slight smoke that passed through a small hole at the top should have been seen by the boy looking after them; two or three of the goats actually came and looked in at us from a rock above, and were driven away by little stones. The next day, the 9th of August, there was great trepidation, and three of the brigands and I were in extreme danger for some little time. All at once Antonino called out, "The soldiers! the soldiers!" They were on the top of the mountain, a quarter of a mile from the cave. Andrea and he bolted out at once and hid themselves behind some rocks near, for they were two old hands at brigandage, and would not allow themselves to be caught like rats in a hole, in the same manner that Giardullo and his band were when they were so cut up some weeks before. I was immediately made to go to the end of the cave, and Pavone, Antonio, and Scope came with me, and every place was cleared from which there was a chance of any thing being seen. Scope told me that, if the soldiers came, he would shoot me at once. I gave them all the advice not to attempt to fire at the troops, but to put their guns down, and then lie flat on the ground, for they might perhaps kill one or two, but in the end must lose their own lives; while, on the contrary, should they give themselves up, they would only have to spend a few years in prison. I never saw any people in such a state of terror. Pavone's teeth were all chattering, and he was as white as a sheet; Scope was the same, and lying on the ground; and Antonio was in such a state of fear and shaking that he kept striking his gun against the rocky sides of the cave, and making a great noise, to the dismay of all.

I sat down on a stone, and, to reassure them, said, "Courage! courage! eat a little;" and, to set the example, took some bread and meat out of my pocket and began eating it. My doing so enraged them to a great extent, and they said, "What a fool you are to begin to eat when you will be dead in two minutes!" I urged them to do as I told them, and all would be right. I had by this time become so despairing of ever escaping from my bondage that I did not care what took place; but in a skirmish with the troops I might have escaped. Had I not been so carefully kept at the extreme end of the cave, with their men hemming me in, I should have now tried to run out and dart down the hill, crying, "The brigands! the brigands!" and they would have been afraid either to follow me or shoot at me, for fear of betraying themselves.

For about three hours we were in this uncomfortable

state, and then, no soldiers appearing, they took heart and went to the mouth of the cave; but I was not allowed to move. When it got quite dark the two brothers returned, and told us that the troops had passed in two companies, one above us, and the other just below, leaving us unnoticed between them. It was a great escape, and I felt most thankful for it; for, if we had been discovered, I should certainly have fallen a victim to the vengeance of the brigands, who had had the strictest orders from Manzo not to let me fall alive into the hands of the soldiers; added to which, one of my keepers, at least, would have gladly seized the opportunity of wreaking his fury upon me. We had now been here for ten days, and orders had been left by Manzo that if he did not return before this time, they were to leave the cave and go to meet him near a fountain some way on the road toward Giffoni. They had had such a fright that it was determined to leave to-night. I was delighted to hear this, for the place had become unbearable from the odor of the sheep's paunches which had been thrown just outside the cave, and I was afraid of being bitten by the swarm of flies which fed constantly on the decaying matter. I also pitied the poor sheep that had hitherto escaped death; for six days the demons had left it without water, and the poor beast suffered so that it gave vent to its feelings by constantly bleating: it did this two or three times while they were in fear of the soldiers. On each occasion Scope went to it, and ground its nose against the rough side of the cave; it was a most painful sight, and I reproached them for allowing the poor animal to be tortured thus. They only remarked that it would not die for two days more, eight days being the time they could exist without water.

Great caution was used as we emerged from our retreat,

where we had now passed ten days, and in about three hours we arrived at the fountain, where we expected to meet their captain. Care was taken not to leave any foot-marks near the water. I remained with them while the other two went to rob a potato-field; they soon returned with a large handkerchief full of potatoes, which were cooked the next day, half of the poor sheep having been boiled in some water, and the potatoes were afterward cut in slices and boiled in the broth, which made the most savory mess I had tasted for months.

During the night I picked up my New Testament, which had fallen out of my pocket while I was sleeping, and early the next morning we moved a quarter of a mile farther on. In the middle of the day I found, to my great dismay, that I had lost my little Prayer-book, which had been the greatest solace all the time of my captivity. Even Pavone felt for me, for religious books are very much respected by these men. He immediately, on my requesting him, went back to the place where we slept, and soon returned, but told me he had not been able to find it; in a few minutes, however, he put his hand in his pocket and gave me the precious book. How pleased I was to see it again! it made me comparatively happy all the rest of the day. There was a scarcity of knives to-day, for the only two they possessed had been lost, one having been left at each of the last two hiding-places, and they had to come to me for my two pocket-knives to slaughter and cut up the sheep.

It was not considered safe to stop with me in this neighborhood, because of the soldiers seen the day before, so Antonino and Scope remained behind to tell Manzo and the band, when they came, where the other three had taken me.

August 10. In the evening we went toward the north

taking five hours to ascend a mountain, which was cultivated in terraces half the way up; the corn had all been cut, and we started a covey of partridges, which went whirring down the hill-side. It was easy walking along a path after we had gone over the summit, and we halted at two springs, making a good meal off the remains of the sheep.

At daybreak we climbed up a mountain covered with wood, and, coming to a suitable place, threw ourselves on the ground and were soon asleep, one keeping guard as usual. When I woke the sun was high, and I could see a town a little to the eastward placed on one end of a curiously flat piece of land, with high mountains on the north and east of it. Between us and the town the ground was much broken, and I thought I recognized Acerno, having caught a glimpse of it once before in the gray of the morning, when Signor Francesco Visconti was with me. I had heard them whispering about a safe place near Acerno the day before, so I boldly told them I could see Acerno, which rather surprised them, and I heard the word *diavolo* pass from one to the other. They told me it was not so, but the town was called Bagnuolo. This confirmed me in my opinion, for any information they volunteered was sure to be false, and they never did even this except to throw me off a scent.

In the evening we descended a long way, and passed over a foaming torrent by a very frail kind of bridge, about six inches wide: all the bed and rocks in it were marble, smooth and polished by the action of the water. We had to ascend another ridge, and then passed on to cultivated ground, where I picked several ears of maize, now getting ripe.

There were also a great number of apple-trees full of fruit, but the greater part very rough and bitter; but at last a tree was found with good-sized apples of a fair kind, with which our pockets were soon filled. The mountain ridge ran round three sides, and another closed in the fourth with a high mountain rising behind it.

In this way a tiny valley was inclosed, well cultivated, and irrigated by a little stream that issued from the precipitous white limestone rock at the northern end; on the eastern side the mountain was cultivated from the bottom to the top, but the western side was covered with broom and small trees, and here we were hid for another fourteen days. It was a most impudent act to choose this spot, only a mile and a half from Acerno, in a cultivated part, with a mule-road right round the little amphitheatre, formed by a ridge about three hundred feet high. At least seventy to eighty peasants passed not three hundred yards from us every morning and evening, as they went to and from their daily work, and we could see company after company of soldiers as they passed backward and forward between Giffoni and Acerno. The place was well chosen, for the troops never thought of looking into a hollow about three hundred yards long and two hundred wide, where people went every day to thresh corn and pick the apples. Every night Antonio brought up bread, cheese, bacon, and fruit, also boiled ears of maize, but in rather small quantities, for the strictest measures were still taken against the peasants, any one found carrying bread at night being liable to be shot; and in the daytime all peasants met by the troops were searched to see if they had more than sufficient to serve for their midday meal, and even this was restricted to a very small quantity. The women, too, going to the springs for water, were obliged to be provided with a pass.

For the first few days I saw two men and a girl employed in threshing corn on the hill-side opposite us. The brigands were quite at home here, and knew the names of all whom they saw, even at a great distance. They told me that these two men were father and son, but they seemed to take great care that we were not seen by them.

It used rather to amuse me to see the contented way the women would carry home heavy burdens, while the men would calmly ride home on the donkeys, which here go by the name of beasts; and I thought of some of my countrywomen, who are so fond of contrasting the status of their sex in England with that of their sisters "abroad," showing a decided predilection for the condition of the latter, based upon the charming external politeness with which they themselves have been treated by a Frenchman or an Italian in some ballroom.

Day after day of the hottest weather passed, but no news of the captain, except that he was gone to take another *galantuomo*. At last, after a week, one evening—it was Wednesday—about ten of the band came up, headed by Generoso, who told me at first that there were no letters or money, but I soon found out from their quiet manner that things were looking better, and I presently found that 6000 ducats had been received, making in all 12,000, and they had got the news that 18,000 ducats more were at Giffoni, and had been there some weeks. Signor Elia Visconti had not sent it all, for Manzo had only asked for 6000, which was the money that he was afraid the five who had given themselves up had stolen, and I now found out the cause of the delay. The letters the five had with them had got destroyed by the peasant who was taking them to Visconti's house. The date of the next letter had been altered by Manzo, and Signor Visconti feared that there was something wrong, and therefore refused to pay the money, as he had done before, when Lorenzo demanded it without any at all.

The brigands were now in good-humor, and told me that

I should be free in a week. I wrote a letter to Giffoni, asking for the money to be sent at once, and in my excitement wrote *July* instead of August, but fortunately found it out just before they went away. I asked why Manzo had been so long away, and was told that he had had much business to transact, and that he was not very far off. I believe he joined them this night in the path below, and went to Giffoni with them: this was Wednesday, the 16th. I expected that they would return from Giffoni on Sunday or Monday, but these days passed without hearing any tidings; food began to fall off; the peasant who had supplied us declared it impossible to obtain any more from the town, on account of the vigilance of the troops, who now examined and searched all persons as they went to and from their daily work. Only about a pound of bread and a few boiled spikes of maize could be got, and this had to suffice for the five men and myself.

One evening Antonio appeared in a magnificent suit of blue cloth, bound and striped with black velvet, with a spread eagle with red eyes, made of the same velvet, on the back. The buttons were gilt, and had on them the *fleur-de-lys* of the Bourbons; he also had got a tremendous stiletto, of which he was very proud. While we were in the grotto he had won from Andrea his revolver, and watch, and gold chain, so that he presented quite a gay appearance: I made him turn round and round in order to admire him, which pleased him immensely.

During these days gambling went on vigorously, and two of the five lost the whole of their expected spoils. During the whole of this time I could not sleep from excitement, and I spent all the nights in watching the stars, which seemed now all in pairs, two and two! Before, they seemed far from each other, but now they seemed much closer;

they seemed to typify the separation from my wife, that I had to undergo all these weary weeks. I always saw the morning star rising with magnificence above the mountains in the east, opposite to where we were, followed once again by the sun, which soon drove us to seek a shelter from his burning rays.

No food now came up, and we lived for two days on nothing but unripe apples. On the 22d of August we went down to the spring below, and spent the next day among the thick underwood at the head of the valley.

August 23. This was Wednesday, and a most important day to me, for at about seven o'clock in the evening Antonio came hurrying up from fetching water with the news that the captain had sent for us. I dreaded hearing that there was another disappointment, and for some time I was afraid to ask. About four men had been sent to us, and among them was Justi, who came and told me that all the money was paid, and that I was to be set free to-morrow. The news was too good for me to believe; and I did not believe it till he had knelt down, and, crossing his arms on his breast, declared, by the Madonna, that it was the case. I felt so intoxicated that I could hardly walk, and a crowd of thoughts rushed suddenly into my mind. I had spent a solitary time, often not speaking for days to the men guarding me, so that I had become almost stupefied, and I quite dreaded the turmoil of civilized life. I would have given any thing to have escaped quietly straight to my home in England.

In about an hour we came to the place where Manzo and the rest of his band were waiting for us, when, to my astonishment, he took no notice of me. I suppose his interest in me had gone now that he had bled me to all the extent he fancied he could, and all he wanted with me was to get rid of me safely, for he had promised that he would do all *he* could to keep me from danger; and I do believe that he thought himself bound by honor as a brigand chief to deliver the *Inglese* safe to his friends.

We walked for an hour or two, passing a little to the north of Acerno, but close to it, and stopped to sleep for two or three hours under some enormous chestnut-trees: this was the first, and, I trust, the last time I shall ever do the same again, for the thin, sharp prickles of the outer covering of the nuts pierced my thin clothing, and, breaking off in the skin, had the most irritating effect on my already tortured body for some days. At about two in the morning we went up the mountain to the east of Acerno, and again stopped and slept till seven or eight o'clock—that is, the brigands did, for not a wink could I sleep. I had not got a night's rest for more than a week, but the exciting prospect of being free kept up my strength. To-day I saw the money counted and divided into 17 shares; it was originally shared by twenty-eight. Thirty had been *in giro* when we were taken, but two were shot by the troops the next day at Monte Corvino; Luigi had fallen over the precipice; five had been taken near Giffoni; one had surrendered himself after the fight on the mountains of Callabritto; one was shot at night by Signor D—— as he was returning from foraging; and the other three belonged to Cerino's band, and, after the quarrel, were not allowed to share any more in our ransom.

The following was the division: Each brigand entitled to a share had 200 Napoleons, which I saw counted out in four sums of 50, this being Manzo's way of reckoning. A thousand ducats were divided among the four men that belonged to Giardullo's late band, and the other thousand kept for the general expenses of the band. This just made up

the whole amount of the last installment of the ransom of
the two Englishmen taken on the 15th of May, thus:

17 shares, 200 Napoleons each	15,980 ducats.
Giardullo's men	1,000 "
Reserved for expenses of band	1,000 "
	17,980 ducats.*

* Though the brigands were very deficient in education, only one tenth being able to read or write, I observed that they could all cast up complicated accounts in a wonderful manner, Pavone and the captain especially being very clever at it. The exchanges used in brigand money transactions are 4·7 ducats to the Napoleon, and 4·25 lire to the ducat. The ducat (very like our guinea, an imaginary coin) is still the favorite unit of calculation in all their receipts and payments, although the merchants and bankers at Naples have adopted the franc in place of it.

CHAPTER XVII.

DIARY OF MRS. MOENS, JULY 31 TO AUGUST 25.

News from the Band.—A Visit from Talarico.—*Otium cum dig.* after an honorable Career.—Talarico's Advice to the Captive's Wife.—His chivalrous Offer.—The five Brigands at Visconti's.—The last Letter from the Captive.—Reduction of the Brigands' Claim.—A gallant Priest.—Another Visit to General Balegno.—His Kindness.—Intense Excitement when the Ransom was all Paid.—Suspense.—Free at last. —Joy too deep for Words.

ON the evening of the 31st of July I walked with my friend's children to a lovely bay two miles from the house. Our path lay along the side of a hill, looking down into the luxuriant vineyards as we gradually descended to the beautiful little bay, with its silver sands sheltered by the lofty rocks. A boiling mineral spring flows into the sea here, and makes the water deliciously warm. We were just going to bathe, when I heard a man's voice calling, "Mrs. Moens is wanted immediately; important news has arrived." I rushed back as fast as I could, and arrived breathless to find that Signor Michele di Majo had come to tell me that there had been an encounter with the brigands, and that two had been captured—their clothes and boots were very much worn, and they were evidently hard pressed. My husband, they said, was concealed in a grotto under the guard of several of the band. I stood in a strong draught while listening to this story, and the consequence was that I was seriously ill for days afterward.

On the 2d of August the celebrated ex-brigand chief, Talarico, paid me a visit. This man, whose story is related by Count Maffei in his "History of Italian Brigandage," had a most successful career; the Bourbon government, finding it impossible to put him down by force, had at last offered him pardon and *a pension* on condition that he should not leave the island of Ischia.* He is an extremely handsome man, very tall, with the smallest and most delicate hands. He sat and talked with us over a bottle of wine, becoming more communicative and animated at every glass.

One story he told amused us much. Having heard that a rich old proprietor had once spoken against brigands, Talarico and some of his men appeared before him suddenly one day as he was walking in his garden, and placing their guns at his breast, made him take them into his house as if they were his friends, order his mule, and ride away with them. On their way they met a poor country doctor: they stopped him, and asked him to dress the arm of one of the band, which he did, extracting from it four bullets. They gave him a handsome present of money, together with a letter, which he was to take from Talarico to a rich tailor. The letter, when opened, contained these words: "Make this man an entire suit of clothes," which, of course, was done immediately, the tailor not daring to refuse.

Talarico evidently considered my husband's position a very serious one. He told me the soldiers would never be allowed to take him alive; he advised my taking the ransom myself, telling me the brigands would not hurt me. I was to ride on a donkey, with the gold concealed in the saddle. He offered to accompany me as guide, if he could get permission from the authorities. I determined to go, as I

* For an account of Talarico, see also the very interesting work of Mr. Hilton, "Brigandage in South Italy," vol. i., p. 250.

could get no pass from the government, and had lost all hopes of the authorities being able to help me. I had wearied General Balegno with visits, and entreaties to keep back the troops, who were pressing the brigands, and preventing them from getting food. He had assured me he had no power to do so, so I made up my mind to follow Talarico's advice, and asked him to write a letter for me to take to Manzo. This he consented to do at once.*

I asked Talarico which he liked best, a brigand's life or an honest man's life. He replied instantly, "Oh, an honest man's career; a brigand's life is this," and he turned his head over the right shoulder, and then over the left, as if fearing an enemy; this gesture spoke volumes. I understood at once the wretched life of continual suspicion, distrust, vigilance, and fear which the brigand leads. His hand is against every man, and every man's hand is against his.

I received a letter on the 1st of August from my friend, Mr. Richard Holme, for whose disinterested and unselfish exertions, involving the greatest danger, my husband and I can not feel sufficiently grateful. His brother, too, Mr. Edward Holme, never omitted an opportunity of sending or bringing me the slightest information that might give me hope or comfort. Alas! I really needed it. It was now twelve weeks since I had parted with my husband. I can only try to feel that he is in God's hands, who will guard and keep him, now and through eternity. I think of all the promises to help the weak, to loosen the prisoner out of captivity, during these long, weary days, and still longer nights, when I can not sleep.

Mr. Holme informed me that immediately on his last arrival at Salerno he saw both the prefect and one of the general's staff officers. Signor Visconti had been requested to

* A copy of this curious epistle will be found in the Appendix, I.

come to Salerno on the following morning to meet him, but had sent no answer. Next morning a letter came from Signor Visconti, stating that, in consequence of the threats of five brigands—who were hovering about his house, saying that they were sent by Manzo for the money—he could not come; but that, as they produced no letter to prove their identity, Signor V. had very properly refused to part with a cent, it being very probable that these men had separated from the main body, and were acting on their own account. They had threatened him in such terms that he dared not leave his house.

Mr. Holme thereupon went to Giffoni, and saw the authorities and Signor Visconti. The latter begged that the money might be at once removed from his house, as he considered his life was endangered. On this point Mr. Holme tried to reassure him, telling him plainly that, unless some equally safe channel were found, he must continue to hold the money, since the brigands, knowing that he had it, would come upon him for the loss of it, if he were not ready at any moment to pay it.

If these five brigands were really not sent by Manzo, Mr. Holme thinks it probable that Manzo will suspect they have either taken the money and escaped, or that they have been taken, in which case he will endeavor to find some other channel of communication.

The 4th of August, our wedding-day, was intensely miserable, only brightened somewhat by hearing that Manzo's mother had got another pass, and had started to see her son. She may bring back news of my husband. I heard also to-day that two brigands had surrendered themselves, and that another had been arrested. Mr. Holme had been with an escort of Bersaglieri to see them, and found that they either knew or would tell nothing of my husband, except that they had seen him a month ago, when he was pretty well. They were part of the five who threatened Signor Visconti.

On the 6th of August I received a letter from Mr. Bonham, telling me that a letter had arrived from my husband so distressing in its character that he would not forward it to me, adding, "He complains of suffering acutely from fatigue and exhaustion, and deficiency of food, and begs that money be sent at once for his ransom." On receiving this letter, Visconti sent off on Thursday morning last all the money he had in the house, for which Manzo has sent a receipt. Manzo's mother saw her son and the band, and implored them to give up their prisoners: some agreed, the majority would not, unless they received 30,000 ducats in all, and they would have an answer to-day. On receiving these letters I sent for Mr. Aynsley and Mr. Holme. After consulting together, we determined that the money ought to be sent without delay, or waiting reference to you; and the money probably is, ere this, at Giffoni. Mr. Moens was not with the band when Manzo's mother and the messengers saw them."

The same day I also received the following letter from Mr. Aynsley:

"Naples, August 5th, 1865.

"MY DEAR MRS. MOENS,—Manzo's mother has just returned from a visit to her son. She says he will accept 30,000 ducats. The balance will be sent at once; Richard Holme takes the money. The £1000 at Visconti's was just a month in reaching them, and you must therefore not be surprised if the money to be sent to-day is as long at the same place before it obtains your husband's liberation.

"In haste, yours very sincerely,

"J. C. MURRAY AYNSLEY."

I determined to go immediately to Naples to learn the contents of the letter which Mr. Bonham spoke of, and started at half past three on the morning of the 7th. I had now become more courageous, and I embarked alone in a little boat to meet the steamer. We rowed for an hour, the sailors, who all knew my story, being most kind to me. The sun was rising from the sea, turning into gold all the rosy clouds that seemed hurrying out of his way; the stars, softly and imperceptibly, were vanishing — and such lovely stars! I had been watching them all the night through my open window. If it were not for the beauty of Nature one might be tempted sometimes to doubt of Heaven, but its surpassing loveliness is an earnest of the Paradise to come.

I arrived at Naples in the midst of a tremendous storm of rain. To my dismay, not a carriage was to be seen; it was impossible to walk, for the streets were running with water. At last I saw a carriage approaching laden with luggage, but no one inside. I rushed to it, and, despite the opposition of the men in charge of it, jumped in and sat down, not paying the least attention to their assurances that it was engaged. Presently a priest came up and informed me that the luggage was his. I made an appeal to his feelings, telling him that I was a foreigner—an Englishwoman, and alone. He smiled, and politely begged me to keep the carriage, ordering his luggage to be taken off, to the great indignation of the porters, who had just piled it up. I went to our consul general, begging him to give me my husband's letter. He refused at first, but I insisted on having it. It was, indeed, very terrible.* What were we to do?

Mr. Bonham immediately sent a telegram to our Foreign

* A copy of this letter will be found in the Appendix, H.

Office, and another to Florence. I determined to hear the result, and then (contrary to the advice of all my friends except Mr. Bonham) to start at once for Salerno, to try and persuade the general to keep back the troops, so that we might attempt to send the money; it is so hard that it should be waiting here with no possibility of paying it. I then went on to Salerno and visited the general. I begged and entreated him, with tears, almost on my knees, to keep back the troops. He listened very kindly, tried to soothe me, but would give no positive answer. I then told him of Talarico's plan, and that I was determined to go myself to the brigands with the money. He held up his hands in horror, and said that it was folly — madness! I told him I was not afraid of the brigands; the only obstacle to our messengers was his soldiers; if they stopped me I should tell them who I was, and I was sure they would not hurt me. He begged me to give up such a wild plan, and to have patience.

I went back to the hotel, and wrote to General Della Marmora again. I received a kind telegram in reply, begging me to keep my mind quiet, but promising nothing.

The general has just sent an aid-de-camp to tell me he can not, consistently with his honor, keep back the troops; he sent a gentleman also who told me horrible stories about the brigands' treatment of women, with the view, I suppose, of dissuading me from adopting Talarico's plan.

Aug. 8. I have just heard from Mr. Aynsley that Manzo's mother has returned. She did not see my husband, but she heard that there was great quarreling among the band about him, Manzo declaring that he will let him go for 30,000 ducats, the others objecting, but being likely to give in. This is, indeed, good news, if true,* as one or two mes-

* It was afterward ascertained that the letters procured and forwarded

sengers more will be able to carry the remainder of the ransom. It has been arranged that if the brigands do not come to meet the messenger, he is to go every day to the appointed place, while Signor D—— waits the result at Visconti's house. My dreadful fear now is that the troops will drive them away from their present position, and then it will be weeks again before we can hear from the band; they are hardly pressed now, and nearly worn out; they said the troops often pass ten yards from where they lie concealed. My husband is not with the main body, but hidden in a grotto, in charge of a small party. Oh, that our government would press the Italian government to keep back their troops, if but for a few hours only, or my husband will yet be sacrificed! He reproaches me in his letter with abandoning him! If we do not within a few days get his freedom, I believe that he will be dead with hunger and exhaustion.

Aug. 9. The brigands are still near Giffoni, and have sent a letter from W——, but Signor Visconti will not give the money, for the letter is dated a *month back!* and he thinks he may not be alive. Faith and patience are tried indeed, and sorely needed here.

After this, nearly a week passed without farther news; the days dragged on heavily; the heat was dreadful, the loneliness oppressive. It was impossible to go out; the general kindly sent me books. I tried to read them, to keep my thoughts a little from brooding over the horrors I imagined. I do not know how I managed to bear this so long. When trouble first comes upon us, we are apt to think it intolerable, little knowing how much deeper and

by Messrs. C—— and Holme on the 31st of July, which only reached Manzo with the £1000 at the beginning of August, were the cause of this reduction in the original claim.

deeper we may sink, and yet be sustained by our Father's hand. I seemed indeed in the Valley of the Shadow of Death; all I know is, that, in the thick darkness that covered me, naught but His hand kept me from falling into despair. On the 16th I heard that Visconti's servant had met Manzo in the mountains, and was made to march three days with him in search of the party who have care of my husband, but without success.

Aug. 21. The brigands have forwarded a letter from my husband acknowledging that £3000 has been paid to them. This is a fearfully exciting day! Will they keep faith and release him? God only knows. This contingency, which I did not fear before, now seems to afford me the greatest possible alarm.

Aug. 22. Mr. R. Holme has just been, with the happy news that the brigands will release my husband directly they have put the money in a place of safety, perhaps the day after to-morrow. I can not read, or walk, or sleep. Can it be true?*

The three next days I passed alone, weary with waiting and waiting for the expected news, till on the evening of the 25th I was almost out of my mind with fear and excitement lest the brigands should not now keep faith. What should we do? I had had so many disappointments that I now lost all hope. When the long and weary day was at an end I went to bed, and, worn out with anxiety, fell asleep. At half past three I was awoke by the joyful tidings that my husband was free! The hideous dream of so many weeks was over, but I could scarcely believe the news was true until Mr. R. Holme came to fetch me, and we drove away together, accompanied by an escort of soldiers, to meet my husband at Giffoni.

* Manzo's Receipt is given in Appendix K.

* * * * * *

"When the Lord turned again the captivity of Zion, we were like them that dream; then was our mouth filled with laughter, and our tongue with singing; then said they among the heathen, the Lord hath done great things for them. The Lord hath done great things for us, whereof we are glad."

CHAPTER XVIII.

DIARY OF MR. MOENS, *Concluded:* AUGUST 24 TO 26.

The sudden Reduction of the Ransom accounted for.—The Soldiers rather too near.—I am still in imminent Danger.—Manzo goes round with the Hat for me.—Parting Civilities.—Interchange of Gifts.—Pasquale's Generosity.—Pavone is affectionate.—I bid him a fond Adieu.—One more Night in the Woods.—Arrival of Tedesco, my Guide.—Manzo's Mother.—My parting Advice to Manzo.—My elegant Appearance.—Kindness of the Peasants.—Crosses on the Mountains.—In sight of Giffoni.—My Reception there.—Kindness of the Visconti Family.—Arrival of my Wife at Giffoni.—We return together to Salerno.

THE morning of the 24th of August was most exciting for me, already in a perfect fever as I was from the want of sleep during the last week. I had been promised my freedom to-day, and expected every moment that Signor Visconti's old shepherd, Fortunato Tedesco, would come up to guide me to Giffoni. Though not so carefully looked after as before, I had still to behave as one of the band, lest my movements should betray them. During the walk of the last night twenty of the brigands went into a field of maize, and each of them had at least twenty or thirty spikes when they returned to us; this will show the mischief done in about ten minutes by these robbers. This was the only food the band had all the rest of the time I was with them, and a most indigestible diet it is when cooked by being simply thrown on the live embers of a wood fire.

To-day Manzo gave me some letters he had kept from me

for a long time. One was from my friend H. C——, in English, which gave me the first intimation I received of his having come out from England to Naples to try and procure my liberation.

There was another from my wife, half in English, which was most painful for me to read, for it showed the anguish from which she was suffering. There were also letters from Mr. Bonham and Mr. Holme; and last, but not least, there was one which gave me the clew to the reduction of the ransom from 50,000 to 30,000 ducats, viz., an official letter from the prefect at Salerno to my wife, stating that the Italian government had not paid and would not pay a ducat toward our ransom. My captors had evidently believed that the prefect in this letter expressed the real intention of his government; but I must say that I sincerely trust the worthy prefect was mistaken, and that the Italian government will, sooner or later, compensate Mr. Aynsley and me for the losses inflicted on us through the negligence of their subordinates. These letters were all sent on to Giffoni on the 3d of July, with the third installment of the ransom.* They were the first I had received for two months, my last dates being the 23d of June, and it was now the 24th of August! No one can imagine the anguish I suffered from not having any news all this time: sometimes the wretches would tell me my wife was dead or gone to England; at other times they would say that she was well and at Naples.

Manzo now asked me for all my letters, and kept all those written in English, but returned me the others; he also asked for my dear little Prayer-book and Fénelon, and quietly put them in his pocket. I had the greatest difficulty in inducing him to let me have them back, for he feared lest I had made any notes in them that might prove injuri-

* See page 209.

ous to the band; but at last, after carefully examining them, he allowed me to take them with me. My notes, which I had made in a small Letts's Diary, I had cut out some days before, and concealed in the inner lining of my waistcoat. I then wrote some more in the little book on purpose for them to tear out. Manzo did this at once on my offering the little book for his inspection. These notes have proved of the greatest service in enabling me to sketch out this narrative, fixing the days on which we changed our hiding-places, and recalling to mind many things that would otherwise certainly have escaped my memory.

Hour after hour I waited for Tedesco, but he did not appear.

There was great gambling going on to-day. I saw Manzo lose seventy Napoleons at one toss. Two others of the band lost all their share, and the money was now nearly all in the hands of the captain, Andrea, Generoso, and Pasquale. We moved a little up the mountain, when all at once we heard in the valley below a great noise of people talking loudly, and the brigands, going to reconnoitre, returned with the intelligence that there was a large force of soldiers surrounding the mountain. This was most unsatisfactory news for me, for Manzo made me follow the band up the mountain, and if it came to a fight, I felt sure that either the brigands (especially Scope) or the soldiers would certainly make me a target, and that I should have the pleasure of being shot after all the ransom had been paid, or have the satisfaction of spending several more days with the band, should it be necessary to take me with them to another neighborhood. I told them that I did not believe the soldiers knew of or were looking for the band, for if they were, they would never make so much noise. I thought of the quiet movements of English troops, contrasted with the hubbub below, where every private was trying to outbawl his comrade. In a short time I heard the joyful news that they were moving away in the direction of Bagnuolo, conveying with them a number of peasants, whom they had arrested for aiding the brigands. All these prisoners were mounted on mules and donkeys, having their feet tied together under the beasts (as I was told by Pavone) to prevent them from escaping. It was the greatest relief to me to see them depart, with their muskets flashing in the sun, for I was so afraid that Manzo would think that there was some connivance between the authorities and my friends, the latter helping to do what they could to exterminate the brigands now that they thought I had been set free.

If the soldiers had by chance seen or got information of the whereabouts of the band, the brigands certainly would have thought this, and would have cut my throat in an instant. I always had the greatest horror of the stiletto in the possession of Pavone, which had taken the lives of two peasants who had come under the term of *infame*. This weapon on one occasion had been lent to Scope, when he was my sole guardian one evening, for the purpose of using against me should I suddenly attack him. This had not been intended for me to see; but as I was always attending to the slightest action on the part of my captors, I had noticed the stiletto passed from the one to the other. At about five o'clock there was a grand consultation about their next movements, Giardullo's late followers taking a great lead, and insisting on their advice being followed, and eventually they got the best of the argument. I could clearly see that these four men would have a great influence in the actions of Manzo's band; and that, having very little money, and being very determined old hands at brigandage, they would not fail to keep the province in a constant state of agitation, and this has very soon proved to be the case.* Manzo and seven of his men had not only to deliver me over to the guide, but to get bread, and (as I distinctly heard) to receive some money. This confirmed me in an idea I had formed that there was another prisoner in their hands, for some of the band were absent, and I could not account for this in any other way. We had a fortnight ago heard that Manzo had gone down for the purpose of taking somebody.

Before they separated, Manzo took off his wide-awake, and, putting some Napoleons in it, went round making a collection for me (as he expressed it), "to go to Naples like a gentleman!" They were not as generous as he expected, and he went to the bag of gold carried by Generoso for the expenses of the band, and made up from the general fund the sum of seventeen and a half Napoleons, which he handed over to me. I on this asked him for a very thick, long gold chain he always wore: he was taking it off to give to me, when he was called away by some one, and I lost the intended gift. Generoso gave me a ring as a keepsake. I asked him for his knife which had taken the lives of two men, and which I wanted to show as a specimen of a brigand's weapon. When open it was more than twelve inches in length, and a terrible cut-throat implement; the handle was of horn, ornamented and inlaid with silver. At first he declared that he had lost it, but I got hold of his jacket and produced it. I told him that we had paid him 30,000 ducats, and he could easily get another, while in England it would be looked on as a great curiosity; at last he consented, and asked me for my tiny penknife, which I gave

* At the present time (Nov. 1) this same band have no less than five captives—M. Wenner, of Salerno, and some of his employés, and a M. Anfrè, a schoolmaster, who had been in their hands once before.

him in exchange. He did not at all like parting with his, and constantly regretted its loss afterward. Pasquale, the man who, not participating in our ransom, perpetually demanded that my ears should be cut off, and had always ill-treated me, now came up, and, to my great astonishment, gave me two more Napoleons, which I accepted with thanks, considering it perfectly right on my part to take all they offered me.

All the rest of the band now went off to the eastward—I believe, from a large map of the province I afterward inspected in England, to the neighborhood of Bagnuolo, and I then saw them for the last time. Before they went, Pavone, who had had the special care of me all the time I was with them, came to me and put up his face for me to kiss him; but this was more than I could stand, and I contented myself with shaking hands with him.

It was now about six o'clock, and I was now told to follow Manzo and his party, and was taken down the mountain toward a place where some cattle were feeding. I was told to sit down while they ran to the herds and had a long talk. They returned without getting any thing, for the peasants refused to carry bread, declaring that it was certain death for them to do so.

I was now taken along the valley and made to sit in places where the expected guides could easily see me, but without any result, though the brigands constantly shouted, in order to attract the attention of the guides, in the manner in which the peasants call one to the other in the mountains.

They then went to the peasants again who were passing near, driving their cattle toward Acerno, and arrangements were made to obtain other guides should Visconti's men not appear. I was most anxious to make my own way to Acerno, and then get some one to go with me to Giffoni.

"Would you not be afraid," they said, "to go alone in these mountains and perish?" to which I replied, "I have not been afraid of you, who are far worse than any others I am likely to meet, and what should I fear with a good conscience?" They began to talk of the knowledge of the country I had shown all the time; but at last the captain told me that I had better wait till the next morning, when guides were sure to arrive. I knew this was a command, and had to make up my mind to another night in the woods; but little sleep did I get, thinking of seeing those from whom I had been separated so long.

August 25. Though I had been promised that the guides would come at daybreak to take me away, five, six, seven o'clock came without their appearance, and I was in despair. Guange and Catane were with me, the former asking me not to speak of him at Naples, for he was well known there. I told him he need not fear my saying any thing that would hurt him, for the authorities knew much more of him than I did, as I did not know whether he was called by a nickname or not.

All at once, at about half past seven, to my intense joy, Tedesco, Visconti's old shepherd, walked up from the place where Manzo and the others were. He was so pleased to see me that he would kiss me, and I had not the heart to refuse him. My first question was to inquire all about my wife, and I was deeply thankful to learn that she was quite well, and had escaped all malarial fever, which is so prevalent in Naples in summer. He told me that he had been hunting every where for the band since the night of Sunday, the 20th, when the £3000 were paid. He had a companion to help him to carry the money, which weighed nearly forty pounds, and was as much as they could carry up the mountains; and that it was a most dangerous task, although they had been promised the protection of both the Italian and English governments. They had run the greatest danger from the troops, who would certainly, he said, have shot **them** had they caught them carrying money **to** the brigands. He told me that he was worn out with the fatigue **and** hunger he had undergone during the last six days, **not** having slept once in a house all that time, and that **he would have** given up the search for the **band** had he not **fallen** in with them this morning, though he had vowed not to return without me. Last night he had slept on the other **side of the mountain opposite** us, not having the slightest idea that we were so close to **him.**

He now went back to Manzo, and sent **an** old woman, who proved to be Manzo's mother, to me; she had brought a small loaf of white bread and a little omelette for me, which luxuries seemed to be most delicious after the coarse fare I had been subjected to lately. It seemed very curious seeing any one in woman's dress, to which I had been **a** stranger for so long a time.

When the **old lady went away Manzo came to** me, and, sitting **down, asked me what I should say** to the prefect when **he questioned me about his band.** I told him that I should **tell** him that he and his band of about 30 men had **been a** match for an army of 10,000 men, and that he had proved himself the cleverer of the two. This pleased him immensely, and he quite rubbed his hands with glee, and immediately gave me two rings, which I put on my fingers in brigand fashion. Contrary to his usual practice, he did not caution me against telling about the band and their proceedings, which greatly surprised me, for the Viscontis had been cautioned **and** threatened in a most violent manner should they say **a** word.

He now returned to his men, and I heard the chinking

sound of their counting money, which I suppose was the sum he was to receive, which I heard mentioned the day before. At about eleven o'clock Manzo asked me if I should like to go; so I threw away all the warm clothing I had been carrying about with me so long, tied up in a handkerchief, and which had served me as a pillow at night since the 19th of June. In answer to my inquiries, Manzo informed me that he was well satisfied with the amount we had paid him. My macintosh coat I put in my pocket, and, refusing the proffered kisses, shook hands all around with them, they parting with me in the most friendly way possible. Generoso added another to my stock of rings, making the number five. I recommended Manzo, for the future, not to take foreigners, but to confine his attention to his own countrymen, which would prove far better for him; for, when a foreigner was taken, it was in all the papers in the world, and it compelled the government to send so many soldiers that the brigands had very little chance of escaping capture.

I now stepped forward, accompanied by Tedesco and the mother of Manzo, all the brigands wishing me a pleasant journey, waving their arms to me while in sight. They were soon lost to view in the wood, and I walked on a free man, having been a captive in their hands 102 days, all which time I never entered any description of house, sleeping always in the open air on the hard ground!

It was one of those fearfully hot days, when, in a southern clime, every thing looks copper-colored, and when the slightest motion requires great exertion; but we had a long journey before us, and it was desirable to get to Giffoni before dark, so on we went in the broiling sun. I felt this very much, for when I was with the band I had never walked once in the sun. Walking in the daytime was only attempted when in a dense forest, where it was impossible for the rays of the sun to penetrate. Up hill and down dale we walked; it seemed so curious to be able to walk in so open a manner, and from habit I kept looking round to see if any one were watching our motions. Tedesco gave me a piece of chocolate, which my late brother captive, Visconti, had kindly sent to me. He had often done so before, but the brigands had always eaten it, and never told me any thing about it. Shirts, too, were sent up two or three times; but these, in the same way, had never reached me, but were worn by the lucky men who fell in with the guides.

I was in a desperate plight as regards dress; and, though I cared little about my appearance when in the woods, I did not quite like showing myself at Giffoni. I had, however, to put on a good face, and make the best of it. My trowsers were all in tatters from catching in the brambles and bushes, and hanging in ribbons at the feet. My coat was covered with the fat and grease of the meat that I had had to carry in the pocket, and all the lining of the skirts was torn to shreds, while constantly sleeping and lying on the dirty ground had quite changed the original color and pattern of the cloth. My wide-awake was dirty and torn. My shirt I had worn day and night since the 19th of June; and my boots were all broken, and many of the seams unstitched. I am quite certain that none of my friends would have been able to recognize me; but I cheered myself with the news that a large warm bath would be ready for me on my appearance at Signor Visconti's house, where my friends had sent every thing that I might require in the shape of dress.

It is almost unnecessary to describe the state of my body. I was covered with sores from the effect of the vermin, through the brigands having steadily refused to allow me to remove my clothing for washing purposes, and never allowing me to stop at a stream for fear of the troops coming upon us before I could rearrange my dress.

In two hours we came to the river running under the hill, where I had spent the last fortnight. I pointed it out to Fortunato. Here we sat down to rest in the shade, for the old woman complained dreadfully of fatigue, and had been lagging behind all the way. While we were sitting here two peasants came up to us, and had a chat with us according to their usual custom, to hear all the news. I was regarded by them with the greatest interest, for every one had heard of the *Inglese* that had been in the hands of the brigands, and they were full of commiseration for me, and opened their eyes very wide when they heard the enormous sum that had been paid, it being the largest sum ever paid in this way. Manzo's mother made me show them the five rings that had been given to me, which she evidently considered reflected great dignity on her as the mother of one who had shown such princely generosity! It had grieved her to the heart when, in starting, I had taken them all off my fingers, because the swelling of the hands while walking made them feel so uncomfortable, besides the ridiculous appearance they presented when worn by me attired as I then was. These two men knew all the band by name, and discussed the generosity of the brigands, who had given me, in their eyes, such magnificent gifts! They were not behindhand in their hospitable offers, wishing to kill a lamb for me from a flock they were tending on the other side of the stream. They wanted to light a fire and cook it on the spot, saying that they knew I had been half starved. I thanked them for their kind offers, which I declined; but I asked them to pick me some grapes and some splendid plums that were hanging quite ripe in the orchard near which we were. They brought a donkey, that I might cross the river on its back, and thus avoid wetting my feet! and we all passed one by one in this manner. On starting again, they wished me a safe journey to England, and, shaking hands with them, I thanked them for their kindness to me, and then we commenced to climb a steep hill, at the top of which was the mule-road on which, while with the brigands, I had seen the soldiers marching along.

This was the road from Acerno to Giffoni, as I had given my opinion to the brigands, who denied so strenuously that I was convinced I was right. The heat was now greater than ever, being reflected from the white crumbling limestone which is common in this part of the country.

A little farther on we came to a large cross, which had been erected on the spot where a peasant had committed a murder, after which he became a member of Manzo's band, but Fortunato did not tell me which one it was; on the cross was a small inscription, stating the name of the victim and the date of his death. We saw other crosses on our way, and at one glen, which looked as dark as the deed committed there, I was told that Carmine Amendolo had waited concealed, and in cold blood had shot a man who had crossed him in love.* I had noticed on several of the brigands' guns little crosses they had cut on them, which were in their idea expiatory of the murders committed with

---

* Mr. Hilton, in his valuable work on "Brigandage in South Italy," vol. i., p. 243, 244, mentions a story told by Marc Monnier which strongly illustrates this custom. A guide to whom a traveler intrusted himself in ascending the Mattese confessed that on various portions of the mountain ridges *he had erected twenty-nine of these crosses!* The morality and religion of such a being indeed belong (as Mr. Hilton says) to the darkest times.

the weapons so marked; and thus the guns or knives are reverenced according to the number of lives taken by them. This was one of the causes why Generoso was so loth to part with the knife he gave to me.

On our way we met several parties of peasants, who all stopped to talk with us. One man we spoke to was introduced to me as the first *ricattato* of the band. He was a poor man, and his family had to pay 100 ducats for his release. I told him he was the first and I the last, but he had been more fortunate, for 30,000 ducats was the price set upon my head. At about half past five o'clock we descended a terrible path in a kind of shelf on the side of the precipitous mountain called St. Salvador, in whose sides are three caves supposed to have been inhabited by the saints in days gone by.

Many a time had I seen the rosy glow of the setting sun on the summit of this mountain during the month of June, when I had been hidden in the neighborhood of Giffoni.

This place, of which I had heard so much, and which took such a great part (through the services of the Visconti family) in procuring my liberation, now burst into view. It appeared to consist of a long, rambling series of dwellings, the whole valley being dotted with little houses, composing two or three distinct villages, each of which had its church. The wide, but now nearly dry bed of the river ran right through the place, and on a conical hill was situated an old Norman castle. The position of Signor Visconti's mansion was pointed out to me, and it was a treat to see Fortunato's look of pride when he told me that we were now on his master's land, which was of great extent on both sides of the valley. I now could recognize the place where I had been from the 8th to the 19th of June, and found that it was not three miles from Giffoni.

When we crossed the river and entered one of the villages (which was composed of the houses inhabited by the peasants attached to the proprietor, who owns the land around, for there are many remains of the feudal system here), our little party was mobbed by all the inhabitants, who poured out to see the foreigner, their *bête noir*, the innocent cause of so many of the villages being depopulated. I was informed that in the provinces of Salerno and Avellino no less than 1500 of the peasants had been arrested and imprisoned for complicity with the brigands while I was in their hands. I was in the most uncomfortable state of mind lest any of the relatives should revenge themselves on my person by making ready use of their knives and stilettos. Many of the young girls were very good-looking, and as we passed the water where they were engaged in washing, they all paused in their occupation to have a good look at the bearded foreigner, who, in return, was gratified with a sight to which he had been long a stranger.

Here I was met by a sergeant of the Carabineers and two of his men off duty, who ordered me, in the roughest way possible, to go to the other end of the village, half a mile out of my road, to the head-quarters of their corps, that I might be examined by the captain; but, as they admitted they had no orders about me, and I was very tired, and anxious to wash off the dirt of three and a half months, and to change my clothes, I refused to go. The sergeant was most impertinent in his manner, and so I told him that, if I was wanted, I should be found at Signor Visconti's house, and walked on. I was soon overtaken by a boy, sent after me to say that if I waited a minute the captain would join me, which he very soon did, accompanied by the syndic of the place. These gentlemen most kindly congratulated me on my escape, and asked me what information I could give them about the brigands. I told them I could tell them nothing that would prove of the slightest use, for I at that time did not know the names of any places which I had been taken to except Acerno. I told them I had been released near that place, and that the band had gone to the eastward.

As we walked on all the gentry of the place came and welcomed me most warmly, and I noticed that most of them carried guns as a protection against the brigands. When we reached the road leading up to Signor Visconti's mansion, a **carriage drove** up, and here I met Mr. Richard Holme, of the firm of Messrs. Cumming, Wood, and Co., of Naples, who had these many weeks been working most indefatigably to procure my release, frequently undergoing the greatest possible risk on behalf of me and Mr. **Aynsley**. It was with the greatest difficulty that I could at first thank him in English, having to supply many words in Italian, and **the excitement of the meeting being** almost too much for me. Signor Michele di Majo, who also had done so much for us, was with **him, and they both seemed as happy as** possible to see their exertions crowned with success.

We now drove through Signor Visconti's property to his house, where I was received with a perfect ovation, all the members of the family and the villagers having assembled in the **court-yard to receive** me as I descended from the carriage. Don Elia, the head of the house, stepped forward and saluted **me, as** did also **my** fellow-captives, Don Francesco and little Tomasino. Nothing could exceed the warmth of their reception of me, **and the kindness** I experienced in their hospitable house — warm baths, a barber, and every thing I could desire were prepared for me; at **ten o'clock a** magnificent supper was ready, and at eleven Mr. Holme returned to Salerno with a letter from me **to my wife,** telling her of my safety, and that the authorities had requested me not to return to Salerno till the next day, as they wished to ask me some questions officially.

I got little sleep that night, though I enjoyed the luxury of a bed; and, rising early, I was ready to receive my wife, who, with Mr. Holme, drove from Salerno, arriving at Giffoni at seven o'clock in the morning.

The pleasure of this meeting I shall not attempt to describe. In the afternoon we returned together to Salerno with grateful hearts, escorted by cavalry sent specially for the purpose by General Balegno.

CHAPTER XIX.

REFLECTIONS ON BRIGANDAGE: SOUTHERN ITALY.

The Ransom all paid to the Band.—No other Persons participate directly.
—The exorbitant Prices charged for Food.—The Peasants the real
Gainers.—Manutengoli.—The real Causes of the Success of Brigand-
age.—The Roots to be eradicated.—Measures proposed.

IN describing the distribution of a portion of the ransom in a former chapter, I was purposely precise, because attempts have been made in certain quarters to suggest that some of the money was kept back *en route*, as a sort of commission from the brigands; but on every occasion on which money was sent up by our friends, I knew what each man had given him, having actually seen it counted out. It may also thus be proved that none of the ransom money paid to Manzo's band went to Rome, or elsewhere in the province of Salerno; for when money is once divided among the men, it is perfectly out of the control of their captain, unless for the actual expenses of food, when all the money kept back by him for this purpose is expended; and then a "whip" is made, according to the necessity of the case, all having to contribute equally. Should any one be without money at the time, he is debited in the captain's accounts, and the amount deducted from the next ransom money.

I do not believe that any articles of food are supplied by *manutengoli* gratis to the brigands; on the other hand, the brigands pay for all they get at most exorbitant prices; and the way in which the Napoleons go for bread, sheep, cheese, bacon, etc., is truly surprising. I often inspected the captain's accounts, and saw clearly from them and the price paid for every thing that five sixths of the money received in shape of ransoms by the brigands go to the peasants, who are thus the persons actually benefited by brigandage! All the time I was in their hands I used to inquire the prices of various articles of food in the towns, and got a very accurate idea of what the brigands paid for them; a *pezzo*, their term for ducat, equal to three shillings and fourpence, was the peasant's ordinary price for a loaf weighing two *rotoli* (equal to about three and a half pounds English); this cost from threepence to sixpence in the towns, according to whether it was made of rye, maize, or wheat, but this made no difference in the price paid by the brigands. A coarse cotton shirt cost them two and a half ducats, or eight shillings and fourpence, and washing one, a ducat, or three shillings and fourpence; each cartridge for a revolver cost the same, and every thing else in proportion.

From a calculation I made when with them, I do not think that a band consisting of from twenty-five to thirty men would spend less than £4000 a year for absolute necessaries, and the rest of their spoils would be lent out among their friends in the country at ten per cent. interest. I recommended them to buy Italian five per cent. stock, as being safer than lending money on personal security! But they said they never lost any, and they feared the stock being confiscated by the government!

When they have got a good sum together by gambling (the ransom money soon gets into three or four hands in this way), and conveyed it to their friends, they give themselves up to the authorities, and in prison enjoy themselves on the extra supply of food paid for out of their savings. They told me that when they buy food for themselves in prison, a profit of 100 per cent. is added to the cost of it by the persons licensed by the governor of the prison for this purpose. While I was with Manzo's band I did not see any traces of *manutengolism*. Food never came up in great quantities; what clothing the men required they bought for themselves from the peasants who brought the bread. I heard that thirty hats and a quantity of shirts were coming up, but I believe that the hats were lost by the surrender of the brigands who were sent for them. I never saw any thing of the shirts. All the money was divided among the band, both in our case and in that of the two Viscontis; although the *manutengoli* are generally supposed to share in the plunder, I do not believe this was done in the case of Manzo's band. It may be that the vigilance and extra measures taken by the Italian government while I was in the hands of the brigands caused the rich proprietors and priests who favored their cause to be very cautious in their dealings with these outlaws. Through Giardullo's revelations several have been convicted, but my impression is that the brigands gain their knowledge of the movements of *galantuomini*, as they call rich men living in the country, and of the troops, from the peasants and *vetturini*, who can give them all the information and aid they require to carry on a successful career; and it is against these classes that the Italian government must direct their efforts, if they intend to put down brigandage.

In the way it is now carried on, the proprietors dare not show their faces out of their houses, for they are carried off from the very villages should they venture to go a step from their own doors. All their lands are left to be cultivated by their laborers at their discretion, without ever being visited by the owners; and subject to the rapacity of these peasants, the master gets a certain proportion of his own produce, the peasants bringing home just what pleases them, and no more. It is the same with the shepherds, who are months together in the mountains with their sheep, and between the shepherds and the brigands I suspect the poor owner of the sheep has a hard time of it.

I may perhaps be allowed to say, on the subject of Italian brigandage generally, that I consider that it can not be suppressed as long as the *interests* of the country people are concerned in its maintenance (as they are at present by the high prices given them by the brigands for food and assistance), or while their *fears of the vendetta* forbid them taking any attitude hostile to the brigands. The readers of Count Maffei's book will understand the terrible position of the unfortunate peasantry who are suspected of having given, or of being likely to give, the authorities any information as to the brigands' movements.*

The first thing to be done to rescue these poor people from the thraldom in which they now live is to open up the country by roads, and the next is to levy the sum paid as ransom for any captive by a rate on the district haunted by the band.

If, in addition to this, a court-martial were held on the spot on any one found with more bread on his person than a specified amount, say sufficient for his midday meal, and if, after a speedy trial, any one thus proved to have any dealings whatsoever with the brigands were hanged, *excepting always any persons who may be rescuing one of their family from the brigands' hands*, it would cause a

* The career of Caruso, as described in General Pallavicini's letter (Maffei, vol. ii., p. 227), affords a striking instance of the enormities committed on these poor unprotected creatures.

state of fear among the peasants at least as **great as** that now excited by the brigands, and the peasants **would** soon betray the causes of this scourge of Southern **Italy into** the hands of the troops, to be dealt with in a different **manner** from that in which they are at present. What punishment is it to a brigand, formerly an idle, good-for-nothing peasant, who has, by murder **or homicide, forfeited** all claims to earning an honest livelihood, to **be confined in** prison, and allowed to buy any quantity **of food and** tobacco with the earnings of brigandage? **What do these** men **glory** in more than idleness and plenty to eat? It is no punishment, but simply *retiring from business,* to spend a few years in the way that suits them best. I often heard the **subject discussed,** and this was the way they always spoke **of it.**

Severe diseases require sharp remedies; **and** no wonder that there is such a dissatisfied **feeling against** the rapidly increasing taxation, **while brigandage, which has** increased in a similar **ratio since the fall of the Bourbons, has** had the effect of decreasing the **produce of the land brought to the** store-house of the proprietors. Were a **local force of armed police** established, like the constabulary in Ireland, **who** would have a knowledge of all those aiding the brigands **and** could watch their movements, it would be of far greater utility than the thousands of Piedmontese troops who are sent to a province where they are perfect strangers, and viewed with **suspicion and dislike by all,** both proprietors and peasants, on account **of the ill feeling that exists** between the inhabitants of **Northern and Southern** Italy.

The military force would **be most useful in following** up the discoveries and measures of the local police, **who would** at once know of the arrival of the brigands in any part **of the country.** These police would know all the inhabitants **of the villages and the surrounding country,** and if any of them were absent at night they could be made to account for being abroad. This would speedily **prevent** all carrying of food during the night. In **fact, a** Curfew Act, such as that which existed not so very long ago in Ireland, would soon produce **the desired** effect.

I can not do better than quote **a passage from** Murray's "Guide to Sicily:" "Whatever the faults of the Bourbon government, **it** had at least this merit, that **it** kept the roads throughout its dominions as secure for the traveler as **those of** Northern Europe. **On** the main land, this was insured by throwing the responsibility of keeping the roads safe on **the several** *commune* **or towns. In** Sicily it was effected by the system **of rural police,** called companies at **arms.** That Sicily is **not so** secure now as it was under the former *régime* is not owing **to the** same causes as disturb the Continental portion of **the** old kingdom. Brigandage is not carried **on** there under the mask of political disaffection. There are no bands of reactionists in Sicily in arms against Victor Emmanuel. Those who have taken to the **road are** of that class which is ever looking **out for** opportunities of robbery and **violence, which has found them in** the unsettled **state of the island since the** expulsion **of** the Bourbons. When we bear in mind the complete subversion of the old political system, under which every thing was done with **the strong** hand, and the police claimed the monopoly of committing outrages against persons and property, and the sudden transition from the most abject political slavery to constitutional liberty, the almost entire change, not only of measures **but of men, that** has **since been** introduced, it **will** hardly be **matter of surprise** that the police machinery has not yet been got into **such** thorough working order as under the Bourbons.

"This body of rural police was established in 1812, during the occupation of the island by the English; for at that time, as for ages previous, the island was so overrun by bandits that stringent measures for their suppression were imperatively demanded. To each of the 24 districts of Sicily a squadron of horse was assigned, by the name of a company at arms, under the command of a captain appointed by the government, but who selected his own men. This system of police was abolished after the disturbances of 1837, and replaced by Neapolitan gensdarmes, who were driven out with the troops in the revolution of 1848; and the *compagni*, being restored, were confirmed in 1849, on the re-establishment of the royal authority. The captains receive 32 tari; the lieutenants, 10 tari; a private, 8 tari, paid monthly. A tari is fourpence. One quarter of this sum is kept back till the end of the year, in order to meet all contingent demands, for both officers and men are held responsible for all highway robberies committed within their respective districts between sunrise and sunset; and the captains have farther to give security of 2000 onze, equal to £1000, to the government on the same account. Out of their slender pay the men have to purchase and keep a horse, and find their uniform; but the government provides them with carbine, sword, and pistols. By living in the country towns and villages they learn all the bad characters; and, if a robbery be committed, they know where to look for the property. It is a singular system of police, peculiar to Sicily, which, by the identity of interests secured by the common responsibility, has in ordinary times secured the safety of the roads."

United Italy is not in half the bad state that is generally imagined; the taxation is only £1 a head, and the interest on its debt is only £10,000,000 to 24,000,000 inhabitants. The pay of laborers in Southern Italy is from 10*d.*

to 15d. a day, and they can live well on 4d. as regards provisions.

But Italy is an agricultural country; its wealth is in the produce of the land, and to develop that wealth must the government direct its exertions. Were the country in a state to allow of the proprietors attending personally to the improvement of their own lands, in the course of a few years the revenue would rise to the legitimate requirements of the state; but as long as the security of the towns only is looked to, and the safety of the producing part of the kingdom made a secondary consideration, Italy will be getting deeper in the mire, and continue to have to borrow money to pay the interest of a constantly increasing debt; and all true lovers of the glorious land will have long to wait to see what they so much desire—a strong, independent, and flourishing United Italy.

APPENDIX.

A (page 70).
Notice posted up in the Hotel Vittoria, Salerno.
AVIS AUX VOYAGEURS.

LE Soussigné avertit messieurs les voyageurs et les étrangers en particulier, qui, craignant les **malvivants**, s'abstiennent peut-être de visiter les monuments de Paestum, **que** la rue depuis Salerne **au dit** lieu de Paestum offre la plus grande sûreté, d'autant plus, que maintenant, grâce à la prévoyance de M. le Lieutenant-Général Avenati, commandant la Division Militaire, il s'est fixé des détachements de troupes sur différents points de la rue, c'est-à-dire, à Battipaglia, Barizzo et Paestum. Quant à la route de Salerne à Amalfi, **elle** est aussi complétement assurée.

V. DE MAJO, *Propriétaire de l'Auberge de la Vittoria à Salerne.*

Translation posted up alongside the above.
NOTICE TO TRAVELERS.

Mr. V. de Majo, proprietor of the Victoria Hotel at Salerno, **begs to inform** travelers desirous of visiting the Temples of Pæstum that the road is now perfectly safe between Salerno and Pæstum, owing to the vigilance of General **Avenati, the** Military Commander of the district, who has **stationed patrols along the** road **at** Battipaglia, Barizzo, and Pæstum. The road from Salerno to Amalfi is also quite safe.

V. DE MAJO, *Proprietor of the Victoria Hotel at Salerno.*

B (page 166).
The Dangers of Signor Visconti's Position.

June 7. When Visconti was about to leave the band, Manzo told him **that** if his father did not consent to forward the money, letters, etc., for me, that they would murder all his family, burn his house, cut down all the **olive** and chestnut trees, destroy his flocks, and do all the damage **they could.** This **put** Signor Visconti in a very awkward position, for the penalty for being in communication with the brigands is twenty years' imprisonment, and Visconti therefore very wisely got the permission of the Italian government, through Mr. Bonham, before undertaking this dangerous office, which he fulfilled so faithfully and **satisfactorily.**

C (page 208).
Reply of Prefect to Inquiry whether the Government would pay Ransom.

"Prefettura de Principato Citeriore, Salerno, li 20 Giugno, 1865.

" Il **sottoscritto è** dolente di dovere assicurare alla S. I. Illma. che non **solo, non è** autorizzato a dare la piu piccola somma per il riscatto dello **infelice** Inglese, che trovasi in mano dei briganti, ma per dovere **di carica deve** impedire con tutti i mezzi che sono in **suo potere, acciocchè non** siano mandati loro denari ed altri oggetti.

"Gradina i sentimenti di **stima ed alta consideratione,**
"**Del Prefetto, Sigismond.**
"Alla Signora Signora Annie Moens, Napoli."

D (page 209).
Translation of a Letter from Signor Visconti to Mrs. Moens.

"HONORED MADAME MOENS,—By last Sunday's post **I received your** very kind letter, containing another addressed to your unfortunate **husband.** I have not yet forwarded **it to its destination, as I have not been** able to **obtain** intelligence **of the spot where** the band **is** actually **to be** found ; but **on the first opportunity I will** not fail to have it conveyed to Mr. **Moens, together with another letter** left here for him by your friend Mr. Holme.

"You have overwhelmed me with so many kind expressions of gratitude **and** acknowledgment, that **I am** ashamed to confess that I do not deserve **them in the** least. I have done nothing for you but write a letter to the **brigand chief,** with the view of impressing on him the idea which **I had formed** of your social position, hoping to move **him from** the **enormous** amount of ransom for which he holds out. But God has not given me this consolation, for the brigands consider **that I am a simple man, easily** to be deceived ; they might, indeed, have **suspected worse of me ; and their** not having entertained any worse supposition **I** attribute to the **mercy** of God, who has so remarkably protected **my** family in restoring to **me my eldest** son quite uninjured, and **even in better** health than when **he** was captured. I trust the Lord will **soon** grant you the like mercies, and also another favor now even more needful—namely, that you may be able to support with patience **and** resignation the anguish and mental suffering which oppress you, the weight of which I can fully estimate, and in which

I heartily sympathize with you. I am not in a position to render you any other services, my dear madam, than those of receiving letters and money, and transmitting them faithfully to their destination; and these services I am resolved to continue to perform for you, although they may —as I greatly fear—compromise me with the government. No thanks or acknowledgment are due to me from you for this, for I seek to do no more than to fulfill the duty of a Christian toward a family suffering (as my own family has suffered) under misfortunes, and especially toward an individual who has shared with my son dangers and every kind of suffering incident to a wild life among men bereft of all the feelings of humanity—an individual, too, whom I greatly respect and esteem, though I have not the pleasure of his acquaintance.

"I have one request to make of you, namely, that you will recommend me to the consul, in whose honorable character and powerful protection I have the greatest confidence; for the little that I do, I do without the formal written authority of the local officials here, having been obliged to content myself hitherto with their simple oral permission.

"Madam, do not abandon yourself to an excess of grief. God will console you when you least expect it—be it by softening the hearts of those savage and unreasoning beings, or by using some of those means of controlling human affairs which are in the power of Him alone. Trust in God with that same confidence which my son assures me your worthy husband has never ceased to display during all his misfortunes.

"Believe me your devoted servant, ELIA VISCONTI."

E (page 231).
Translation of a Letter to Signor Visconti from Manzo.

"SIG. D. ELIA VISCONTI,—I can do nothing more, because my band require absolutely 50,000 ducats, otherwise they wish to take his life; therefore then, with many tears of my mother, and many prayers of my mother and Fortunato Tedesco, they had compassion; they cried so much that they wanted to take him with them. I interceded with my band, because they wished to take away his life; thereupon they said they would have 30,000 ducats, with what I have already received, without deducting a centime—30,000 ducats, otherwise we shall take his life.
"CAPITANO MANZO."

F (page 247).
Were the Brigands connected with Francis II.?

On the 17th of May, Carmine Amendolo showed me the commission he had received, signed by "Tardio." This Giuseppe Tardio was a native of the province of Salerno, and had been a law student, but at the age of twenty-five he went to Rome, and there organized a band to make the vain attempt to restore Francis II. to the throne of his fathers; with these he returned to his province, and signed proclamations as "Captain commanding the Bourbon army."

This commission of Amendolo's was written on the back of a *carte de visite* of Francis II., and officially stamped with the arms of the house of Bourbon.

He also had had another commission making him sergeant, and another raising him to the rank of adjutant, in consideration of his great services; these were written on letter-paper, also signed by Tardio, and stamped with the official seal of the deposed monarch. The latest date of these documents was July, 1863. I do not think that any others of the band had similar documents, or they would have been certain to have shown them to me, as they did any thing that they had in the shape of writing.

Amendolo was caught in August while trying to hide himself in a ditch, and dragged out by the soldiers. Having his gun with him at the time, he stands but little chance of getting off with his life.

On one occasion I was asked by all whether I was not a relative of Francis II., for the band had heard something of the kind from the peasants. I believe that some letters were written to the ex-king at Rome concerning me, and this, being talked about in the towns, had soon spread through the country.

It was with the greatest difficulty that I could persuade them that I had nothing to do with the Bourbon race.

G (page 289).—*A Brigand Song.*
1ª CANZONETTA.

Appendix.

Io gli diedi la mano	Se ne vene lu sargente
La bella non senteva	Co nu magro de fune
Le diedi un bacio d' amore...	C' attacca a dui a dui
Oimò! che son tradita.	A lu carcere ci porta.

Tu rondinella cara
Non sei tradita ancora.
Io son quel giovinetto
Che sempre a te pensava.

Quannu furun 'ntribunale
Si scrive na sentenza
O cielo che spartenza
Che ne sara di me.

Un giorno jetti pe mare;
Li spezzano le vele
Questa nennella mia
Sempre appresso mi steva.

In questo camerone
Ci stanno 'nquantitate
Di muonici e di prievesti
Carcerati 'nquantità.

Una stanza ordinata;
Le sedie preparate:
I beccamorti subito
Preparano la bara.

Vurria reclamare
Diletto pressidente,
Ora pietosamente
Damme la libertà.

2ª Canzonetta.

Il pertusillo è vostro
Il demaniale è nostro
Addio Madà—nfa—nfa
Addio Monsù—nfu—nfu
Canta il gallo e farà cucuricù.

Noi belle donne
'Npietto avite le zizzarelle
Addio Madà—nfa—nfa
Addio Monsù—nfu—nfu
Canta il gallo e farà cucuricù.

Le zizzarelle son vostre
Il demaniale è nostro
Addio Madà—nfa—nfa
Addio Monsù—nfu—nfu
Canta il gallo e farà cucuricù.

La giardiniello è vostro
Il demaniale è nostro
Addio Madà—nfa—nfa
Addio Monsù—nfu—nfu
Canta il gallo e farà cucuricù.

La boscherillo è vostro
Il demaniale è nostro
Addio Madà—nfa—nfa
Addio Monsù—nfu—nfu
Canta il gallo e farà cucuricù.

Quel ch' è nostro è vostro
Quel ch' è vostro è nostro
Addio Madà—nfa—nfa
Addio Monsù—nfu—nfu
Canta il gallo e farà cucuricù.

H (page 296).

The last Letter from the Captive to his Wife, dictated verbatim by Manzo.

"31 Juglio, 1865.

"O moglia ingrata, O moglia crudele, come mi avate abandonato, con quale coraggio mi volete fare morire per denaro, uno povero nomo cosi abandonato da tutte! O moglia ingrata, come mi ai abandonato, cosi come io nonne vi so niente! Mi volete far morire per denaro. O moglia, movetevi a compassione e pietà verso di me, povero, afflitto e sventurato! Che m'avate cosi abandonato da tutte, ho veduto la mia morte con miei occhi a poco a poco, movetevi con compassione, fatelo per cinque piaghe di Jesu Christo nonne mi fate morire cosi, a poco a poco. O moglia carissima movetevi a compassione, mandate il denaro, portatevi a piedi al nostro consule Inglese e al nostri concittadini; pregate che mandassino il denaro che se movessero a compassione di uno disgrazziato giovane Inglese, che non mi facessero morire nel boschi del regno di Napoli, movesse a compassione e pietà che non mi abandonassero, non mi facessero morire nel boschi, che le mia carne sarebbe mangiata dal animale salvatici, mandate il denaro, avate pietà della mia carne. Non credete che mi riscattate colle forze pubbliche queste è la piu peggiore cosa per mi chi vogliono il denaro per mio riscatto, non mai la forza mi riscata, morto non vivo, chi vogliono il denaro, non la forza per mio riscatto si voi non mandate il denaro, certo sono morto; e mandate presto il denaro, perche io non posso soffrire piu. O carissima moglia, io scrivo a voi nuovo; non posso soffrire piu, sono tre parte morto con fame, tre giorni senza cibo e poi un poco di carne crude; sono si debole che è difficile per me di camminare; se volete di rivedermi è importante assai che mandate il denaro subito, subito non in si poce somme, ma in piu grande. Non tengo lettere di voi dopo il 23 Junio; sono molto lontano; il capitano ha ricevuto il denaro, e subito quando il denaro è pagato sono liberato. Non credava che i nostri amici erano si crudeli contro me, non hanno una scintilla di pietà verso me.

"Credetemi se il denaro non è pagato presto presto, è securo che io morro; sono si debole, sono spesso due giorni senza cibo e aqua, che fate, carissima, che lasciatemi cosi? Mandatemi due camice di cotone del paese, e uno nuovo pajo di calzone forte, e due pajo forte di calzetta di lanata oscura. Se non potete mandare il denaro, sono pieno di pidocchi e sono coperto di piage. Addio, addio, carissima mia, ho lasciato ogni speranza di rivederti. Vostro sempre amante e affezionato marito,

"W. J. C. M."

On the back was written in English.

"Trust in God only keeps me alive. I have told them to send you my books if I die. Adieu, dearest A."

I (page 315).

Letter written by a celebrated Brigand Chief to Manzo in behalf of the Captive, and given to Mrs. Moens.

"Mio degno Signore,—Voi siete l'uomo esimio, e che fate risplendere il vostro nome da per tutto, senza commettere vilezze ed azzioni vituperose, percio, adesso siete l'arbitre della vita d'un forestiere, che non avendo mezzi geme quale belva, senza potersi giovare, e la moglie raminga senza potergli dare aiuto perche priva di mezzi ed ancorchè volesse farvi giungere una somma per riparare ai vostri bisogni, con chi? e con qual mezzo? percio usate a costui gentilezze, carita, e commiserazione con rimandarlo libero a cosa sua; imitate un Baldarelli, un Caliglieri, i Capozzoli, ed il celebre Talarico, che si decanta per generosità. Finisco con espormi a vostri comandi, e mi dico

"Vto. amico aff^to^ P. L."

K (page 321).

Copy of Manzo's Receipt.

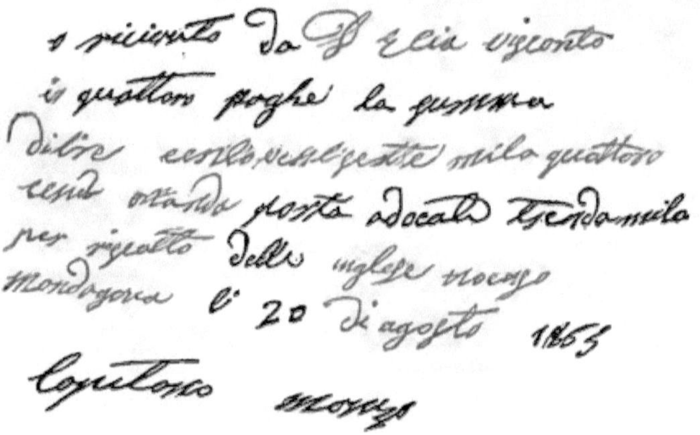
i ricievuto da D. Elia viconto
i quattoro poghe la summa
di lire cento [illegible] milo quattoro
cento ottanta posta a docati [illegible]
per riscatto dello inglese mocens
Mondragone li 20 di agosto 1865
Capitano Manzo

Translation.

"I have received from Don Elia Visconti, in four payments, the sum of a hundred and twenty-seven thousand four hundred and eighty livres, being thirty thousand ducats, for the ransom of the Englishman Moens.
"(Signed)   Captain Manzo.
"Mondogerio, the 20th August, 1865."

L.

Names of Brigands Arrested, Tried, and Shot in 1865, in the Provinces of Salerno.

1. Spinelli, an under **captain**.
2. Mayaldi.
3. Pallotta.
4. Saccoccia.
5. Antonio Maratea, *alias* Giardullo, captain.
6. Carmine Amendolo.
7. Vincenzo Pizza.

Twelve others, belonging **to Manfro's** and Palumbo's bands, were captured in a house of a priest in the province of Avellino, after an obstinate fight with the troops.

The total number taken and tried in the two provinces of Avellino and Salerno during the year was about 70.

M.

The *Names of the Manutengoli who were Arrested in* 1865.

The two Brothers Caggiano, of St. Rufo.
The Priest Pagano and his nephew, of the same place.
The Priest di Vincenzo and all his brother's family, of Castel-Cività.
Don Nicola Budetta, of Montecorvino Rovella.
The Baron Giacomo Perrotta and his brother (a priest).
Don Francesco and Don Domenico Copeta.
Don Vincenzo and Don Eusebio Castagna.
Dottore Antonino Cubicciotti.
Signor Benedetto Cozzi.
Don Giovani-battista **Rocco**.
Don Alfonso Adelizzi **and** his brother, all of Campagna d'Eboli, implicated with the band of Giardullo.
The Syndaco of Sicignano (Pro. of Salerno).
The Syndaco of Senerchia and **all** his family **(Pro. of** Avellino).
Dottore Andrea Marano, of Montella.

N.

Number of Soldiers in the two Provinces in March and April, 1865.

6000 regulars, besides the Carabineers **and National Guard.**

Number of Soldiers in the two Provinces in July and August, 1865.

9000 regulars, besides the Carabineers and National Guard (called out specially).

O.

Names of the Persons seized and held to Ransom in 1865 *by Manzo and Giardullo, and amounts of Ransoms demanded and paid.*

	Francs demanded.	Francs paid.
1. The Brothers Salvatore, cheese merchants, of Eboli	106,250	38,038
2. Don Francesco **Comelli**, railway engineer	212,500	45,000
3. Signori Perito and Gallotta, Canons of Eboli	85,000	28,475
4. Adamo Postiglione, **visitor to Eboli**	51,000	15,300
5. Signori Achilli Bellelli and **Salvatore Magnone**	170,000	51,000
6. Signori Francesco and Tomasino Visconti	170,000	109,250
7. W. J. C. Moens and Rev. J. C. Murray Aynsley, England	212,500	127,500
8. Signor Wenner (and *employés*); son of Signor Alberto Wenner, calico-printer of Salerno	1,062,500	*125,000
	2,069,750	536,563

or, £82,788 demanded, and **£21,462** paid to the brigands of the province of **Salerno for** eight captives, many other smaller amounts having been also paid during this time for persons of less consequence.

* Taken in September, 1865, and now in February, 1866, **still with Manzo's band, who** ask the whole sum of £42,500 for their ransom.

THE END.

Valuable & Interesting Books

PUBLISHED BY HARPER & BROTHERS, NEW YORK.

☞ HARPER & BROTHERS *will send their Books by Mail, postage free,* **to any part** *of the United States, on receipt of the Price.*

☞ HARPER'S CATALOGUE *and new* TRADE-LIST *may be* **obtained gratuitously** *on application to the Publishers personally,* **or by** *letter, enclosing Five Cents.*

Napoleon's Life of Cæsar. The History of Julius Cæsar. By His Imperial Majesty NAPOLEON III. A new Elegant Library Edition, with wide Margins, on Superfine Calendered Paper, with Portrait, &c. Vols. I. and II., Cloth, Beveled Edges, price $3 50 **each.**

Carlyle's Frederick the Great. History of Friedrich II., called Frederick the Great. By THOMAS CARLYLE. With Portraits and Maps. 6 vols., 12mo. Price per Vol., $2 00.

The Story of the Great March: Diary of General Sherman's Campaign through Georgia and the Carolinas. By Brevet Major GEORGE WARD NICHOLS, Aid-de-Camp to General SHERMAN. With a Map and Illustrations. 12mo, Cloth, $2 00.

Governor Foote on the War and the Union. War of the Rebellion; or, Scylla and Charybdis. Consisting of Observations upon the Causes, Course, and Consequences of the late Civil War in the United States. By H. S. FOOTE. 12mo, Cloth, $2 50.

Harper's Pictorial History of the Great Rebellion. By ALFRED H. GUERNSEY and HENRY M. ALDEN. Part I. From the Beginning of the Conspiracy to the Close of the Peninsular Campaign of 1862. With more than Five **Hundred Illustrations.** 4to, $6 00.

Abbott's Sketches of Prison Life. Sketches of Prison Life, Showing how we lived and were treated at the Libby, Macon, Savannah, Charleston, Columbia, Charlotte, Raleigh, Goldsboro, and Andersonville. By A. O. ABBOTT, late Lieutenant First New York Dragoons. Illustrated. 12mo, Cloth, $2 00.

Brackett's United States Cavalry. History of the United States Cavalry from the Formation of the Federal Government to the 1st of June, 1863. To which is added a List of all the Cavalry Regiments, with the names of their Commanders, which have been in the United States Service since the breaking out of the Rebellion. By ALBERT G. BRACKETT, Major First United States Cavalry, late Chief of Cavalry of the Department of Missouri, Special Inspector of Cavalry, Department of the Cumberland. With Illustrations. 12mo, Cloth, $2 00.

Draper's American Civil Policy. Thoughts on the Future Civil Policy of America. By JOHN WILLIAM DRAPER, M.D., LL.D., Author of a "Treatise on Human Physiology," and of a "History of the Intellectual Development of Europe." Crown 8vo, Cloth, $2 50.

Thirty Years of Army Life on the Border. Comprising Descriptions of the Indian Nomads of the Plains; Explorations of New Territory; a Trip across the Rocky Mountains in the Winter; Descriptions of the Habits of different Animals found in the West, and the Methods of Hunting them; with Incidents in the Life of different Frontier Men, &c., &c. By Colonel R. B. MARCY, Author of "The Prairie Traveler." With numerous Illustrations. Post 8vo, Cloth, Beveled, $3 00.

Kinglake's Crimean War. The Invasion of the Crimea: its Origin, and an Account of its Progress down to the Death of Lord Raglan. By ALEXANDER WILLIAM KINGLAKE. With Maps and Plans. 2 vols. Vol. I. Maps. 12mo, Cloth, $2 00.

Abbott's Napoleon Bonaparte. The History of Napoleon Bonaparte. By JOHN S. C. ABBOTT. With Maps, Woodcuts, and Portraits on Steel. 2 vols., 8vo, Cloth, $10 00.

Szabad's Modern War. Modern War: its Theory and Practice. Illustrated from Celebrated Campaigns and Battles. With Maps and Diagrams. By EMERIC SZABAD, Captain U.S.A. 12mo, Cloth, $1 50.

Noyes's the Bivouac and Battle-field. The Bivouac and Battlefield; or, Campaign Sketches in Virginia and Maryland. By Captain GEORGE F. NOYES. 12mo, Cloth, $1 50.

Russell's American Diary. My Diary North and South. By WILLIAM HOWARD RUSSELL, LL.D. 8vo, Cloth, $1 00.

General Scott's Infantry Tactics; or, Rules for the Exercise and Manœuvres of the United States Infantry. Published by Authority. 3 vols., 24mo, Cloth, $3 00.

Butterfield's Camp and Outpost Duty. Camp and Outpost Duty for Infantry. With Standing Orders, Extracts from the Revised Regulations for the Army, Rules for Health, Maxims for Soldiers, and Duties of Officers. By Major-General DANIEL BUTTERFIELD, U.S.A. 18mo, Cloth, 60 cents. (Suited for the Pocket.)

Alison's Life of Marlborough. Military Life of John, Duke of Marlborough. With Maps. 12mo, Cloth, $1 75.

Story of the Peninsular War. By General CHARLES W. VANE, Marquis of Londonderry, &c. New Edition, revised, with considerable Additions. 12mo, Cloth, $1 50.

Carleton's Buena Vista. The Battle of Buena Vista, with the Operations of the "Army of Occupation" for One Month. By Captain CARLETON. 12mo, Cloth, $1 25.

Alison's History of Europe. First Series.—From the Commencement of the French Revolution, in 1789, to the Restoration of the Bourbons in 1815. (In addition to the Notes on Chapter LXXVI., which correct the errors of the original work concerning the United States, a copious Analytical Index has been appended to this American Edition.) SECOND SERIES.—From the Fall of Napoleon, in 1815, to the Accession of Louis Napoleon, in 1852. A New Series. 8 vols., 8vo, Cloth, $16 00.

Motley's Dutch Republic. The Rise of the Dutch Republic. A History. By JOHN LOTHROP MOTLEY, LL.D., D.C.L. With a Portrait of William of Orange. 3 vols., 8vo, Cloth, $9 00.

Motley's United Netherlands. History of the United Netherlands: from the Death of William the Silent to the Synod of Dort. With a full View of the English-Dutch Struggle against Spain, and of the Origin and Destruction of the Spanish Armada. By JOHN LOTHROP MOTLEY, LL.D., D.C.L., Author of "The Rise of the Dutch Republic." 2 vols., 8vo, Cloth, $6 00.

Hildreth's History of the United States. First Series.—From the First Settlement of the Country to the Adoption of the Federal Constitution. SECOND SERIES.—From the Adoption of the Federal Constitution to the End of the Sixteenth Congress. By RICHARD HILDRETH. 6 vols., 8vo, Cloth, $18 00.

"They do honor to American Literature, and would do honor to the Literature of any Country in the World."

THE RISE OF
THE DUTCH REPUBLIC.
A History.

By JOHN LOTHROP MOTLEY.

New Edition. With a Portrait of WILLIAM OF ORANGE. 3 vols. 8vo, Muslin, $9 00.

We regard this work as the best contribution to modern history that has yet been made by an American.—*Methodist Quarterly Review.*

The "History of the Dutch Republic" is a great gift to us; but the heart and earnestness that beat through all its pages are greater, for they give us most timely inspiration to vindicate the true ideas of our country, and to compose an able history of our own.—*Christian Examiner* (Boston).

This work bears on its face the evidences of scholarship and research. The arrangement is clear and effective; the style energetic, lively, and often brilliant. * * * Mr. Motley's instructive volumes will, we trust, have a circulation commensurate with their interest and value.—*Protestant Episcopal Quarterly Review.*

To the illustration of this most interesting period Mr. Motley has brought the matured powers of a vigorous and brilliant mind, and the abundant fruits of patient and judicious study and deep reflection. The result is, one of the most important contributions to historical literature that have been made in this country.—*North American Review.*

We would conclude this notice by earnestly recommending our readers to procure for themselves this truly great and admirable work, by the production of which the author has conferred no less honor upon his country than he has won praise and fame for himself, and than which, we can assure them, they can find nothing more attractive or interesting within the compass of modern literature. —*Evangelical Review.*

It is not often that we have the pleasure of commending to the attention of the lover of books a work of such extraordinary and unexceptionable excellence as this one.—*Universalist Quarterly Review.*

There are an elevation and a classic polish in these volumes, and a felicity of grouping and of portraiture, which invest the subject with the attractions of a living and stirring episode in the grand historic drama.—*Southern Methodist Quarterly Review.*

The author writes with a genial glow and love of his subject.—*Presbyterian Quarterly Review.*

Mr. Motley is a sturdy Republican and a hearty Protestant. His style is lively and picturesque, and his work is an honor and an important accession to our national literature.—*Church Review.*

Mr. Motley's work is an important one, the result of profound research, sincere convictions, sound principles, and manly sentiments; and even those who are most familiar with the history of the period will find in it a fresh and vivid addition to their previous knowledge. It does honor to American literature, and would do honor to the literature of any country in the world.—*Edinburgh Review.*

A serious chasm in English historical literature has been (by this book) very remarkably filled. * * * A history as complete as industry and genius can make it now lies before us, of the first twenty years of the revolt of the United Provinces. * * * All the essentials of a great writer Mr. Motley eminently possesses. His mind is broad, his industry unwearied. In power of dramatic description no modern historian, except, perhaps, Mr. Carlyle, surpasses him, and in analysis of character he is elaborate and distinct.—*Westminster Review.*

It is a work of real historical value, the result of accurate criticism, written in a liberal spirit, and from first to last deeply interesting.—*Athenæum.*

The style is excellent, clear, vivid, eloquent; and the industry with which original sources have been investigated, and through which new light has been shed over perplexed incidents and characters, entitles Mr. Motley to a high rank in the literature of an age peculiarly rich in history.—*North British Review.*

It abounds in new information, and, as a first work, commands a very cordial recognition, not merely of the promise it gives, but of the extent and importance of the labor actually performed on it.—*London Examiner.*

Mr. Motley's "History" is a work of which any country might be proud.—*Press* (London).

Mr. Motley's History will be **a standard book of reference in historical literature.**—*London Literary Gazette.*

Mr. Motley has searched the whole range of historical documents necessary to the composition of his work.—*London Leader.*

This is really a great work. It belongs to the class of **books in** which we range **our** Grotes, Milmans, Merivales, and Macaulays, as the glories of English literature in the department of history. * * * Mr. Motley's gifts as a historical writer are among the highest and rarest.—*Nonconformist* (London).

Mr. Motley's volumes will well repay perusal. * * * For his learning, his liberal tone, and his generous enthusiasm, we heartily commend him, and bid him good speed for the remainder of his interesting and heroic narrative.—*Saturday Review.*

The story is a noble one, and is worthily treated. * * * Mr. Motley has had the patience to unravel, with unfailing perseverance, the thousand intricate plots of the adversaries of the Prince of Orange; but the details and the literal extracts which he has derived from original documents, and transferred to his pages, give a truthful color and a picturesque effect, which are especially charming.—*London Daily News.*

M. Lothrop Motley **dans** son magnifique tableau de la formation **de notre République.**—G. GROEN VAN PRINSTERER.

Our accomplished countryman, Mr. J. Lothrop Motley, who, during the last five years, for the better prosecution of his labors, has established his residence in the neighborhood of the scenes of his narrative. No one acquainted with the fine powers of mind possessed by this scholar, and the earnestness with which he has devoted himself to the task, can doubt that he will do full justice to his important but difficult subject.—W. H. PRESCOTT.

The production of such a work as this astonishes, while it gratifies the pride of the American reader.—*N. Y. Observer.*

The "Rise of the Dutch Republic" at **once, and by acclamation, takes its** place by the "Decline and Fall of **the Roman Empire,**" as **a work which,** whether for research, substance, **or style, will never be superseded.**—*N. Y. Albion.*

A **work upon which all who** read the **English language may congratulate themselves.**—*New Yorker Handels Zeitung.*

Mr. Motley's place **is** now (alluding to this book) with Hallam and Lord Mahon, Alison and Macaulay in the Old Country, and with Washington Irving, Prescott, and Bancroft in this.—*N. Y. Times.*

THE authority, in the English tongue, for the history of the period and people to which it refers.—*N. Y. Courier and Enquirer.*

This work at once places the author on the list of American historians which has been so signally illustrated by the names of Irving, Prescott, Bancroft, and Hildreth.—*Boston Times.*

The work is a noble one, and a most desirable acquisition to our historical literature.—*Mobile Advertiser.*

Such a work is an honor to its author, to his country, and to the age in which it was written.—*Ohio Farmer.*

Published by **HARPER & BROTHERS,**
Franklin Square, New York.

HARPER & BROTHERS will send the above Work by Mail (postage paid (for any distance in the United States under 3000 miles), on receipt of the Money.

www.ingramcontent.com/pod-product-compliance
Lightning Source LLC
Chambersburg PA
CBHW020323240426
43673CB00039B/899